THE SOCIAL CONTRACT

IN AMERICA

AMERICAN POLITICAL THOUGHT

Wilson Carey McWilliams and Lance Banning, Founding Editors

THE

Social Contract

IN America

FROM THE REVOLUTION

TO THE PRESENT AGE

Mark Hulliung

University Press of Kansas

Published by the University Press of Kansas (Lawrence, Kansas
66045), which was organized by the Kansas Board of Regents and is
operated and funded by Emporia State University, Fort Hays State
University, Kansas State University, Pittsburg State University,
the University of Kansas, and Wichita State University

Library of Congress Cataloging-in-Publication Data
Hulliung, Mark.
The social contract in America :
from the revolution to the present age /
Mark Hulliung.
p. cm. — (American political thought)
Includes bibliographical references and index.
ISBN 978-0-7006-1540-7 (cloth : alk. paper)
1. Social contract—History. 2. Civil society—United
States—History. I. Title.
JA84.U5H84 2007
320.1'10973—dc22
2007008031

British Library Cataloguing-in-Publication Data is available.

Printed in the United States of America

10 9 8 7 6 5 4 3 2 1

The paper used in this publication meets the minimum requirements
of the American National Standard for Permanence of Paper for
Printed Library Materials Z39.48-1992.

Contents

Preface and
Acknowledgments

The purpose of this book is to investigate the place of theories of the social contract in American history. Where previous studies have typically concentrated on the Revolution and the Founding, I shall provide an account stretching from the revolutionary period to our own time. The first chapter deals, inevitably, with the Revolution and Founding; the second with theories of the social contract in antebellum America; the third, on land reform, begins with the period prior to the Civil War but ends with Henry George at the close of the nineteenth century; the fourth, on the fate in America of Edmund Burke's anti–social contract, ends in the 1950s; the fifth, on the Declaration of Independence, culminates in the 1960s and stretches from there to the present day; the sixth, on the end of the social contract, reaches the "rights revolution" of the 1970s and carries the story forward to the ambiguities and uncertainties of our own time.

Theories, not a single *theory,* will be my concern, for the social contract was not one but several, and each variation had its incarnation in America. Mine is a study of the Americanization of Hugo Grotius and Samuel Pufendorf as well as of the more widely recognized John Locke. I shall re-create the struggles between claims of alienable versus inalienable rights; of consent given once and for all versus consent reaffirmed with each new generation; of the sovereignty of the people of the various states versus the sovereignty of the people of the nation—and many another duel between alternative readings of the social contract.

There is no shortage of books that profess to recover America's public philosophy. Unfortunately, more often than not, the authors of such studies come to their subject preoccupied with a current ideological conflict that they read back into the past, imposing their own viewpoint upon the dead. Historians understandably look for the nearest exit when someone stands up and starts declaiming about our public philosophy. The argument of this book is that historians should consider staying in the room because a case can be made on strong historical grounds that for many years the theory of the social contract played a special role in American history—that it was enlisted by advocates of seemingly every major cause and figured in virtually all major controversies, and that its opponents, in the course of struggling mightily to remove it from the center of public discourse, frequently had trouble disentangling themselves from its web. The social contract may not be our public philosophy—or no longer so—but it is probably as close as we have ever come to having one.

Most of my attention will be devoted to the heyday of contested versions of the social contract: the period from the Revolution to the Civil War. Until 1861 theories of the social contract unquestionably supplied Americans with many of the most powerful and widely used resources in their intellectual arsenal. Before the Civil War even the writers seemingly least sympathetic to social contract theory were frequently forced to resort to its language.

After the Civil War the social contract still had its moments of grandeur, in Henry George, for instance, whose thought was not only vital to land reformers but exercised surprising influence over the very Progressives who eventually scorned him. As late as 1963 Martin Luther King Jr., in the course of demanding full citizenship for African Americans, invoked the social contract language of the preamble of the Declaration of Independence.

There is no denying, however, that the social contract was on the wane in postbellum America, its sporadic renewals frequently achieved at the cost of fragmentation and dilution. In our public discourse, assertions of natural rights lived on in the late-nineteenth and twentieth centuries but were increasingly divorced from the rest of the old theories of the social contract—the state of nature, the contractual agreement, the higher moral law. The social contract suffered demotion again when efforts to shape "public opinion" took the place of the prior concern for securing the consent of the governed, sometimes self-consciously so, as in the case of Herbert Croly and some other Progressives. Only the philosophers in the academy, cut off from direct contact with workaday politics, continue nowadays to speak seriously of the social contract, and even they tellingly resort to reasoning in the mode of a Kantian "as if." "Consent," "natural rights," or "state of nature" do not appear as entries in the index of John Rawls's *A Theory of Justice*.

Another postbellum story is that of the outright decline of theories of the social contract in the face of intellectual movements such as Progressivism. John Dewey's argument that natural rights and the social contract are outdated and must be replaced with a Progressive philosophy is familiar to us all. What is unfamiliar to us is Dewey's confidence that Progressivism would succeed where the social contract fell short. In today's world Progressivism, too, is in danger of sounding more like the voice of the past than the prospect of the future.

IN WRITING THIS BOOK I HAVE FOUND MYSELF deeply indebted to many scholars. Whatever novelty exists in the exploratory chapters that follow consists especially in the sweep of my account. Insofar as I have succeeded in setting forth a worthwhile overview of American history without sacrificing specificity, it is because so many able scholars have paved the way and eased my burden. The labors of Bernard Bailyn, Eric Foner, George Fredrickson, Thomas Horne, Isaac Kramnick, Pauline Maier, Patrick Riley, Daniel Rodgers, Gordon Wood, and Michael Zuckert proved invaluable to me in my undertakings, and to mention them is only to scratch the surface. I hope that my notes indicate some of my other debts.

I wish also to express my appreciation of the work of R. R. Palmer, a man before my time, a man whom I never met but whose historical writings remain, to my mind, a model of the kind of work that needs to be done. I dedicate this book to him—to his habit of insightful analysis, to his capacity for synthesis, to his insistence upon studying America in comparison with Europe—and to all the historians and political theorists whose publications are written, like his, not merely for the present day but for the years to come.

THE SOCIAL CONTRACT

IN AMERICA

■
Prologue: Remembrances of Things Past

In 1991 Democratic presidential candidate Bill Clinton called for a "New Covenant," a "new compact," a renewed American social contract. In 1994 Newt Gingrich, rallying the Republicans to electoral victory in congressional races, took up the theme of a "Contract with America." In 1995 Supreme Court Justice Clarence Thomas issued a dissenting opinion that was set forth in terms of a theory of the social contract.

It is far from obvious that any of these three public figures had a serious understanding of theories of the social contract and the role of such theories in American history. Metaphors, perhaps, were all they offered the public. Yet they would not have been attracted to the imagery of social contract were it not that such language continues to evoke warmly supportive responses. My argument is that present-day politicians, jurists, and speechwriters occasionally speak of a social contract because, once upon a time, not so many years ago, seemingly everyone did. Overwhelmingly, from the Revolution to the Civil War, theories of the social contract provided a standard vocabulary of public affairs. The greatest debates, the most meaningful struggles, were frequently carried out by pursuing one or another theory of the social contract.

The mistake of Clinton's speechwriters was to believe, apparently, that they were dealing with *the* rather than *a* theory of the social contract, or perhaps they thought that any such theory has been at home in America.

1

Unknowingly, they drew upon a particular version of social contract theory, and unfortunately they chose one that is especially unsuitable for the events of American history. Clinton spoke favorably of "a covenant between people and their government" and made the historical claim that "our founding fathers outlined our first social compact between government and the people."[1] He did not understand that at the time of the Revolution it was consistently the Loyalists, far more so than the Patriots, who spoke of a contract between the rulers and ruled, governors and governed, government and the people—the Loyalists of America made this claim, and so did their mentors, the governing Whigs of England, who defended the acts of Parliament that infuriated the colonists. The eighteenth-century Whigs in Parliament and their Loyalist counterparts in the colonies believed the people had, in effect, signed away their rights once and for all to a sovereign Parliament in 1688 (see chapter 1).

It was John Locke's social contract, defeated in 1688, that triumphed at the time of the American Revolution, and Locke explicitly disallowed the notion of a contract between government and people. The sovereign people owe nothing to the rulers; the rulers owe everything to the governed, said Locke's disciple Tom Paine, and, after 1776, so said many Americans who supported the Revolution. There is a social contract by which the people bind themselves to one another, but no subsequent political contract. The rulers hold power temporarily, as mere "trustees" of the people; a second contract must be disallowed on the grounds that it contradicts the sovereignty of the people. What the people give they can take away whenever they please, because they are bound by no contract between governors and governed.

The notion of the second contract, a contract of "submission," was borrowed by England's establishment Whigs from the writings of Samuel Pufendorf, who was as widely influential in his day as he is now forgotten by all save a few scholars. Today, historians recognize his pioneering efforts as a social contract theorist in his massive treatise of 1672, *Of the Law of Nature and Nations;* he is equally credited as the author who a few years later wrote a brief and very popular book titled *On the Duty of Man and Citizen.* Having begun with natural rights, Pufendorf quickly swallowed them up into a philosophy of duties, so strongly stated that one might as well be reading Cicero's *On Duties.* Natural rights, like the social contract, appear only to disappear a moment later in the thought of Pufendorf.[2]

When Clinton's speechwriters dusted off their college notes on the social contract, they misread their Locke and backtracked to positions duplicating those of Pufendorf, a thinker Locke refuted. Clinton's speech on an American social contract inadvertently reproduced Pufendorf not only in its talk about a contract between government and people but also in its substitution of duties for rights. The overriding theme of the speech was responsibilities and duties, so much so that when the ardent natural rights advocate Thomas Jefferson made a brief appearance in Clinton's hortatory prose, it was in the guise of a statesman speaking of a "debt of service" we all owe our country.

Perhaps Clinton meant to remind the citizenry of President Kennedy's line: "Ask not what your country can do for you; ask what you can do for your country." Or perhaps Clinton was trying to counter the "rights revolution" of the previous two decades, during which Democrats phrased everything from environmental protection and clean air to assistance to the disabled in terms of a rhetoric of rights.[3] Even if one is sympathetic to his motive, whatever it was, his social contract bears no resemblance to the American historical reality of popular sovereignty and natural rights. There were duties in Locke's world without the curtailment of rights, but Clinton's writers had lost contact with the author of the *Second Treatise of Government*, the one person they presumably had to keep in mind if they wished to celebrate and renew the American social contract.

Only one sentence of Clinton's speech on a New Covenant flows comfortably from American history. "To turn America around, we've got to have a new approach, founded on our most sacred *principles* as a nation," Clinton announced. Throughout their history, whenever Americans have spoken about their social contract, they have discussed their "principles" of government. In this regard they have decisively distanced themselves from their English origins, for the intent of most mainstream English thinkers of the eighteenth century and beyond has been to avoid raising the risky topic of first principles, which they have habitually associated with the Levellers of the Puritan Revolution. Quite recently the renowned English philosopher Michael Oakeshott began his frequently cited essay "Rationalism in Politics" with this quotation from the seventeenth-century French moralist Vauvenargues: "Les grands hommes, en apprenant aux faibles à réfléchir, les ont mis sur la route de l'erreur." For Oakeshott, as for so many of his English predecessors, questions of principles are best left unasked.[4]

The typical strategy of English writers has been to write everything disruptive out of their history—whether by pretending the Stuart monarch "abdicated" the throne in 1688; or by deleting the Puritan Revolution from historical memory; or by conjuring up a common law dating from time immemorial, thereby denying the significance of the Norman Conquest.[5] In America, by contrast, Benjamin Rush boasted that his ancestor had served in Cromwell's army and swelled with pride at the thought that "the republics of America are the fruits of the precious truths that were disseminated in the British Parliament [of the 1640s]."[6] Rush and the rest of the revolutionary and founding generation were as eager to speak publicly about the "principles" of government as the English have been to maintain a discreet silence.

No doubt Clarence Thomas regarded his dissenting opinion in 1995 as far more attuned than Clinton's to the social contract as it has actually figured in American history. "I start with some first principles," was his promising beginning, soon followed by another sentence that is faithful to the American tradition of the social contract: "Our system of government rests on one overriding principle: All power stems from the consent of the people." So far, so good, but then Thomas uttered words that are truly astonishing: "The ultimate source of the Constitution's authority is the consent of the people of each individual State, not the consent of the undifferentiated people of the Nation as a whole." If we add Thomas's assertion that "the United States" is a plural noun, what he offers us is a replication of the social contract as it was understood by the Southern slave owners.[7]

Thomas presumably did not realize he had sided with the antebellum South, and he may have forgotten that the position he rejected on who the "people" are—the people as the nation—had been upheld by the likes of John Marshall, Joseph Story, and Daniel Webster (see chapters 2 and 6). He took one side of an antebellum controversy without acknowledging that his thought had anything to do with the constitutional debates of the period leading up to the Civil War.

"Original intent," apparently, is Thomas's excuse for ignoring the antebellum character of his position. Rather than confront the Federalists of the first party system and the Whigs of the second, he wraps himself up in what he convinces himself was the position of James Madison in 1787. A peculiar Madison it is that Thomas offers us, a Madison supposedly arguing in the

Federalist for the states' rights position that would not be his until years later, 1798, when he and his *Federalist* coauthor Alexander Hamilton had become enemies. In truth the Madison of 1787 was so suspicious of the states that at the Constitutional Convention he had repeatedly argued for a federal veto over state laws.[8] After losing that debate Madison accepted the milder but still vigorous and tenacious version of quasi-nationalist argument that he articulated in the *Federalist.* Undaunted, Clarence Thomas pointed to a passage by Madison in the *Federalist* explaining that ratification would be decided by the people of the states, the only passage he could find where Madison could be misread to sound like the Antifederalists.[9]

Thomas imagined that there has been only one version of the social contract, the states' rights variant, and persuaded himself that it spoke through his mouth without his mind ever offering an interpretation. All of his reasoning was based on suppressing the competing doctrines of the social contract that have played a prominent role in American history.

Representative Newt Gingrich wanted to "restore our historic principles" in 1994 by issuing a contract that would "help repair a fundamental disconnection between citizens and their elected officials." He spoke at length about an "ongoing revolution" and—shades of Benjamin Rush!—told the voters that "the lesson of the English Civil War and the American Revolution was that political freedom is ultimately based on the courage and preparedness of those who would remain free." Rights are easy to find in his writings, and they are "inalienable rights." Gingrich's position on the right to own firearms is especially interesting: "The Second Amendment is a political right written into our Constitution for the purpose of protecting individual citizens from their own government." The right of revolution cannot be denied.[10]

Gingrich, wanting to be better informed about American history than most politicians, read and commented on two of Gordon Wood's studies, *The Creation of the American Republic, 1776–1787* (1969) and *The Radicalism of the American Revolution* (1991). The more recent of those books is evidently the one that truly attracted him because in it Gingrich found what he took to be a pleasing account of the Jeffersonian and Jacksonian periods. After reading Wood's second book, Gingrich concluded that small government and a populist uprising against the elites were common to 1830 and 1994. The Republican Party is the modern incarnation, in his estimation, of Jeffersonian and Jacksonian democracy.[11]

In Gingrich's understanding of American history, as in Clarence Thomas's, we encounter a depiction of antebellum America in which the Whig Party is never mentioned; the names of Daniel Webster and Joseph Story are absent from the index; and the speeches they delivered to answer Southerners on some occasions, Jacksonians on others, have disappeared without a trace. Gingrich attempted to annex the social contract tradition without examining or even mentioning the great battles waged over the definition of its terms.

We may conclude that recent attempts to recover the social contract tell us more about ourselves than about the past. Scraps from previous ages occasionally come our way in the speeches of contemporary political figures; now and then a piece from one of the competing social contracts is unearthed or alluded to, but the larger story is never told, let alone the fact that the social contract was for many years the heart and soul of political discourse.

What is needed, and what I shall provide, is a sustained effort to retrieve the history of the social contract in America. The period before the Civil War, we shall find, was especially rich in competing efforts to claim the contract (chapters 1 and 2). In later history the theory of the social contract was less significant, but its life did not end in 1865. So long as there was open land, Locke would continue to answer American needs. The natural right to land would remain a dominant theme until the end of the nineteenth century, and its last act would be one of its greatest: Henry George's trip to Ireland and England (chapter 3). The Declaration of Independence, with its brief manifesto in favor of consent and natural rights, would remain a remarkably powerful document as late as 1963, the date of Martin Luther King's "I Have a Dream" speech (chapter 5). The social contract, natural rights, and popular sovereignty have been slow to exit American history.

European history is another story entirely and serves to underscore the distinctiveness of American political thought. Kant's social contract was merely an "as if" proposition, and he disallowed a right of revolution. The consent of the governed was not his concern; all that mattered was that the rulers should be urged to govern in such a manner that the ruled, if enlightened, would presumably approve.[12] After Kant came Hegel, whose historicism marked the demise of the state of nature, natural rights, the social contract, and the very notion that humans can will a new political order into being. Germany, then, has been less than hospitable to theories of the social contract, and the same may be said of England, where Jeremy Bentham ridiculed both the Declaration of Independence and the French Declaration of the Rights of Man and of the Citizen. English Whig and liberal historians may have disagreed with Bentham's analytical method, but Thomas Babington Macaulay and his fellow students of the past made it their special mission to blame doctrines of a social contract and natural rights for much of what went wrong in the French Revolution and to credit the absence of the same for the wonders of 1688.[13] America stands alone in its preoccupation, well into the nineteenth century, if not later, with the social contract.

Why scholars have not paid more attention to the social contract in America is something of a mystery. One answer is that we see what we are looking for, and, until recently, we have been looking for or bemoaning the loss of civic virtue in American history. It was the final ten pages of Wood's *The Creation of the American Republic, 1776–1787*, the section entitled "The Decline of Classical Politics," that caught the eye of an entire generation of scholars. Lost along the way were the previous six hundred pages, which feature many thoughtful analyses of the social contract during the Revolution and the Founding.

A decade before the appearance of Wood's first book, R. R. Palmer published volume one of *The Age of the Democratic Revolution* (1959). Despite occasional salutes from scholars, Palmer's noteworthy study has received relatively little serious attention in recent years. Much is lost if we overlook his work—much that is directly relevant to an examination of the social contract in America. His chapter "The American Revolution: The People as Constituent Power" remains rewarding reading. Although Palmer did not speak of social contract theory, his study begs for a continuation along that line of inquiry. There is also much to be gained from following his procedure of studying America in relation to Europe. For our purposes, the "Atlantic Crossings" that matter most are those between England, Ireland, and Scotland on one side and America on the other.[14]

Unfortunately, the most famous efforts to compare America with Europe have done more to impose European categories on America than to understand the meaning that events in America had for Americans. Marx on the left, Gentz on the right, and Tocqueville in the middle missed the significance of American revolutionary ideology—the theory of the social contract. If the American Revolution did not feature a third estate rising up against a nobility, then to Marx and Marxists it sadly was not a revolution.

If to counterrevolutionary Friedrich Gentz there was no social revolution, then the American Revolution was happily not a revolution; rather, it was something infinitely better, an encore performance of 1688 (chapter 4). Tocqueville, too, taking the French Revolution as a measuring rod, proclaimed the American Revolution a nonrevolution.

Marx, Tocqueville, and Gentz—European socialist, liberal, and counterrevolutionary—ignored or downplayed the American revolutionary ideology of 1776, 1787, and thereafter, which is why, or at least one of the reasons why, Bernard Bailyn's *The Ideological Origins of the American Revolution* (1967) is a very important book. It is possible, however, that even Bailyn had difficulty coming out from under the shadow of the Europeans. The title of his book is somewhat problematical. To discuss the ideological origins suggests, perhaps, that we should study the ideological alongside the social origins and the economic origins, when presumably his point, and certainly mine, is that the American Revolution was a revolution precisely because of its ideology.

Palmer's older study had the virtue of treating the American Revolution as a revolution, in contradistinction to Louis Hartz, who four years earlier had followed the Europeans in denying that the Revolution was a revolution. Even Palmer, however, turned mainly to an economic argument—the amount of confiscated Loyalist property—rather than to the American ideology of the social contract to make his case.[15]

Possibly we resist discussing theories of the social contract and their role in American history for fear of falling back into an old-fashioned intellectual history of abstract, disembodied ideas. If so, we are mistaken, because the ideas in question were far from abstract. Ministers, politicians, jurists, and journalists were the speakers in debates that everyone knew involved nothing less than the definition of America, its aspirations, its viability as a political entity. Studying these debates, moreover, is a good way to reach out to social historians: their issues concerning slaves, women, labor movements, and the like will frequently be ours, too. Not only intellectual but cultural and political history is my pursuit in the essays that follow.

In recent years there have been signs that the study of the social contract in American history has begun.[16] I will build upon this edifice and reach chronologically beyond the Revolution and the Founding, where most of the work is now being done, to the antebellum era and to later periods.

Unquestionably, the place to begin is with the American Revolution, a time when the intellectual battles between Loyalists and Patriots and within the ranks of the Patriots themselves were played out by revisiting the social contract theories of Grotius, Pufendorf, and Locke (chapter 1). After that I shall turn to the repeated claims of a natural right to the land, which throughout antebellum history had the effect of renewing the most radical versions of Locke's thought (chapter 3). This is not to say, however, that there was a shortage of antebellum public figures, in either the North or the South, who wanted to tame the social contract and construct a more conservative political edifice. But what is striking is that during the struggle between the North and the South, both sides, in their efforts to refute their opponents, returned to the theme of popular sovereignty and made their ultimate arguments in terms of contrasting understandings of the American social contract (chapter 2). Never was the revolutionary beginning decisively overturned, and sporadic attempts to Americanize Burke's repudiation of the social contract always fell short (chapter 4).

The one document that towers over American history is the Declaration of Independence, that great tribute to the doctrines of natural rights and consent that were central to American discourse as late as Dr. King's speech of 1963. Those excluded from the promise of American life—women, African Americans, laborers—always turned to the Declaration, and so did the person who was arguably the greatest American statesman: Abraham Lincoln. Appeals to the Declaration have been central to American history.

Efforts of antebellum Southerners and postbellum Progressives to downplay Jefferson's words are likewise of paramount importance in American history. And no account of the history of the Declaration of Independence would be complete without a word or two on the reasons for its relative disappearance from public life after 1963 (chapter 5).

Fragments of the social contract tradition lived on after the Civil War, but never with the old vigor. The great conflict that tore the nation in two led to a reaction against a theory that highlighted the problematical nature of political obligation. Conservatives had had their fill of such a dangerous mode of thinking, and Progressives, like their European counterparts, viewed the social contract as a historical relic. Did another political language succeed in replacing the theory of the social contract or are we lost at sea in a storm of political incoherence (chapter 6)?

For many years Americans frequently fought their greatest political battles by wielding one or another version of social contract theory. Until we have come to terms with the importance of the social contract in American history and the significance of its possible demise, something essential will be missing from our accounts of the past and our comprehension of the ambiguities of the present. We need more than unreflective remembrances of things past; we need historical understanding in order to learn who we were and who we are.

ONE

■

Principles, Forms, Foundations

Social Contracts in Revolutionary America

From 1764 to 1776 the colonists in America recapitulated the history of social contract theory from Grotius to Pufendorf to Locke. During that brief, hectic period rebels borrowed one or another of the various theories of the social contract to debate fellow rebels; rebels did the same to challenge loyalists; and loyalists to call rebels to account.

Thomas Paine's astonishingly successful pamphlet of early 1776, *Common Sense,* offered a radical Lockean justification for its claim that the time had come to declare independence. Some Americans applauded Paine because he said what they had long thought, others because they were finally convinced that the time had come to move from a moderate to a radical position. As early as December 1765, at New London, Connecticut, the cry had gone up at a mass meeting for the colonists to reject the Stamp Act and "reassume their natural rights and the authority the laws of nature and of God have vested them with."[1] Other Patriots, by contrast, were reluctant rebels, and moved slowly "from resistance to rebellion," stopping at each step to invoke a pre-Lockean contract that sanctioned disobedience but not revolution.[2]

The Loyalists, for their part, may be the forgotten persons of American history, but not for want of intellectual acuity on their part. Two months after the appearance of Paine's pamphlet, the Loyalist "Candidus" published a formidable rebuttal exhorting British Americans to recognize the *Plain Truth*, that there was not an ounce of "common sense" to be found in Tom Paine's ravings. "Candidus" (possibly James Chalmers) and other Loyalists were very good at diverting attention from discussions of the social contract to safer matters; or at setting forth alternative, less lethal versions of the contract; or, when necessary, at raising doubts about the very notion of government by contract.

The social contract, its varieties and its critics, quit the quiet of the study and entered the tumult of public life during the dozen years leading up to the American Revolution. Theories of the social contract would not return to the study for many years thereafter.

THE LOYALISTS WERE WHIGS, NOT TORIES, and as such they could not deny the right of resistance or categorically reject all notions of a social contract. Their position contrasted with that of the notorious Tory Robert Filmer, who, Bible in hand, had uncompromisingly asserted a century earlier that "it is not possible for the wit of man to search out the first grounds or principles of government." Filmer's firm belief was that all theories of the social contract, not excepting that of the absolutist Thomas Hobbes, failed to safeguard political stability.[3] No Whig of any variety could feel comfortable saying the same.

The Loyalists in America were well versed in the pamphlet literature of that faction of the English Whigs who were political insiders throughout most of the eighteenth century: the parliamentary and court Whigs, Robert Walpole and his successors. Only Jonathan Boucher of Maryland denounced Locke and sided with Filmer. Not so Samuel Seabury, Thomas Hutchinson, Daniel Leonard, Joseph Galloway, or James Chalmers, among others. Their dedication to the ideology of court Whiggery was steadfast, and even in Boucher's case there are unmistakable signs of a court Whig, at heart, driven to despair by the revolutionary actions of his fellow colonists.[4]

Filmer was long irrelevant in eighteenth-century England, where political debates—to the limited extent that they existed—were between Whigs in and out of power, court and country Whigs, conservative and "real" Whigs. The Loyalists in America borrowed all the stratagems of the court Whigs in the mother country, beginning with the favorite device of changing the topic of conversation from the philosophical "principles" to the institutional "forms" of government. The Loyalists knew full well that the Patriots shared their fascination with the "form" of the English Constitution: its happy mixture of monarchical, aristocratic, and democratic elements that by common admission made England the freest nation on the face of the earth.

Rather than examine the problematical grounds of political obligation, the court Whigs and Loyalists sought to take advantage of the high esteem in which the English constitution was held in America and on the European Continent. Frequently they quoted Montesquieu's *The Spirit of the Laws* on the wonders of checks and balances in England, or they highlighted passages from Jean Louis Delolme's *The English Constitution,* which in the expurgated English translation contained none of the French edition's complaints about rotten boroughs and infrequent elections. How could anyone rebel against the most magnificent political achievement of all human history, the constitution of England?[5]

That court Whigs and their American Loyalist followers should ritualistically eulogize the English Constitution is only to be expected; what is remarkable is that the Patriot Stephen Hopkins of Rhode Island mimicked the Loyalists by speaking in 1764 of "this glorious [English] constitution, the best that ever existed among men."[6] Many other Patriots sprinkled their pamphlets with equally effusive comments about the English constitution, so powerful throughout the eighteenth century was the glowing image of England's political institutions.

To the bitter end, the colonists upheld the virtues of the English constitution, but they eventually learned how to turn the British model to their own advantage. No view was more popular among the rebellious Americans than John Adams's verdict, delivered a year prior to the break, that "we enjoy the British constitution in greater purity and perfection than they do in England," with its miserable placemen, pensioners, and corruption.[7]

The Loyalists needed intellectually formidable allies and found them in such major figures of the Scottish Enlightenment as David Hume and Adam Ferguson. The *Essays* of Hume were widely known and offered the Loyalists a respectable defense of patronage, whether wielded by Prime Minister Walpole earlier in the century or by George III, later. "We give to this influence what name we please," remarked Hume; "we may call it by the invidious appellations of *corruption* and *dependence;* but some degree and some kind of it are . . . necessary to the preservation of our mixed government." More ominously, Hume warned that a successful campaign to reform and eliminate so-called corruption "would introduce a total alteration in our government, and would reduce it to a pure republic."[8]

Loyalists in America rallied to Hume. Not only had he defended the honor of the British constitution at home; his writings could also be used to argue that the popular governments of Massachusetts and other colonies were seriously unbalanced and in need of stronger executive authority, a more aristocratic upper house, and a lower house cut down to size. The constitution was indeed in trouble—but in America, not in England. In their search for a conservative anchor, court Whigs and their Loyalist counterparts went so far as to contemplate the introduction of bishoprics in New England, land of dissenting, anti-establishment Protestantism.[9]

James Chalmers was one of the Loyalists who thanked Hume for pointing out that without royal influence "our Constitution would immediately degenerate into Democracy." The novelty of Chalmers's position was that in *Plain Truth* he went on to quote approvingly from Hume's "Of the Original Contract." This essay contained virtually every criticism of the theory of the social contract that would become common stock in nineteenth-century European thought: Governments, good and bad, usually have their origins in acts of violence; all governments would fall if judged in terms of whether the governed had granted their consent; promises are binding insofar as social union already exists but have nothing to do with the creation of social union; and political obligation existed under the absolutist government of France just as surely as under England's constitutional government. If other Loyalists had joined forces with Candidus in a concerted attack on the social contract, the American rebels would have met their match.[10]

By and large the Loyalists did not have the stomach to follow Hume and Candidus in rejecting social contract theory outright. One reason they hesitated was that as good court Whigs they had been raised to believe that evasion rather than repudiation was the preferable tactic. Not to speak about the social contract or the grounds of political obligation in the presence of the unwashed populace was the message they received from Sir William Blackstone, who wrote in his *Commentaries* (1765–1769), "It is well if the mass of mankind will obey the laws, when made, without scrutinizing too nicely into the reasons of making them."[11] A few years later Adam Ferguson sounded the same theme: "It is dangerous to enfeeble government by speculations, . . . [and] laudable to conceal from an unthinking multitude the source of government—the obedience due to authority ought never to be canvassed by the people."[12] Edmund Burke, throughout the American troubles, counseled his parliamentary colleagues to forget their rightful claims and speak solely about the practical consequences of any given policy. In 1780 he opened a speech with the statement that "it is always to be lamented when men are driven to search into the foundations of the commonwealth."[13] It is safe to conclude that the Loyalists could not directly attack the social contract without sinning against their English mentors.

In truth the Loyalists were caught in a painful dilemma. Except for Hume, court Whigs in England neither renounced the social contract nor embraced it because to renounce it was to be a Tory, whereas to embrace it was to be a radical Whig. In England the ensuing strategy of benign neglect met with considerable success, but not in the colonies, where the rebels forced the Loyalists to move beyond discussions of "forms" of government to debates over "principles." The absence of radical Whigs in England's Parliament shielded the court Whigs; the presence of radical Whigs in the American legislatures, and on the streets, forced Loyalists to climb the precarious ladder of abstraction.

Samuel Seabury of New York is an excellent example. In common with other Loyalists, he began with a repetition of Blackstone's affirmation of parliamentary sovereignty and then drew out the consequences for the colonists—that they must answer to Parliament even when it acted unwisely and seek remedies within the established constitutional structure, not in the streets.[14] Before long, however, the American context caught up with him and he found himself shouting to his fellow British Americans about "principles" in a most un-court-like fashion: "You must obtain a knowledge of the first principles, at least, of civil government; from *them* you must deduce your reasonings; to *them* you must conform your conduct." In defiance of the unseemly words emanating from the Continental Congress, Seabury was forced to speak a language unfamiliar to court Whigs. "My business," he explained, "is to detect and expose the false, arbitrary, and tyrannical PRINCIPLES upon which the Congress acted."[15]

The day of ignoring principles was gone. Little by little, Seabury felt obliged to replace false principles with true. The same may be said of Thomas Hutchinson of Massachusetts, whose contempt for the "loose principles" of the rebels obliged him to speak about correct principles and reasonable inferences from principles.[16] To meet their needs the Loyalists had to avail themselves of the principles of the social contract, but in their case the appeal would be to the pre-Lockean and conservative contracts of Hugo Grotius and Samuel Pufendorf. Admired by absolutists on the Continent, in England Grotius and Pufendorf were successfully transformed by the Whigs into champions of the constitutional settlement of 1688.

Both Grotius in his *The Law of War and Peace* (1625) and Pufendorf in his *The Law of Nature and Nations* (1672) sought to end the wars of religion and establish a new basis of political order by turning away from ambiguous biblical texts to the pure light of nature. These enormously influential theorists of the social contract emphasized human nature, including the human will, which over time had called into being different governments in various nations.[17] Desiring peace and stability, individual humans had frequently agreed to alienate their rights to other persons; entire peoples had likewise agreed to alienate their rights to the existing governmental authority.[18] Grotius explained that "as a general rule rebellion is not permitted by the law of nature."[19] There is no basis, he held, for the view that a king, having violated his trust, may be removed.[20] Pufendorf concurred: "Those persons are not to be endured who assert . . . that a King, when he degenerates into a tyrant, may be deprived of his crown, and brought to punishment by his people."[21] Right is on the side of the constituted authority, not the "constituent authority," Grotius argued, except in those rare cases where the people stipulated otherwise when signing what Pufendorf later called "the original contract."[22]

The triumphal Whigs of the Glorious Revolution sensed that they had everything to gain and nothing to lose in siding with Grotius.[23] Was England not this exception of which he had spoken, a singular land blessed with an original contract holding royalty in check? Against the more radically minded in their ranks, the Grotian Whigs of 1688 successfully contended that the way to avoid bloodshed and buy off the Tories was to invoke the conservative contract of Grotius. Jean-Jacques Rousseau later famously complained that Grotius simply rationalized any and every status quo, adding "ought" to "is."[24] To the Whigs, however, that was Grotius's great virtue because English history, in their view, was a record of the triumph through the ages of the constitutional government they cherished. From a Grotian standpoint, Whiggish limited government should obviously continue in England because it had always been. Residues of Grotius may still be found in Bishop William Warburton's popular essays of the mid-eighteenth century, marked by the theme that whatever is is right, and in Adam Ferguson's comment in 1776 that "we must take the world as it goes."[25]

All the great disruptions of English history, especially the Puritan Revolution, were conveniently forgotten by the Whigs. James II, they announced, had "abdicated" the throne. The myth of historical continuity was successfully launched, and the familiar Whig story of the steady, non-revolutionary unfolding of English liberty emerged victorious in 1688. The social contract survived, but only as metaphor or as a completed episode, admitting no sequel.

Samuel Seabury spoke as a disciple of Grotius when he proclaimed to the rebels that "every person owes obedience to the laws of the government under which he lives, . . . because, if *one* has a right to disregard the laws . . . , *all* have the *same* right; and *then* government is at an end." Much as he admired the settlement of 1688, Seabury wanted never again to risk established liberties in an effort to remove an objectionable monarch. The time for overt acts of consent was long past, he added.[26]

Neither Seabury nor Hutchinson denied the reality of natural rights, but both, in the manner of Grotius and Pufendorf, minimized their contemporary significance.[27] All government entails the "abridgement" of natural rights, said Hutchinson; otherwise the contract turns into a "rope of sand." Our existing laws, moreover, postdate the contract and address new concerns; to ask that laws be measured against the beginning is inevitably to destroy even the mildest government.[28] Seabury made the same argument by conjuring up a picture of rebellion, economic collapse, unemployment, robbers, highwaymen, and political anarchy: "We should then taste the sweets of *natural* liberty, and see the *natural* rights of mankind exemplified in dreadful instances."[29]

Another strategy employed by the Loyalists was to borrow Pufendorf's notion that the contract of "association" (the social contract) was followed by a second contract of "submission" to the newly constituted government (the political contract).[30] Loyalists found Pufendorf's argument to their liking because they could have their contract and yet nullify its radical implications. Hutchinson echoed Pufendorf in holding that, after the final contract is signed, we are no longer permitted to decide what is and is not ours by natural right.[31] Joseph Galloway, in a pamphlet of 1775, condemned the "untenable principles" of the rebels, lauded "the learned Pufendorf," affirmed that "in the constitution of all societies two covenants are essential," and concluded that "men . . . surrender up their natural rights [when they] enter into society."[32]

Locke's name came to mean so much in the years immediately preceding the Revolution that the Loyalists sometimes plotted to steal the *Second Treatise* from the rebels. A favorite tactic was to fail to understand that Locke had rejected Pufendorf's contract of submission. Another ploy was to confuse Locke's words about the legislature as the supreme power in the government with Blackstone's doctrine of parliamentary sovereignty.[33] In truth, of course, Locke's position was that the people can remove the legislative power, for government is held as a revocable trust rather than an irreversible contract of submission.[34]

One can hardly blame the Loyalists for wrongly appropriating Locke since their hero Blackstone had been guilty of the same offense. It was from Blackstone that the Loyalists derived their theme of parliamentary sovereignty, and perhaps from Blackstone, again, their misleading account of Locke. Certainly Blackstone was willing to compliment Locke whenever he could do so without potentially stirring up the spirit of rebellion: "As Mr. Locke has well observed, where there is no law, there is no freedom." But when Blackstone addressed the state of nature he expressed his concerns by citing Pufendorf. His discussion of property as based on occupancy and contractual agreement is also borrowed from Pufendorf and is at odds with Locke's notion of mixing one's labor with the land. In his polite and eclectic manner Blackstone praised Locke while gently chiding him for carrying "his theory too far." Even if there is something to be said for Locke's theory, "we cannot adopt it, nor argue from it, under any dispensation of government at present actually existing."[35] Blackstone absorbed Locke into conservative Whiggery, and the American Loyalists, pressed on all fronts by rebel Lockeans, followed his example and amplified it to meet the challenge they faced.

The Loyalists, in sum, discovering that they could not escape from the theory of the social contract, tried valiantly to make the most of it for their cause. Despite occasional misleading efforts to take advantage of Locke's name, theirs was the social contract of Grotius and Pufendorf. Samuel Seabury, frightened by the street politics of the rebels, concluded that "the *tyranny* of a mob is the *freedom* of America."[36] A century earlier his forebear Pufendorf warned that "the multitude act not by rational motives" and will never understand the complexity of governmental affairs.[37] Loyalists seconded Pufendorf, who maintained that the contract of association begins with the people but soon yields, necessarily and properly, to the contract of submission that places public life beyond their reach.

IT IS TEMPTING BUT MISLEADING TO SAY that whereas the Loyalists enlisted the assistance of Pufendorf, the Patriots adopted Locke. No doubt *Common Sense* and the Declaration of Independence do avail themselves of Locke's justification of revolution. But it is important to realize that as the Patriots slowly progressed from resistance to revolution, they made frequent use, explicitly and implicitly, of Pufendorf's theory of the social contract.

Pufendorf's text was sufficiently ambiguous for many Whig pamphleteers to exploit it in 1688, no matter that it had long served German princes as a justification of royal absolutism. American Patriots likewise found Pufendorf to their liking when the time came in 1765 to start thinking about political principles that justified disobedience. Against his will the absolutist Pufendorf became a Whig, first in England and then in America, where Patriots competed with Loyalists to claim his authority.

For this ironic outcome Pufendorf had only his own inconsistencies to blame. Although preoccupied with order, he sounded on occasion like a Whig who wanted to combine order with freedom: "By the submission of their wills, made on the part of the subjects, their *natural* liberty of choice is not extinguished," he wrote; "they are still able, *de facto*, to resume what they once gave, and to deny and withdraw their obedience which they promised." At times Pufendorf also spoke of a "reciprocal promise" between sovereign and subjects.[38]

Pufendorf, indeed, was far more useful to the Whigs of 1688 than Locke, whose fate was to win each philosophical battle with Pufendorf but to lose the war for influence in England's public affairs. Locke had deliberately eliminated both Pufendorf's contract of submission and his original contract: the former because of its absolutist meaning, the latter because of its implication that the consent of the people was a thing of the past. Many Whigs in 1688, afraid of the potentially radical thrust of Locke, preferred to accuse James II of breaking the "original contract." Throughout the eighteenth century Whigs continued to speak approvingly about an original contract, secured in 1688.

English Whigs were equally enamored of the double contract, redefined to meet their needs. In Whig thought the second contract of Pufendorf's scheme, the contract of government, conferred a permanent obligation on the rulers as well as on the ruled. No king could ever again overstep the bounds, as James II had, because Parliament would rightfully stop him from transgressing. The double contract, despite its past association with monarchical absolutism, had become a doctrine of parliamentary sovereignty. The contract between governors and governed ruled out divine right on one side and the dangers of popular sovereignty on the other. With the help of Pufendorf, the Whigs secured their cause without risking revolution.[39]

By the early eighteenth century Pufendorf had made a decisive American appearance in John Wise's "A Vindication of the Government of New England Churches" (1717). "I shall Principally take Baron *Puffendorff* for my Chief Guide and Spokesman," he informed his audience, and then proceeded to offer a sophisticated application of arguments drawn from *The Law of Nature and Nations*. Pastor of a church in Ipswich, he nevertheless held that "Civil Government in General . . . must needs be acknowledged to be the Effect of Humane Free-Compacts and not of Divine Institution."[40] The state of nature that figured for little in Grotius was written large in Pufendorf—and in Wise. If there is a difference between the German and the British American, it is that for Pufendorf's portrait of a distressing state of nature, Wise substituted an account that featured free and equal men, fair-minded in their relations with one another and determined to enter into contractual union without sacrificing all their original freedom.

Hobbes, in Pufendorf's view, overstated our natural asociability, but Aristotle had gone to the opposite extreme when he declared that we are by nature political beings: in truth, without the fear of punishment, most of us would be a threat to our fellows.[41] Not so the natural persons of Wise, whose "self-love" was more than offset by a "sociable disposition" and "love to Mankind." Although Wise retained Pufendorf's second contract, the governing authorities were thereby put on notice that they must dutifully serve the governed or face the consequences.[42] These arguments, set forth by Wise during an early-eighteenth-century debate between Congregationalists and Presbyterians, were no less relevant to later quarrels with England.

If the colonists could imbibe Pufendorf from the sermons of their religious ministers, they could do the same from political treatises imported from England. Lord Bolinbroke's writings, appreciated both by Adams and Jefferson, loved by North and South, were one of the many English sources from which the colonists learned to apply Pufendorf to their political quarrels with the mother country. "The prince and the people take, in effect, a sort of engagement with one another; the prince to govern well, and the people to honor and obey him," wrote Bolingbroke in a pamphlet of 1749. He further Anglicized Pufendorf by conceding, somewhat reluctantly, that "by the principles of the [Glorious] Revolution, a subject may resist, no doubt, the prince who endeavours to ruin and enslave his people."[43] What made Bolingbroke all the more attractive to the colonists was that—a frustrated political outsider—he constantly harped upon the theme of the corruption of the once grand British constitution. Taken to the extreme, his analysis might vindicate their ultimate rebellion; taken in moderation, his English version of Pufendorf surely justified their many prior acts of resistance.

Quick to assert their natural rights but slow to accept Locke's potentially radical doctrine, the colonists found ample use for the middling views of Pufendorf in his English guise. In their protests of 1765 Connecticut's Sons of Liberty sounded like Locke's offspring, but at the last moment they withdrew to the safer position that "it is the duty of every Person in the Colonies to oppose [the Stamp Act] by every *lawful means*."[44] Because Saturday and Sunday nights were holy, Boston's orderly rioters refrained from resisting on those evenings.[45] Pufendorf had placed his bets on the rulers, and so in their fashion did the colonists when they interpreted their rioting as proof of the failure of the constituted authorities to govern adequately. Resistance in America was originally not a call for an overthrow of government, not a proclamation of the sovereignty of the people, but a simple request for the rulers to return to their senses.

Pufendorf might have tolerated such modest resistance, as might Francis Hutcheson, major figure of the Scottish Enlightenment, well known to the colonists both for his Whiggish version of the two-contracts theory and his willingness to sanction limited resistance. Citations of Hutcheson's writings of the 1730s were dear to the colonists in the earlier phase of their rebellion, despite the Scotsman's un-Lockean claim that when an individual chose civil society over the state of nature, he did so "not only for himself but for his posterity . . . [who] are bound therefore, whether they consent or not."[46] Resistance but not revolution was what the colonists originally had in mind, so they chose to pursue their goals through Whiggish adaptations of Pufendorf.

For so long as the colonists conceded the sovereignty of Parliament, for so long as they looked for ways to limit the reach of Parliament rather than to demand full autonomy, for so long as they petitioned Parliament to regulate trade but not to levy taxes, and for so long as they cited chartered contracts negotiated with a king long ago, they could not graduate from Pufendorf to Locke. But when the colonists finally started giving serious thought to independence rather than resistance, their pamphlets discussing imperial rule and parliamentary sovereignty gave way to the new language of inalienable popular sovereignty and inalienable rights.

Samuel Adams, agitator extraordinaire, released a pamphlet in 1772 that was an almost perfect recapitulation of *The Second Treatise of Government*. Unlike Pufendorf but in keeping with Locke, Adams argued that "it is not in the power of Man to alienate this gift [of freedom], and voluntarily become a slave."[47] Life, liberty, and property are ours by natural right, and remain ours in perpetuity after we have signed the social contract.

Locke's social contract had at last truly arrived in America in the pamphlets of resisters transformed into revolutionaries. No longer British Americans, the former colonists were ready for Paine's *Common Sense* and Jefferson's Declaration of Independence.

"Revolution Principles" and Forms of Government

When Benjamin Franklin remarked in 1773 that Americans were "zealous whigs, friends of liberty, nurtured in revolution principles," his historical reference was to 1688.[48] Before 1776 Americans always meant the Glorious Revolution when speaking of "revolution principles"; after 1776 they invariably meant their own revolution.

Prior to 1776, whenever American writers discussed "forms" of government, they inevitably worshipped at the shrine of the historically sanctioned British Constitution; after 1776 their concern was with whatever forms of government the American people, exercising their bold new "revolution principles," chose to institute by acts of human will. The English and Americans, having parted company at the point of a gun, could agree on one thing at least: that for better or for worse the year 1776 was no mere repeat of 1688.

Adam Ferguson convinced himself in 1776, as Burke would in 1789, that the outbreak of revolution in the eighteenth century signified a "second civil war," a return to the worst days of the Puritan Revolution, that "period so full of horror" that we should "not call [it] to recollection."[49] Ferguson's ill-tempered pamphlet of 1776, titled *Remarks on Dr. Price's Observations on the Nature of Civil Liberty,* underscores the great divide of political culture that crystallized in 1776 between America and Great

Britain, two nations henceforth separated by a common language spoken in sharply contrasting ideological accents. To Ferguson, the triumph in America of Locke's radical social contract was a disaster, although the far greater potential disaster was that his fellow Englishman Richard Price—dissenting minister; political outsider; radical Whig; friend of Jefferson, Franklin, and Adams—was advocating the American cause in the mother country and applying its principles to England.[50]

Recording Ferguson's disgust with America's "revolution principles" is a promising way to display the profound importance of 1776. "Nothing but sedition, and the worst of principles, could prompt the Americans to so destructive a rebellion," he believed. Time and again Ferguson denounced America's "miserable principles," its "destructive principles," its "seditious principles." Nor did he refrain from concluding that "the iron hand of war must root out principles so dangerous, so destructive to the peace of mankind."[51]

Ferguson's tirade against Price and the Americans moved on to its climax. America, he continued, must be "taught that her riotous seditions will not pass unpunished." "Rather let their towns be desolated," "rather let [Americans] be impoverished," than permit them to continue sinning against the cherished English constitution and empire. "To such a people, the sword only can teach a sense of duty."[52] Drive them inland, he advised, away from their cities, and there they would experience not the yeoman arcadia and golden age of Price's dreams—and theirs—but a dreary backwoods and backward society.[53]

The seeds of Ferguson's outrage may be traced back to his most famous work, *An Essay on the History of Civil Society* (1767). In the opening pages Ferguson attacked the notion of a state of nature to prepare the reader for his view that humans must be understood as they are found in recorded history. Against Rousseau's conjecture that humans had once been animals, perhaps related to the orangutan, Ferguson dogmatically postulated that "when [the natural historian] treats of any particular species of animals, he supposes that their present dispositions and instincts are the same as they originally had."[54] Rousseau's ultimate objective in searching for the man of nature was to show the high price we pay for "progress"; Ferguson's was to applaud the move from hunting to pastoral to commercial society. The general point of Rousseau's system was, in a reversal of Grotius, "to test the facts by right."[55] Ferguson, by contrast, like Grotius, frequently simply added "ought" to "is." When the Americans began talking, as Rousseau had, about popular sovereignty, natural rights, and the social contract, Ferguson feared for civilization itself.

From historical hindsight, Ferguson's pamphlet of 1776 perfectly prefigures Burke's *Reflections on the Revolution in France*. Ferguson passionately condemned Price's *Observations on the Nature of Civil Liberty, the Principles of Government, and the Justice and Policy of the War with America* (1776); Burke lambasted Price's *A Discourse on the Love of Our Country* (1789). Both polemicists use Rousseau as a bogeyman, and both express horror that Price advocated popular sovereignty—the right of the people to choose their own governors, to "cashier" them for misconduct, and to frame a government for themselves. Everything Burke argued against the French Revolution had been previously argued, in outline at least, by Ferguson against the American Revolution.

If Burke warned from day one that the French Revolution was evil incarnate, that was because, as the example of Ferguson proves, he and many other Whigs were preconditioned to be ready, willing, and able to turn quickly into ardent counterrevolutionaries (the new Tories) the moment they were faced with the doctrines of popular sovereignty, natural rights, and social contract. It is doubtful whether the traveler Arthur Young's firsthand revelations of the oppression of the French people under the Old Regime, had they been available in 1789, would have tempered Burke's strident rhetoric.[56] His overriding concern was the same as Ferguson's: to prevent revolutionary "principles" from gaining respectability in England.[57]

America's "principles" of revolution were eventually forgotten in England, but only because the English government became preoccupied with a far more dangerous revolutionary foe: France. The citizens of the new republic of America, unlike the people of England, took their time before giving up on the French Revolution, waiting until 1795 or thereabouts to abandon hope; and even then they did not stop speaking proudly about their own "revolution principles."[58]

It is a matter of striking symbolic significance that the Americans offered citizenship to two great dissenting radical English Whigs, Richard Price and Joseph Priestley, the former upbraided by Ferguson and then by Burke, the latter forced to accept the American invitation when his house was burned during the French Revolution. Recent immigrant Tom Paine, author of *Common Sense*, was the man of the hour in revolutionary America, but when he returned to England and published *Rights of Man* at the outset of the French Revolution, he was forced to choose between leaving the country or going to jail. Radical Whiggery and revolutionary principles, treated as alien presences and harshly suppressed in England, were welcomed in America, their natural home.[59]

AMERICANS LOVED TO TALK ABOUT THE "principles" of government and usually drew a clear line separating them from "forms." Benjamin Rush in 1777 stated a commonly held view: "It is one thing to understand the *principles,* and another thing to understand the *forms* of government. The former are simple; the latter are difficult and complicated. . . . Mr. Locke is an oracle as to the *principles,* Harrington and Montesquieu are oracles as to the *forms* of government."[60]

Locke himself had sketched the path of reasoning the Americans would follow: "Politics," he wrote, "contains parts very different the one from the other, the one containing the original of societies and the rise and extent of political power, the other, the art of governing men in society." *Two Treatises of Government,* he added, belonged in the first category.[61]

From the first days of the conflict with England, the colonials spoke about the distinction between, and the interrelationship of, principles and forms of government. James Otis in 1764, in *The Rights of the British Colonies Asserted and Proved,* cited Locke for principles, James Harrington for forms. "The incomparable Harrington" offered a rich discussion of political institutions and their relationship to property—of what is "true in fact and *experience,*" but not of what is *right.* For the latter we must consult the theorists of natural right, Otis explained. Not Grotius or Pufendorf, however: "It is their constant practice to establish the matter of right on the matter of *fact:* this the celebrated *Rousseau* expressly says of Grotius." For advice on "the natural rights of colonists" Otis turned to Locke and thus to the principle that sovereign power lies "*originally* and *ultimately* in the people." Otis may have been too timid to ask anything more of Parliament than seats for a few Americans, but in his theoretical discussion he does not shy away from the conclusion that "the form of government is by *nature* and by *right* . . . left to the *individuals* of each society."[62]

The distinction between principles and forms was, in some ways, the same as that between theory and practice. Certainly Blackstone accepted that formulation, and so did the Americans, but with a difference. Blackstone was not unwilling to concede that Locke might have been correct in principle when he wrote that the people have the right to remove the current government; in practice, however, the idea was an absurdity.[63] John Adams ("Novanglus"), speaking of "revolution principles" in 1775, would have none of this, neither from the pen of Blackstone himself nor from that of his Loyalist stalking horse, Daniel Leonard ("Massachusettensis"): "How [revolution principles] can be in general true, and not applicable to particular cases, I cannot apprehend," wrote Adams on the eve of the Revolution.[64] After the Revolution and Founding, Jefferson set forth what might be called a standard American formulation: Locke's *Two Treatises* should be read for theory, the *Federalist* for practice.[65]

Even as the Americans became preoccupied after the Revolution with creating new forms of government, they never lost sight of the primacy of principles. "I am not disposed to unreasonably contend about forms," Richard Henry Lee wrote in 1787, at the very moment that his countrymen were preoccupied with the "form" of the new federal constitution; all would be well if "deliberate and thinking men" made it their duty to "establish and secure governments on free principles."[66] Later, despite a new focus on sectional conflict, John Taylor of Virginia in 1820 made known his opinion that "to fight for forms only, is to fight for shadows."[67]

When the Americans placed principles above forms, they ranked their education in Grotius and Locke above their classical education. In the modern world of the social contract, Plato's and Aristotle's famous discussions of the best form of government were no longer the primary concern of political theorists; instead, the leading question was whether the government was legitimate. "A people can select the form of government which it pleases," Grotius had written, "and the extent of its legal right in the matter is not to be measured by the superior excellence of this or that form of government, in regard to which different men hold different views, but by its free choice."[68] By the time we reach Locke, the proper question for a social contract theorist to ask had unambiguously become one of legitimacy: whether the people willed the government into existence and whether they continued to grant it their consent.

Otis in 1764 was a transitional figure insofar as he still assumed there was one best form while admitting that we might never reach agreement on its definition.[69] England's radical Whigs, in this matter as in others, were ahead of the Americans: "My intention," Richard Price explained in a typical statement, "has been merely to shew what is requisite to constitute a state or a government free, and not at all to define the best form of government."[70] Eventually the Americans caught up with their radical English brethren: the social contract, in its constructive phase after 1776, allowed the sovereign people of the various states to make different but equally legitimate choices about forms of government.

Still, the Americans did take their forms of government seriously because without a workable form their all-important principles would come to nothing. In their discussions of forms of government the Americans were arguably more thoughtful and realistic than the radical Whigs of England. Price and Priestley were so preoccupied with principles that they either expressed indifference to forms or ritualistically and unreflectively genuflected to England's mixed government.[71]

John Adams, on the American side, by contrast, spent a lifetime thinking about forms of government. "It is the form of Government which gives the decisive Colour to the Manners of the People," Adams told Mercy Warren two days before the appearance of *Common Sense*.[72] Immediately after reading Paine's pamphlet, Adams responded with his unforgiving *Thoughts on Government*. Instead of combining "simple" principles with "complex" forms, as was essential for stability, the rabble-rousing Paine, Adams lamented, had unconscionably called for simple forms to contrast with England's complex political structure.[73] Adams hastened to make the case, against Paine and Pennsylvania, for a bicameral rather than a unicameral legislature and for a strong executive armed with a veto.[74] Other Americans, obliged to create new state governments after 1776 and a new federal government in 1787, had no choice but to engage in a prolonged discussion of forms of government.

Yet, no matter how much emphasis the Americans placed on forms, they understood full well that whatever institutional structure they chose had no validity unless enacted by the sovereign people in accordance with "revolution principles." Slowly but surely they felt their way to the devices of special conventions and popular ratifications by which the constituent power of the people called into being new constitutions. From 1776 to 1777 eleven new state constitutions were written, but only two hailed from conventions rather than legislatures, and none were passed on to the voters for ratification. A turning point came in 1780 with the Massachusetts constitution, the first based on both convention and popular ratification. By the time the delegates met in Philadelphia to debate a federal constitution, they could draw upon a wealth of learning at the level of state government.

Europeans gazed in wonder as the Americans, by constitutional convention and popular ratification, put Locke's social contract into practice.

Consent, assumed and passive in England, was active and meaningful in America. The people were sovereign before the contract and continued to be so afterward. Government, instituted to protect rights, was to be held as a revocable trust; anything like parliamentary sovereignty was out of the question. Not since the Levellers had the world seen anything like this, and that chapter of English history had been effectively erased from memory by good Whigs. Well might the Americans boast of having introduced a new order of the ages, a *novus ordo seclorum*.[75]

The dispute between Federalists and Antifederalists was over which side was truer to the "principles" of the Revolution. How far America had moved from the mainstream conservative Whiggery of England was particularly evident when a Pennsylvania Antifederalist, upholding the right of the people of each state to suggest amendments to the proposed constitution, called himself "an Old Whig"—revealing that new Whiggery in America was, remarkably, already old. "No man, reasoning upon *revolution* principles, can possibly controvert this right," he contended, not when the revolution in question was that of 1776 rather than the far less revolutionary event of 1688.[76]

The Federalists also claimed "revolution principles"—in the first place to justify overruling the Articles of Confederation, in the second to defend themselves against the charge that their proposed national government was a return to the English model, and in the third to confer legitimacy upon the new federal constitution.

Faced with the problem that only by unanimous decision of the states could the Articles of Confederation be amended, Alexander Hamilton and James Wilson overcame the doubts of their fellow delegates at Philadelphia by explicitly calling upon revolutionary "principles." Legalistic scruples making change impossible could be cast aside if the members of the Constitutional Convention acted on the premise that they were the agents of the sovereign people. No human law, in Locke's world, is above the people.[77]

James Wilson's speech to the ratifying convention of Pennsylvania is an excellent example of how the Federalists countered the charge that they were, in effect if not in intent, advocating the creation on American soil of a British-style constitution. The similarities were superficial, Wilson argued, considering that in England only the House of Commons was representative; America alone enjoyed "the glory and the happiness of diffusing this vital principle [of representation] through all the constituent parts of government." Wilson went on to ask, "What is the nature and kind of that gov-

CHAPTER ONE

ernment, which has been proposed for the United States, by the late convention?" His answer was that "in its principle, it is purely democratical; but that principle is applied in different forms, in order to obtain the advantages, and exclude the disadvantages of the simple modes of government."

Most of all, Wilson explained, it was the question of sovereignty that differentiated the American from the English constitution. "The idea of a constitution, limiting and superintending the operations of legislative authority, seems not to have been accurately understood in Britain. . . . The British constitution is just what the British parliament pleases." America offered a contrasting and superior model: "To control the power and conduct of the legislature by an overruling constitution, was an improvement in the science and practice of government reserved to the American States. . . . In our governments, the supreme, absolute, and uncontrollable power remains in the people. As our constitutions are superiour to our legislatures; so the people are superiour to our constitutions. . . . The consequence is, that the people may change the constitutions whenever and however they please." The new federal constitution was anything but a copy of the English constitution; it was the fulfillment, not the betrayal, of 1776.[78]

Revolutionary "principles" were also of vital importance to the Federalists when they searched for a way to legitimize their bold new constitutional proposal. Arriving in Philadelphia, the delegates were more than a little skeptical about the conduct of the people in the state governments over the past several years: the repudiation of debts, Shays's Rebellion, the uprisings of countryside against cities. Gouverneur Morris and James Madison were among the founders who feared that established property rights were in danger of being overturned by an unruly mob. But as they left Philadelphia, the same actors realized that taking their scheme to the people for ratification was the way both to succeed and to be true to their own earlier philosophy of government. And so we find Madison in the *Federalist* pleading for the new constitution in the name of popular sovereignty: "The federal and State governments are in fact but different agents and trustees of the people. . . . The adversaries of the Constitution seem to have lost sight of the people. . . . They must be told that the ultimate authority resides in the people alone."[79]

Alexander Hamilton, also in the *Federalist*, appealed directly to the public in the name of popular sovereignty: "It has not a little contributed to the infirmities of the existing federal system [the Articles of Confederation] that it never had a ratification by the PEOPLE. Resting on no better foundation than the consent of the several legislatures, it has been exposed to frequent and intricate questions concerning the validity of its powers." "The fabric of American empire," Hamilton urged, "ought to rest on the solid basis of THE CONSENT OF THE PEOPLE."[80]

Anyone familiar with his writings of the revolutionary period had no reason to doubt that Hamilton was a sincere devotee of the theory of the social contract: "The fundamental source of all your errors, sophisms and false reasonings," he had written in response to Loyalist Samuel Seabury, "is a total ignorance of the natural rights of mankind."[81] No matter how sympathetic Hamilton had become in the intervening years to the effectiveness of British-style government, he remained a good Lockean in 1787 and could therefore legitimately claim ratification and popular sovereignty for the Federalists.

Hamilton realized, as did Madison, that a political scheme that stressed the natural rights of individuals was excellent for enhancing the powers of the central government. Much as French revolutionary intellectuals would soon use natural rights arguments to strike down the corporate bodies of feudalism, the Federalists before them pursued a parallel strategy to diminish the powers of the states. "The great and radical vice in the construction of the existing confederation is in the principle of legislation for states . . . in their corporate or collective capacities, and as contradistinguished from the individuals of whom they consist," wrote Hamilton. The new constitution "must stand in need of no intermediate legislations." Hamilton and Madison agreed that "a legislation for communities, as contradistinguished for individuals . . . , is subversive of the order and ends of civil polity."[82]

Locke was a favorite of Federalists, Pufendorf of Antifederalists. "I would recommend to your perusal, Grotius, Puffendorf, Locke," wrote a young Alexander Hamilton. He then proceeded to make such a strong argument for "the sacred rights of mankind" that it soon became clear that Locke was his primary inspiration.[83] One might say of his Antifederalist opponents that although they, too, had gone to school with both Pufendorf and Locke, the difference was that they took the German theorist much more seriously. Whereas Federalists upheld Locke's view that there was no second contract between the rulers and the ruled, the Antifederalists sometimes restored Pufendorf's argument. "A constitution is a compact of a people with their rulers," wrote "Brutus" of New York. "Federal Farmer," similarly, opined that "the bills of rights and the state constitutions are fundamental compacts . . . between those who govern and the people of the same state." "In the year 1788," he added, "the people of the United States make a federal constitution, which is a fundamental compact between them and their federal rulers."[84] Years spent before the Revolution talking about royal charters of colonists with king made it difficult to relinquish overnight the notion of a contract between rulers and ruled.[85]

Less cosmopolitan than the Federalists and more wary of innovation, some Antifederalists probably clung to Pufendorf in his guise as an English Whig precisely because that particular political orientation had stood the test of time. A Maryland Antifederalist, for instance, was quite certain that "there is nothing solid or useful that is new." Patrick Henry complained that "this [proposed] government is so new that it wants a name."[86]

And yet, when all was said and done, the backward-looking Antifederalists did win a major victory with the passage of the Bill of Rights, the first ten amendments to the federal Constitution. While their notion of a contract between rulers and ruled lost out at the constitutional convention to Locke's single contract and government as a trust, they succeeded shortly thereafter in establishing what was in certain respects an American variation on the English Bill of Rights (1689). In response to Federalists who used notions of popular sovereignty and a focus on individuals to diminish the powers of the states, the Antifederalists countered with the Bill of Rights to protect the states from federal intervention.

Although Federalists such as James Madison eventually thought it politic to concede the Bill of Rights, they had trouble understanding how it fit into the new world they had called into being. A bill of rights, they thought, was appropriate for a country ruled by an overbearing king, or a country where the dominant belief was that a contract existed between ruler and ruled. One Federalist remarked, "Here liberty originated with the people. Why then should the people by a bill of rights convey or grant to *themselves* what was their own inherent and natural right?" Benjamin Rush found it "absurd" to suggest that "our natural rights . . . are the gift of those rulers whom we have created." Alexander Hamilton thought that anyone anxious for a bill of rights might do well to realize "that the Constitution is itself . . . A BILL OF RIGHTS," but of the newest kind, not a grant from the rulers but a recognition of what the sovereign people owed itself.[87]

What was the significance of the Bill of Rights of 1791? Looked at from one angle, it appeared to be a return to Pufendorf's second contract between rulers and ruled; a return also to the English tradition of rights reluctantly conceded by the rulers to the ruled in the Magna Carta, the Petition of Right of 1628, and the Bill of Rights of 1689. But looked at from another angle, the American Bill of Rights was far more than a return to the past—was itself, indeed, an institutionalization of the new "revolution principles" because the bold principle of popular sovereignty was implied in the ninth amendment: "The enumeration in the Constitution, of certain rights, shall not be construed to deny or disparage others retained by the people." Whereas the English "people" of Whiggish imagination had safeguarded certain rights by alienating others, the American "people" alienated none of their rights when specifically safeguarding several.

Federalists and Antifederalists, as time would tell, shared enough common ground to give the new political structure a good chance to survive. Devotion to the "principles" of the Revolution was the underlying common denominator. On inalienable natural rights and the sovereignty of the people, all were in agreement.

Principles and Foundations

Reluctant revolutionaries but revolutionaries nonetheless, the Americans often commenced with traditional conceptions and then transformed the old ideas into something new and remarkable. Long before the Americans began to dwell on "principles" of government, Niccolò Machiavelli had done so in his *Discourses on Livy* and Montesquieu in *The Spirit of the Laws*. Similarly, the ancient Roman historians and their neoclassical admirers had addressed the topic of "foundations" well in advance of the American "founders." The Americans were well versed in their Plutarch, Livy, Machiavelli, and Montesquieu and drew freely upon their famous writings, borrowing at will their words and images. Hamilton and Madison in the *Federalist,* for instance, assumed the moniker "Publius," the Roman who with Lucius Brutus had expelled Tarquin and founded the Roman republic. But by the time the Americans were done, they had transformed the political vocabulary by forcing the old words "principles" and "foundations" into the novel mold of "revolution principles."

Whatever allusions to texts and authors we find in John Dickinson's *Letters from a Farmer in Pennsylvania* were probably well known to his contemporaries because his pamphlet of 1767 was the most frequently read of any American publication that appeared prior to Paine's *Common*

Sense. One writer on whom Dickinson briefly commented was the famous and infamous author of the *Discourses on Livy.* Dickinson tipped his hat courteously to Machiavelli's call for a periodic *ritorno ai principii,* a return to and renewal of the first principles of government: "*Machiavel* employs a whole chapter in his discourses, to prove that a state, to be long lived, must be frequently corrected, and reduced to its first principles."[88] Neither Dickinson, however, nor anyone else during the years before and after 1776 took Machiavelli at his word. Americans had their own ideas, derived from the theory of the social contract, about political principles, their establishment, and their renewal. To play a part in American thought, Machiavelli would have to adapt to the Americans, not they to him.

James Wilson of Pennsylvania availed himself in 1774 of Machiavelli's phraseology, but his purpose was to argue for a Lockean conception of government. True enough, Wilson spoke in favor of a constitution that would be "frequently renewed, and drawn back, as it were, to its first principles." Unlike Machiavelli's, however, the principles in question were those of "natural rights" and the axiom that "all power is derived from the people." Wilson further proclaimed that "all men are, by nature, equal and free: no one has a right to any authority over another without his consent." Machiavelli's quotable "return to principles" had been appropriated by Wilson for the philosophy of Locke.[89]

Exactly the same may be said of the Virginia Bill of Rights of 1776. Toward the end of the document, in article 15, we read "that no free government . . . can be preserved . . . but by . . . frequent recurrence to fundamental principles." For a moment we seem to have encountered Machiavelli, but the preceding fourteen articles make it abundantly clear that the principles in question are Locke's revolutionary principles. Article 1 tells us that "all men are by nature equally free and independent and have certain inherent rights, of which, when they enter a state of society, they cannot by any compact deprive or divest their posterity"; article 2, that "all power is . . . derived from the people; that magistrates are their trustees and servants"; article 3, that the people have an "unalienable and indefeasible right to reform or abolish" the government.[90] Machiavelli yields constantly to Locke.

No doubt the Americans of the Revolution and early republic welcomed Machiavelli's endorsement of citizens' militias over professional armies. Nevertheless, such affinities with Machiavelli on particular points, undeniable though they are, cannot hide what counts for much more: the Americans' total repudiation of everything Machiavelli said about the laying of "foundations." Citing the likes of Numa, Solon, and Lycurgus, Machiavelli posited that "to found a new republic, or to reform an existing one, must be the work of one man only."[91] Well versed in the classics, the Americans readily understood Machiavelli's references.[92] John Adams, for instance, wrote to an acquaintance in 1776, "You and I, my dear friend, have been sent into life at a time when the greatest lawgivers of antiquity would have wished to live."[93] Yet Adams would have agreed with James Madison in 1787 that "the glory of the people of America" was that "they have not suffered a blind veneration for antiquity" to dictate their constitution-making.[94] Madison dutifully noted that "in every case reported by ancient history . . . , the task of framing [government] has not been committed to an assembly of men, but has been performed by some individual citizen." If, he continued, the ultimate fate of the constitutions drawn up by Solon and Lycurgus teach us the frailty of all governments, they also give us reason "to admire the improvement made by America on the ancient mode of preparing and establishing regular plans of government."[95] Founding, in the American experience, was an act of, for, and by the people.

James Wilson made the same argument: "The United States exhibit to the world the first instance . . . of a nation . . . assembling voluntarily, deliberating fully, and deciding calmly, concerning the system of government, under which they would wish that they and their posterity should live. The ancients, so enlightened on other subjects, were very uninformed with regard to this."[96] A collective and deliberative founding is the distinctive glory of America, and one that accords perfectly with the theory of the social contract.

Madison, Wilson, and other Americans knew that in Machiavelli's account of Roman history, the republic was founded upon and sustained by means of a religion invented by the great legislator and subsequently manipulated by the ruling elite to control the masses.[97] Here once again the Americans rejected Machiavelli and sometimes looked to Locke for enlightenment. Acceptable to many Americans was Locke's teaching that religion should be kept pure and intolerance kept at bay, and that the best way to accomplish those ends was to avoid the constant intrusion of religion into politics.[98] In the land of the social contract, all that is most important is subject to human choice, and religion is no different. Patrick Henry might not accept Jefferson's and Madison's ideas about rigorously separating church and state, but he was strongly in favor of freedom of religion.[99]

By natural right, matters of religious affiliation and conscience are for each person to decide on his own.

Religion and founding were not the only points of disagreement with Machiavelli. Even as Americans began to come to terms with the reality that their polity would presumably be a republic, they could never accept Machiavelli's republic. In his world politics was from the top down: The rulers were the active party charged with imposing "form" upon the inert "matter" of the populace; the people's virtue, when it existed, had trickled down from the political leaders; and if the people remained virtuous for a while after the corruption of their rulers, it was only because they were mindless creatures of habit.[100] It is tempting to conclude that Machiavelli's republican citizens were almost as permanently infantile as Filmer's monarchical subjects.[101]

Completely different was the American world of popular sovereignty and the social contract. In the newly emerging nation, the people willed the constitution into and out of being and placed their governors on permanent probation. It was only a matter of time before the Americans would stop speaking of the king as their father and England as their mother. The old parental imagery took its time in dying, but as early as 1765 Adams inquired, "Is there not something extremely fallacious in the common-place images of mother country and children colonies?"[102] By 1776 Tom Paine had bluntly declared that "the colonies come of age," and "a government of our own is our natural right."[103] In the society of Locke's aspirations, individuals reaching maturity assume responsibility for the care of their natural rights, and peoples do so as well. Machiavelli's notions of principles and foundations were rendered largely irrelevant by America's commitment to the public philosophy of the social contract.

For insight into the "principles" of government the Americans turned more frequently to Montesquieu than to Machiavelli. We usually think of Montesquieu's influence in America in terms of his discussions of forms of government—his thoughts on the British constitution, for instance, or his examination of the prospects of varying kinds of confederate republics. There is, however, an additional if relatively neglected dimension of his thought that attracted attention in the new world—his distinction between the "nature" and the "principle" of each type of government: "There is this difference between the nature of the government and its principle: its nature is that which makes it what it is, and its principle, that which makes it act. The one is its particular structure, and the other is the human passions that set it in motion."[104] Somewhat anachronistically, no doubt, we may say that Montesquieu was distinguishing between the political institutions and the political culture of a country.

John Adams displayed an appreciation of Montesquieu when he wrote that "the foundation of every government is some principle or passion in the minds of the people."[105] Much later he offered an understanding of the events of his youth that again drew upon Montesquieu's way of thinking: "The Revolution was effected before the war commenced. The Revolution was in the minds and hearts of the people. . . . This radical change in the principles, opinions, sentiments, and affections of the people was the real American Revolution."[106]

Benjamin Rush was also very appreciative of Montesquieu's comments on principles, not least because he was unconvinced that American principles were firmly established. "We have only finished the first act of the great drama," he wrote to Richard Price in 1786. "We have changed our forms of government, but it remains to effect a Revolution in our principles, opinions, and manners so as to accommodate them to the forms of government we have adopted."[107] Not surprisingly, Rush took a particular interest in Montesquieu's discussion of how education should aim to support the principle of government. "The laws of education . . . prepare us to be citizens," Montesquieu had written, and Rush accordingly devoted some of his writings to painstaking schemes of education that would turn out good American citizens.[108]

Thomas Jefferson complained in 1789 that "we were educated in royalism" and expressed hope that the younger generation would correct the fault of its elders. Looking back from the perspective of 1819 on his prolonged struggle with Hamilton and the Federalists, he claimed with satisfaction that "the revolution of 1800 . . . was as real a revolution in the principles of our government as that of 1776 was in its form."[109] Over the years Jefferson came to despise Montesquieu because the Frenchman had praised the English constitution; nevertheless, in his discussion of America's successful adoption of principles suitable to its new government, Jefferson was deeply indebted to Montesquieu's method of thinking about politics.

Adams, Rush, and Jefferson were all, in slightly different ways, making the same point. In their judgment the best way to shore up abstract and novel Lockean "revolution principles" was to complement them with the right kind of political education. The "principles" Montesquieu spoke of in *The Spirit of the Laws* should be deliberately enlisted in the service of America's revolutionary "principles." For without good citizens, the social contract cannot hold.

Neither Machiavelli nor Montesquieu was of much use to the Americans when they contemplated the problem of building a proper "foundation" upon which to rest their new constitutions. Nor, by and large, did the Americans turn to the revered Roman conception of foundation, effectively summarized by Hannah Arendt: "At the heart of Roman politics, from the beginning of the republic until virtually the end of the imperial era, stands the conviction of the sacredness of foundation, in the sense that once something has been founded it remains binding for all future generations."[110] Such reverence for the past counted for little in the new America.

"History is little else than a recital of the follies and vices of kings and noblemen," Benjamin Rush suggested in 1777.[111] Jefferson, predictably, agreed: As part of his denunciation of Hume's conservative-leaning historical writings, Jefferson argued that "history, in general, only informs us what bad government is." Public figures and writers more moderate than Jefferson made good use of English history, but without offering eulogies of custom and tradition. John Jay, for example, noted that "the history of Great Britain . . . gives us many useful lessons. We may profit by their experience without paying the price which it costs them."[112] Madison, in the *Federalist*, wrote that "the experience of Great Britain, which presents to mankind so many political lessons, both of the monitory and exemplary kind, . . . has been frequently consulted in the course of these inquiries."[113] John Adams's massive treatise, *A Defence of the Constitutions of the United States*, was likewise premised on the notion that history provides a laboratory from which we may draw useful lessons. Yet, despite their attention to the experiments of the past, Adams, Madison, and Jay were as far removed from Roman or Burkean veneration for tradition as were the radicals Rush and Jefferson.

Not only did the founders refuse the Roman and English injunction to bow down before the past, they went so far as to make a virtue of their unprecedented acts. "The birthday of a new world is at hand," wrote Paine in his famous pamphlet; he then proceeded to boast that "we have it in our power to begin the world over again."[114] Twenty-five years later Jefferson, swelling with pride, told Priestley that "we can no longer say there is nothing new under the sun. For this whole chapter in the history of man is new."[115] Madison, the most cautious of founders, did not shy away from congratulating his fellow citizens on the novelty of the proposed new constitution: "Hearken not to the voice which petulantly tells you that the form of government recommended for your adoption is a novelty in the political world." Americans should be proud that "they accomplished a revolution which has no parallel in the annals of human society. They reared the fabrics of governments which have no model on the face of the globe."[116]

Loyalist Jonathan Boucher had voiced his aversion to the spirit of "novel experiment in the world." In particular he was opposed to any and all efforts "to build up a Constitution without any *foundations*."[117] How he would have shuddered, and deemed his dire predictions vindicated, had he learned of Jefferson's repeated claims that "the earth belongs to the living"—a view that might reasonably be understood as a deliberate proposal for a political order without foundations. In 1789, then in 1816, and finally in 1824 Jefferson argued for a very radical version of the Lockean social contract, never finished, always in need of renewal.

"Can one generation bind another, and all others, in succession forever?" asked Jefferson. "I think not. The Creator has made the earth for the living, not the dead." The world of Jefferson, we can say in retrospect, was the exact opposite of Burke's. Jefferson had contempt for organic analogies: "The rights of the whole can be no more than the sum of the rights of individuals." For ancestors and for the duties of one generation toward another, Jefferson again had no use: "By the law of nature, one generation is to another as one independent nation to another." As Jefferson saw it, "the dead have no rights. They are nothing." "No society," he added, "can make a perpetual constitution. . . . The earth belongs to the living generation. . . . Every constitution, then, naturally expires at the end of 19 years," a generation.[118]

Quite consistently, Jefferson the opponent of foundations was also the opponent of the very notion of revered founding fathers. "Some men look at constitutions with sanctimonious reverence, and deem them like the arc of the covenant, too sacred to be touched. They ascribe to the men of the preceding age a wisdom more than human." Jefferson believed that "the generation now in place . . . are wiser than we were, and their successors will be wiser than they, from the progressive advance of science."[119]

The task of taming this radicalized Lockean social contract without retreating to Grotius or Pufendorf fell to James Madison, recipient of Jefferson's original letter on the topic of the uncompromising rights of the living generation. Having just struggled with all his might to put a new federal constitution into place, Madison was not pleased to hear that the next generation would be invited to dismantle his carefully laid foundation. In the *Federalist* he wryly remarked that "the experiments are of too ticklish a nature to be unnecessarily multiplied." Frequent appeals to the people would "deprive the government of that veneration which time bestows on everything, and without which perhaps the wisest and freest governments would not possess the requisite stability."[120] When Madison replied directly to Jefferson's proposals in a private letter, he modified his friend's radicalism by invoking Locke's notion of tacit consent. Until consent is explicitly withdrawn, we can and must assume it exists. "Is it not doubtful whether it be possible to exclude wholly the idea of an implied or tacit assent, without subverting the very foundation of Civil Society?"[121] Madison offered a Lockean solution to the problem presented by Lockean political philosophy.

There were limits, however, as to how far Madison could carry his scheme for toning down the words of the master since he, too, as a loyal Jeffersonian, had to accept the right of revolution. In Jefferson's letters, where he could freely speak his mind, the future president had famously proclaimed that "the tree of liberty must be refreshed from time to time with the blood of tyrants." Federalists might worry about Shays and draw the lesson that a strong federal government was necessary; Jefferson, by contrast, responded by saying, "God forbid that we should ever be twenty years without such a rebellion."[122] What Jefferson uttered in flamboyant phrases other Americans stated less dramatically but with equal clarity. Once the right of revolution had entered American thought, it was slow to take its leave, making its presence felt even in such rather conservative figures of the antebellum age as Joseph Story and Daniel Webster (chapter 2).

Inviting the Antifederalists to accept the new constitution, Hamilton confirmed that "if the representatives of the people betray their constituents, there is no resource left but in the exertion of that original right of self-defense." It speaks volumes about the debates of 1787 that a figure as eager to build a powerful government as Hamilton felt obliged to legitimize the proposals of the Philadelphia convention by assuring the Antifederalists that their right of revolution would remain intact and, indeed, be more effective at the national than at the state level. The right of revolution "against the usurpations of the national rulers may be exerted with infinitely better prospect of success than against those of the rulers of an individual State," wrote Hamilton in the *Federalist*.[123]

If the assertions of a natural right of revolution show Americans' indebtedness to Locke, so does their belief in a natural right to emigrate. Pufendorf had allowed for emigration, but purely as a prudential matter, a method of removing discontented and dangerous subjects ignorant of public affairs and unappreciative of the superior wisdom of the rulers. He spoke of "the privilege of quitting the state."[124] Locke broke with Pufendorf by transforming emigration into a natural right: "For every man's children being by Nature as *free* as himself . . . may choose what society they will join themselves to, what Commonwealth they will put themselves under." Elsewhere in the *Second Treatise* we read that "a child is born a subject of no country or government. He is under his father's tuition and authority, till he come to the age of discretion; and then he is a free man, at liberty what government he will put himself under."[125]

To make certain that few persons avail themselves of their freedom to emigrate, Locke insisted that to inherit property in a particular country is to give one's consent to its government. Nevertheless, the point has been established: Everyone has a natural right to leave the country and to seek citizenship elsewhere.[126]

Because James Otis took Locke for his philosophical mentor in his pamphlet of 1764, we should not be surprised to hear him say that "it is left to every man as he comes of age to choose what society he will continue to belong to."[127] Nor should we be taken aback by Richard Bland's comment, two years later, that we never forfeit our "natural right of quitting the Country" of our birth, in order "to enter into another society" more respectful of our rights.[128] Jefferson followed suit in 1774 with his pronouncement that "our ancestors . . . possessed a right which nature has given to all men, of departing from the country in which chance, not choice, has placed them, of going in quest of new habitations, and of there establishing new societies, under such laws and regulations as to them shall seem most likely to promote public happiness." On another occasion, at a much later date, Jefferson asserted, "I hold the right of expatriation to be inherent in every man by the laws of nature, and incapable of being rightly taken away from him even by the united will of every other person in the nation."[129]

That which Otis and Jefferson asserted before 1776 continued to be widely proclaimed after independence. In keeping with the changing times, the citizens of Pennsylvania included in their new constitution of 1776 the provision that "all men have a natural inherent right to emigrate from one state to another that will receive them, or to form a new state in vacant countries."[130] James Wilson, one of the original justices of the Supreme Court, cited Locke approvingly in the early 1790s and then offered his own commendation of the right to emigrate.[131] When St. George Tucker, a Jeffersonian, published his revised version of Blackstone's *Commentaries* in 1803, he explicitly deleted the provisions forbidding a "right of expatriation."[132] Englishmen might be Englishmen by virtue of birth, but Americans were Americans by virtue of free choice of citizenship. It was Locke's social contract, not quotations from ancient Greek and Roman texts, that transformed Americans from subjects into citizens.[133]

AFTER "REVOLUTION PRINCIPLES" CAME to the fore in 1776 Americans spoke a language in which "principles" frequently triumphed over "foundations," just as they did over "forms" of government. Despite occasional protests from conservatives of both North and South, principles remained the trump card of political disputes throughout the antebellum period, which is another way of saying that the theory of the social contract refused to fade from American public life, unlike the European scenario.

Arch-Jeffersonian Joel Barlow's comments in the early 1790s nicely captured the American situation by contrasting it with England's. Pufendorf's compact between king and people, contended Barlow, had been brought back into English usage by the likes of Edmund Burke in order to rationalize the status quo. In truth, however, Barlow continued, even Pufendorf was too much for Burke, whose fear of any kind of social contract eventually drove him simply to proclaim that royalty served "the general good." Quite the opposite was America, where the social contract reigned and Locke's principles were not only widely embraced but had become the very foundation of government. "Only admit the original, unalterable truth, *that all men are equal in their rights,* and the foundation of every thing is laid."[134]

Romans honored their foundations by building upon the past; Americans by constructing a *novus ordo seclorum* stretching into the future. Romans religiously worshipped the past; Lincoln and other Americans anticipated the age to come insofar as it would fulfill the ideals enunciated in Locke's philosophy, proclaimed in the Declaration of Independence, and cherished by the "founders."

Americans found themselves in a most peculiar situation: The more they came to revere the "founders," the more they risked losing the meaning of the Founding, which was about great ideals rather than great persons, the future rather than the beginning.

■

Social Contracts in Antebellum America

During the first two-thirds of the nineteenth century, when theories of the social contract were in danger of dying out in Europe, they flourished in America. Throughout the antebellum period the names of Grotius, Pufendorf, and Locke persistently wended their way into pamphlets, editorials, essays, and legal commentaries. Prerevolutionary battles fought among advocates of competing theories of the social contract did not come to a close in 1776; despite Locke's apparent victory with the signing of the Declaration of Independence, Grotius and Pufendorf staged periodic comebacks during the years preceding the Civil War. At the very time, then, that nineteenth-century Europeans were turning away from theories of the social contract, Americans were preoccupied with deciding which contract was the correct one. Was it that of Grotius, Pufendorf, or Locke?

Admittedly, the social contract was at times sharply criticized in both the Northern and the Southern states. Unlike the situation in Europe, however, the naysayers in America never succeeded in marginalizing the theory of the social contract. On the contrary, it was the anticontractualists who sooner or later retreated. In antebellum politics the trump cards were always held by the theorists of the social contract.

Nothing is more misleading than the claim that John Locke won an easy, preordained victory in American history.[1] For although there is no denying that the likes of Sam Adams and Tom Paine were ready to ride Locke to victory in 1776, many other Americans justified the break with England in terms reminiscent of Pufendorf. The more the colonists demanded legislative autonomy in the early 1770s, the more in consequence they turned away from the lawgiving Parliament and toward the king, which led them to speak of a contract between king and people. Then, when all else failed, the day came when they either had to back down or accuse the king of violating the contract of government. On April 23, 1776, Justice William Henry Drayton, addressing a gathering in Charleston, declared South Carolina released from obedience to George III, who had "endeavored to subvert the constitution of this country, by breaking the original contract between king and people."[2]

If the rebellious colonists eventually did, in fact, seek refuge in Locke during the summer of 1776, one reason was that they had no other choice. Neither Grotius nor Pufendorf nor their popular eighteenth-century offspring, Jean Jacques Burlamaqui and Emmerich Vattel, offered the upstart Americans an effectively articulated argument for revolution and independence. In 1776 Locke provided the only suitable option, but soon thereafter a great many Americans, wanting to bring revolutionary upheavals to a close, neglected the *Second Treatise*. It is telling that Locke was published in America in 1773 but never again for the next 164 years. By contrast, Burlamaqui, who offered a nonrevolutionary, Whiggish revision of Pufendorf, was reprinted six times before the Civil War.[3]

Nevertheless, newly arisen problems had a way of repeatedly restoring Locke to prominence in antebellum America. Unceasing calls for yet another state constitutional convention; the search for justification of an unheard-of, classics-defying, expansive, and ever-expanding republic; and efforts to Americanize Blackstone without sacrificing "revolution principles" were numbered among the ways the *Second Treatise of Government* was revitalized at the very moment when some Americans were looking for a safer approach to public affairs.

Blackstone

In the aftermath of the Revolution, American legal commentators found themselves faced with a demanding task. To accept the English common law, rather than suffer the chaos that would follow its abandonment, was essential.[4] No less important, however, was the need to reissue Blackstone in a form compatible with the principles of the American Revolution. James Wilson of Pennsylvania in his lectures on law (1790–1791) and St. George Tucker of Virginia in his annotated edition of the *Commentaries on the Laws of England* (1803) conjured up a Blackstone compatible with the revolutionary "principles" of 1776.

Annexing Blackstone to the American revolutionary cause was no simple undertaking. The author of the *Commentaries* had wanted nothing to do with revolution, which to his mind was inseparable from the bloodletting of the mid-seventeenth century. Even 1688, in his estimation, needed to be downplayed. Accordingly, Blackstone endorsed the fiction that the king had "abdicated" and recommended that the record of the proceedings of the parliamentary convention be permitted to collect dust rather than that anyone should risk a dangerous reexamination of the work of "our ancestors." The wisdom of the elders was particularly evident, he believed, in their refusal to regard 1688 as a "total dissolution of the government, according to the principles of Mr. Locke: which would have . . . levelled all distinctions of honour, rank, offices, and property."[5]

As they emerged from 1776, Americans could react only with horror to Blackstone's contention that, "though a philosophical mind will consider the royal person merely as one man appointed by mutual consent . . . , yet the mass of mankind will be apt to grow insolent and refractory, if taught to consider their prince as a man of no greater perfection than themselves." An Americanized Blackstone had to be purged of his monarchical prejudices, and freed also from his aristocratic prejudices in favor of the gentry, whose calling he thought it was "to watch, to check, and to avert every dangerous innovation" emanating from the people.[6]

No one was better qualified than James Wilson to Americanize Blackstone. Perhaps the most able legal mind of his age, one of only six signers of both the Declaration of Independence and the Constitution, second only to Madison in his intellectual contributions to the federal convention, a major actor in securing ratification of the U.S. Constitution in Pennsylvania, principal architect of the new Pennsylvania state constitution of 1790, and justice on the Supreme Court—James Wilson's résumé commanded respect. A symbolic confirmation of his stature was the presence of President George Washington and Vice President John Adams in the audience when he delivered his inaugural address as professor of law at the College of Philadelphia.

At the outset Wilson informed his audience that Blackstone "deserves to be much admired; but he ought not to be implicitly followed." Inevitably, "many parts of the laws of England can . . . have neither force nor application here. . . . Such are the parts which relate to the monarchical and aristocratick branches." Present here but absent in the "Transatlantick world," Wilson observed, was the master idea of the social contract. Americans had no choice but to expurgate the *Commentaries* because Blackstone had treated popular sovereignty and the right of the people to abolish their constitution, in Wilson's accurate paraphrase, as "a political chimera, existing only in the minds of some theorists."[7]

Wilson indicated what measures were necessary to convert Blackstone's writings into a form suitable for Americans. All the passages in which Blackstone suggested that civil rights were purchased by abridging natural rights[8] should be expurgated. The American position must be that natural rights, "instead of being abridged, may be increased and secured in a government which is good and wise."[9] Much of what Blackstone said about civil rights could be kept in place, but only after his text had been suitably altered to conform to the dictates of a strong natural rights philosophy.

"Customs owe their original to common consent," affirmed Blackstone, and so does the common law.[10] Wilson concurred but pointed out that Blackstone either did not mean what he said or was guilty of gross inconsistency.[11] If the laws were based on consent, how could Blackstone write that a law is "a rule of action dictated by some superior being"?[12] Wilson took pride that in his account of the law, "the will of a superior is discarded."[13] How, again, if Blackstone thought the common law was grounded in consent, could he write that "the power of parliament is absolute and without control"?[14] Americans should keep Blackstone's common law based on consent while cleansing it of unfreedom by rejecting his notions of parliamentary sovereignty and law as command.

Much of what was wrong in Blackstone, explained Wilson, could be traced back to Pufendorf, a major source of the *Commentaries*. Grotius was equally objectionable: All his erudition was aimed at robbing the people of their sovereignty. Locke was the best source because he looked beyond the Parliament, if need be, to the people.[15] In Blackstone's pages Locke had been absorbed into conservative Whiggery; in Wilson's pages Blackstone was absorbed into Locke's potentially radical Whiggery.

St. George Tucker, like Wilson, thought it necessary for Americans to avail themselves of the resources of the common law. But he also insisted, as had Wilson, that the American Revolution brought forth principles "irreconcilable to the principles contained in the *Commentaries.*" A new edition of the *Commentaries,* "translating them into a different work," was needed. Useful in this process of revision was Locke, whose *Treatise of Government* is "a work with which every American ought to be perfectly acquainted."[16]

Locke, remarked Tucker, "contends that all power is vested in the people," a view "controverted by some, . . . among whom it is sufficient to mention the learned Grotius and the author of these *Commentaries.*" Just as Americans had looked to Locke for their principles of revolution, they must again look to him in postrevolutionary times as they strove to make the common law safe for democracy. With Locke in mind, Americans must abrogate "every rule of the common law . . . founded on the nature of regal government, in derogation of the natural and unalienable rights of mankind; or, inconsistent with the nature and principles of democratic governments." Nineteenth-century America must continue the work of reducing Locke's theory to practice.[17]

Conventions

"Between 1829 and 1880," wrote historian Daniel T. Rodgers, "it was an unusual political year which did not witness the calling of a revisory state constitutional convention somewhere in the United States. In the space of a single decade, 1844 to 1853, . . . more than half the existing states summoned a constitutional convention into being."[18] To which we may add that each such convention, by its very calling, and before the participants sat down for their first meeting, paid homage in advance to Locke's notion of popular sovereignty. Once the members of the conventions assembled, their proceedings again brought Locke to the fore, as squabbles frequently broke out between different kinds of Lockeans and sporadically between Lockeans and anti-Lockeans.

Constitutional conventions popularly ratified are direct outgrowths, intellectually, of social contract theory—or, rather, of one version of social contract theory: Locke's. Grotius and Pufendorf fared well, Locke poorly, at the Convention Parliament of 1688, which refused to admit that it was a constitutional convention and never went to the people. American constitutions, by contrast, being willed into being by the sovereign people, could find their original rationale only in Locke—or in his predecessors, the unmentionable Levellers, one of whom, John Wildman, eventually befriended Locke.

When the members of a state convention met, they frequently found themselves arguing over the suffrage: whether it should pertain to the landed classes only—those with a "stake" in society—or a much larger number of citizens, perhaps all adult white males. Property or numbers was often the issue, and either position could be argued by offering variations upon Lockean themes. Or, if sufficiently frightened, the party of property might actually dare to criticize Locke's premises, albeit usually without conceding a retreat from revolutionary principles.

The Massachusetts convention of 1820–1821 was remarkable for its cast of characters, which included John Adams, Justice Joseph Story, and up-and-coming public figure Daniel Webster. It was noteworthy also for the quality of its debates on topics ranging from state-supported religion to the legitimacy of a senate representing property rather than numbers. Voices of members requesting an expansion of democracy were countered by eloquent responses from conservatives. Throughout the proceedings the theory of the social contract was rarely out of sight and never out of mind. After all, the constitution being considered for revision was the 1780 document of John Adams, in which the social contract figured prominently in the preamble: "The body politic is formed by a voluntary association of individuals. It is a social compact, by which the whole people covenants with each citizen, and each citizen with the whole people."[19]

Reformers wished to delete the provisions of the 1780 constitution that imposed public support of religion and religious tests of office. James Prince held that "the rights of conscience" should be enumerated among our "unalienable and natural rights." Repeatedly he argued that "in forming or revising the social compact, we ought wholly to exclude every principle which by possible construction may interfere with the consciences of men."[20] Leverett Saltonstall answered for the conservatives by saying that "there is no more hardship . . . in being obliged to contribute towards the support of a minister than any other teacher. . . . The right of society in both cases rests on the same foundation—the right to tax for the common good."[21] It was Saltonstall's good fortune that Adams had ended the preamble's dedication to the social contract with the statement that the purpose of the agreement was to institute a government such that "all shall be governed by certain laws for the common good."[22] Thus, Saltonstall did not have to turn his back on the social contract to arrive at a political morality of the public good.

Dealing with the suffrage, conservative-leaning Warren Dutton held that "there was no question of right; it was wholly a question of expediency." Having limited the range of natural rights, Dutton argued the case for the inexpediency of universal suffrage. Only harm, a democratic form of despotism, could come from a world in which "men without a dollar" would "determine the rights of property, or have any concern in its appropriation."[23] The elderly John Adams joined in the defense of property during the discussion of the future of the senate: "The constitution declares that all men are born free and equal," but "no man pretends that all are born with equal property." The great object of government is "to render property secure. . . . It is the foundation upon which civilization rests."[24]

The constitution of 1780 stated that "all men are born equally free and independent, and have certain natural, essential, and unalienable rights." Those words cheered the democrats of 1820 but did not separate them from the conservatives who nodded in agreement and then quoted the constitution's guarantee of "life, liberty, and *property.*"[25] No less than the reformers, the conservatives spoke in the tones of Locke, to the frustration of the democrats who would not have their way until they learned to demand the vote as a natural right.[26]

Discussions in the Virginia convention of 1829–1830 were noteworthy for the brilliance of the speeches delivered in favor of conflicting ideological positions.[27] Democratic reformers such as John Cooke, Philip Doddridge, and Alexander Campbell frequently and forcefully updated the arguments of the *Second Treatise of Government.* Some conservatives such as Benjamin Watkins Leigh countered by cleverly enlisting Locke in their cause, whereas others such as Abel Upshur worked up the courage to challenge the theory of the social contract.

The reformers loved to quote from the Virginia Declaration of Rights of 1776, especially its call for a "frequent recurrence to fundamental principles." Cooke noted that the constitution of Virginia predated the Declaration of Rights, which explained why the established order was so defective. All the reformers asked was that a new or revised constitution be enacted that would fulfill the ideals of the Declaration. Those ideals, stemming from Locke and Sydney, might be unrealistic in Europe, but they were quite practical in Virginia. Campbell joined Cooke in claiming Locke for the reform position, as did William Naylor and Charles Mercer.[28]

In staking out the conservative position, Leigh did not deny natural rights, nor did he reject the state of nature, provided that it was understood as pertaining to the past. The problem was one of misappropriation:

"Locke has had a singular fate. He was a zealous advocate of mixed monarchy . . . ; his notions of practical Government are exhibited in the Constitution he made for North Carolina, with its [noble titles]; yet from his book has been deduced . . . the *divine right of democracy.*"[29] Properly understood, Locke was the teacher of moderation, not revolution.

Upshur went further than Leigh—much further. "There are no original principles of government at all," he told the delegates. "Principles do not *precede*, but spring out of government." History, he added, knows nothing of a social contract or original equality. Upshur's speeches led an angry Mercer to draw an analogy with Filmer—unfairly, because Filmer could never have written, as Upshur did, that "every government is legitimate which springs directly from the will of the people."[30] Upshur did not hearken back to Filmer but forward to a later phase of Southern thought, when slavery was the issue and the theory of the social contract was called into question.

Expansion

Although the exceptional size of America opened the door to unprecedented opportunities, it also posed serious problems of ideological justification. For one, how could the new federal constitution be defended against Antifederalist charges that a government ruling a large nation would inevitably be guilty of the sins of "consolidation" and incipient despotism? For another, by what rationale could antebellum America proceed with its program of westward expansion and yet remain a single free nation rather than splitting into several? In 1787 the solution proposed by supporters of the new constitution was a marriage of revamped federalism with Lockean social contract theory, a union so successful that it was revisited at a later date when Americans decided to pursue their "manifest destiny."

The United States became a republic by default rather than premeditation. To understand their accidental republic, the perplexed former colonists turned to Montesquieu and soon found themselves embroiled in a dilemma. The passage in which Montesquieu identified England as a "republic hiding under the form of a monarchy" escaped their attention, and in consequence Americans missed his notion that a modern commercial republic could exist on a national scale.[31] What they kept was his scheme of classification—his initial division of governments into small city-state republics, medium-sized monarchies, and large-scale oriental despotisms. After reading the earlier portions of *The Spirit of the Laws*, the Antifederalists became obsessed with the thought that under the proposed federal constitution their country could not remain a republic but would soon degenerate into an oppressive monarchy or a despotic state.

Montesquieu had observed that in the city-states of antiquity the citizens shared a common culture. John Jay was quick, therefore, to state in the *Federalist* that Americans are "one united people—a people descended from the same ancestors, speaking the same language, professing the same religion, . . . very similar in their manners and customs."[32] Unfortunately, Jay's generalization did not even fit his own ethnically diverse New York, much less America in general.

Antifederalists such as "Brutus" of New York agreed that "in a republic, the manners, sentiments, and interests of the people should be similar" and used that observation to oppose the proposed constitution: "The United States," he explained, "includes a variety of climates. . . . Manners and habits differ."[33] "Agrippa" of Massachusetts elaborated the same point, arguing that Southerners living in warm climates were naturally "more dissolute in their manners" than puritanical Northerners. Paraphrasing Montesquieu, Agrippa concluded that "no extensive empire can be governed upon republican principles. . . . The very great empires have always been despotick."[34] George Mason of Virginia similarly posed the question: "Is it to be supposed that one National Government will suit so extensive a country, embracing so many climates, and containing inhabitants so very different in manners, habits, and customs? . . . Popular governments can only exist in small territories."[35] America could healthily consist of thirteen republics loosely affiliated, but those thirteen could never be absorbed into one republic without suffering disastrous consequences.

Federalists answered by rejecting the old-fashioned federalism of the Antifederalists, which was grounded in early-modern notions of treaties and alliances. Consolidation was wrong, the Federalists admitted, but the Antifederalists were equally wrong to continue applying the language of international relations to internal American affairs at a time when the United States needed enough unity to become an effectively governed, free-standing nation. A new federalism—in which the states would be sovereign in some matters, the federal government in others—was essential.

According to the Federalists, this new constitution would be the fulfillment of a grand ideal and not simply a clever political bargain because, if ratified, it would be the incarnation of Locke's inalienable popular sovereignty. Happily for the Federalists, their Antifederalist opponents were more than advocates of the old federalism of allied sovereign states; Antifederalists were also proponents of the new idea of the sovereignty of the people—within the several states. After the Federalists finished bowing to the sovereign peoples of the thirteen states in all matters concerning the states, they insisted upon what could not easily be denied: the sovereignty of the people of the entire United States in matters concerning the well-being of all Americans. In the United States, as in no other country, social contract and federalism became inextricably entwined.

They remained inseparable throughout the antebellum age. Federalism and social contract constantly reinforced one another as Americans pushed westward, slowly but surely annexing the entire width of the continent. The critics of expansion soon discovered that their classically inspired wisdom gave few Americans pause. Admonitory analogies with Roman imperialism and the consequent decline of the republic were deemed irrelevant. Webster's injunction "You have a Sparta, embellish it!" was rebuffed.[36] Neither Spartans nor Romans knew anything of federalism, social contract, consent, or the union that might be built on the basis of their constructive fusion.

By the early 1780s Americans were already forging westward in significant numbers and with the tentative blessing of luminaries such as George Washington and Ben Franklin.[37] But how far might America expand without either becoming a despotic empire or breaking up into multiple free countries? Over the course of antebellum times, public figures on several occasions announced an outer limit beyond which the nation could not reach and yet remain one free nation—the Mississippi during the Revolution, the Rocky Mountains for Jeffersonians in 1803, the Pacific in the 1840s—and each time, sooner or later, the limit was waived. "More! More! More!" was the title of an editorial by John O'Sullivan, coiner of the phrase "manifest destiny." We must not stop, he urged his countrymen, until "the whole boundless continent is ours."[38]

Federalism and consent triumphed in unison at the Founding, and at a later date their marriage came to the fore again as a justification of continentalism. John Quincy Adams announced in 1824 that "a government by federation would be found practicable upon a territory as extensive as this continent."[39] Why should the Rockies stop America's march to greatness when federalism permitted the territories to be absorbed into the union in the form of healthy new states rather than as Roman-style downtrodden provinces? Expansion need not entail centralization or exploitation. Each time, moreover, that the inhabitants of a territory signed a contract among themselves to form a new state and then petitioned the union to enter by free consent, the twin causes of greatness and liberty were purportedly well served, under the auspices of federalism allied with social contract.

There remained the problem of conjuring up a suitable rationale for disposing of the Indians. For these purposes Americans turned again to writers in the natural law tradition, sometimes Locke but perhaps more frequently Vattel's chapter "on the cultivation of the soil." It was Vattel's view, expressed in *The Law of Nations or Principles of the Law of Nature* (1758), that peoples "who inhabit fertile countries, but disdain to cultivate their lands, and choose rather to live by plunder, . . . deserve to be extirpated as savage and pernicious beasts." In the same paragraph he called for "the establishment of many colonies on the continent of North America," an objective that antebellum Americans gladly accepted after replacing the word "colonies" with "states."[40]

Nothing more powerfully underscores the ubiquity of discourse in the tradition of natural law and natural rights than the efforts of the Cherokee Indians to save themselves from Andrew Jackson by signing their own social contract and writing their own constitution.[41] The eventual sad fate of the Cherokees at the hands of Jackson also reminds us that in spite of the universalistic thrust of Locke's thought, white American males have been adept at excluding various groups from the social contract.

The Social Contract in the South

In 1765 Christopher Gadsden of South Carolina called upon all the "true sons of liberty," South and North, to support the "Common cause." "There ought to be no New England man, no New Yorker, *etc.* known on the Continent, but all of us Americans." Overriding all differences, he was convinced, was a shared American belief: "We should all endeavour to stand upon the broad common ground of . . . natural and inherent rights."[42] Decades later, during the peak of the antebellum era, his fellow South Carolinians denied both of his major premises: the oneness of Americans and the doctrine of inalienable rights. This reversal marked a change not only for South Carolina but for the entire South, and at the center of these developments stood contested theories of the social contract.

Antebellum Southern encounters with theories of natural rights and social contracts were many, varied, complex, and tangled. After a strong Lockean start, some Southern intellectuals discovered that the best way to seek protection, whether from the tariff or the antislavery agitation, was to backtrack to pre-Lockean versions of the social contract. Other thinkers, or the same ones on other occasions, eventually launched an all-out assault on inalienable rights, the state of nature, and the social contract. And from the time of the Antifederalists down to the Civil War, Southerners were adept at turning to their own ends the novel American marriage of federalism and social contract.

Jeffersonians of the post-1800 South returned to federalism and the social contract with a vengeance when they became alarmed that John Marshall and the seemingly defeated Federalists were successfully continuing their pursuit of "consolidation" through the judiciary, the one branch of the federal government still under their control. St. George Tucker, a loyal Jeffersonian, was as concerned to secure the rights of states as he was to make Blackstone compatible with Locke; hence he urged that the common law be left to the individual discretion of the several states and never placed at the disposal of the federal government.[43] It fell to John Taylor of Caroline, Virginia, however, to offer the most systematic Jeffersonian case against the Federalist judiciary. None other than Jefferson himself heaped lavish praise upon Taylor's *Construction Construed and Constitutions Vindicated* (1820). "This book," wrote Jefferson, "is the most effectual retraction of our government to its original principles which has ever yet been sent by heaven to our aid."[44]

Taylor began by sharing his worry that "we are exchanging the pure principles of the revolution for the garbage of [judicial] aristocracy." Throughout *Construction Construed* he expressed his affiliation with Locke's rights of "life, liberty, and property," "the rights of mankind," and the notion that the rulers are the "trustees of the people." The "natural right of self-government," he proudly asserted, "might have slept forever in theory, except for the American revolution." It is not the "forms" but the "principles of our Constitutions" to which we must return if the rights of states are to be upheld.[45]

If Locke is center stage in *Construction Construed*, Grotius, Pufendorf, and Vattel are the anonymous singers we hear in the chorus. The titles of their books addressed "the law of war and peace," "the law of nature and nations," and "the law of nations" because their primary concern was with re-creating stability after the splintering of Christendom into squabbling, autonomous nation-states. Taylor had reason to borrow their language of international relations in 1820, a time when he was busily setting forth strong claims for states' rights. Returning to his Antifederalist days, he asserted that "the federal is not a national government; it is a league between nations." Each state is a nation, he proclaimed, and the rights of nature of which he spoke were frequently the "natural rights of nations, . . . [which] are more universally recognized than the rights of individual men."[46]

Early in his book Taylor decided that he had to come to terms with the word "sovereignty." Originally it was a religious term, "stolen from the attributes of God, and impiously assumed by Kings."[47] Taylor was tempted to toss out the word because he shared with early-modern federalists an aversion to the centralizing implications of sovereignty, but as an advocate of the newfangled philosophy of Locke, he elected to keep it and attribute sovereignty to "the people."[48] New-style Lockean natural rights and the old-style federalism of treaties and alliances could work effectively in tandem, provided everyone acknowledged that "we the people of the United States" referred to the people of each state, not the nation.[49] The Constitution was an alliance of states, or, more accurately, the peoples of the various states.

In his earlier writings Taylor had maintained that "the [state] constitutions consider a nation [that is, a state] as *made of individuals*."[50] Now, in 1820, arguing for the sovereignty of the states, Taylor added that "the term 'union' has never been applied to describe a government *established by the consent of individuals*." The only proper and binding social contracts, then, were those signed within states; the federal Constitution or union, by contrast, was a mere alliance of states. Natural rights, too, pertained to individuals and states but not to the government in Washington: "The states," he wrote in *Construction Construed*, "are armed with their original national [and natural] rights; [the Federal] congress with [merely] conventional rights."[51]

To Taylor's mind, the "more perfect union" of 1787 was little more than a slight amendment of the old union, which the Articles of Confederation had called a "league of friendship" among sovereign states.[52] The major difference was that the league of 1787 was not of state governments but of the sovereign peoples of the states. Perhaps more than any other thinker, Taylor combined federalism and social contract into an ardent states' rights philosophy, based on "revolution principles," that the South would follow even unto civil war.

John C. Calhoun took over for the deceased Taylor during the nullification crisis that followed passage of the tariffs of 1828 and 1832. The events unfolding before his eyes, Calhoun remarked, were reminiscent of the American Revolution. "There are, indeed, many and striking analogies between that and the present controversy." Not only the events but "the very arguments resorted to at the commencement of the American Revolution . . . are almost identically the same."[53] Calhoun was correct, possibly more so than he knew, for the arguments being made in South Carolina truly did recapitulate both the resistance theme of 1765 and the revolution theme of 1776.

Before the Revolution, Americans had turned to resistance if possible, revolution if necessary. Similarly, when a committee of the legislature of South Carolina called for a nullification convention in 1832, the authors were willing "to seek a remedy even in Revolution itself," but, they hurriedly added, "we cannot bring ourselves for one moment to believe that the alternative presented to us is revolution or slavery." Nullification, they believed, was the answer. "The right to nullify is universally admitted to be a natural or sovereign right," opined the delegates. By resorting to nullification they were stopping short of secession, short of revolution—were returning to the old politics of resistance, the old Whig notions of contract, which had sufficed in 1765 and could again save the day in 1833. When they called a convention of the people to settle a dispute beyond the jurisdiction of any "earthly tribunal," the nullifiers sounded like the children of Locke, but in nullifying rather than seceding, they chose a conservative Whig act of resistance rather than a revolutionary Lockean "appeal to heaven."[54]

Calhoun agreed that nullification was the best way to press the claims of South Carolina while keeping its revolutionary hotheads under control.[55] The better to serve his state without sanctioning secession, he cited Magna Charta, James II's violation of the "original contract," and the writings on rights of the nonrevolutionary Burlamaqui.[56] All along his position had been that South Carolina sought "reformation, and not revolution," the legitimacy "not of setting aside the provisions of the Constitution . . . , but the right to maintain and preserve them" from the usurpations of the federal government. Unlike Taylor, who did not distance himself from the revolutionary language of 1776, Calhoun updated the "constitutional," reformist, and "safe" rhetoric of 1765.[57]

Calhoun wanted to play it safe—to hold on to the security of the old ways, the old patterns of thinking—and so did many other Southerners at a later date when the issue changed from nullification to the even more inflammatory question of slavery. Reared on the social contract, Southerners were reluctant to abandon it. Under attack from the North, Southern spokespersons discovered that they could have their social contract and slavery, too, if they backtracked from Locke to Grotius and Pufendorf. "By nature . . . ," wrote Grotius, "no human beings are slaves." Nevertheless, "it is not in conflict with natural justice that slavery should have its origin in a human act, that is, should arise from a convention." Not only the parents but the children and "their descendants forever" were rightfully slaves if the first generation entered into a contract of master and slave.[58] Similar arguments may be found in Pufendorf.[59]

After the Virginia legislature met in 1831–1832 to discuss the Nat Turner revolt, Thomas R. Dew took up his pen to vindicate slavery. "Grotius says that, as the law of nations permits prisoners of war to be killed, so the same law has introduced the right of making them slaves." Pufendorf, he added, concurred.[60] Leading Southern politician and polemicist James Henry Hammond followed Dew's lead in utilizing the social contract to defend slavery: "If we travel back with the philosophers who refer all human institutions to an original contract, I will still engage to find a place for slavery there. Let it be regarded as a compact between the master and the slave."[61] Albert Bledsoe, James Henry Thornwell, and Edward B. Bryan were numbered among the many Southerners who affirmed the contract of slavery while seeking to render it less offensive by suggesting that the master owned the slave's labor but not the man.[62]

The more deeply one delves into Southern thought, the more obvious it is that its theme, occasionally explicit, usually implicit, was "Whatever is, is right."[63] Slave owners could not abide Locke's statement that "at best an argument from what has been to what should of right be, has no great force."[64] Radicalized Lockeans such as Jefferson and Paine deemed history of no moral value, Paine going so far as to suggest that the past was guilty of "working to *un-make* man."[65] In response, Southern thinkers revived Grotius, who had turned history into the standard of right. Whatever practices were common in "better times and better peoples," Grotius asserted, were sanctioned by the law of nature.[66] Classically educated, Grotius did not doubt that the Greeks, Romans, and Hebrews were the "better peoples." Southerners were happy to agree because all three of those peoples had practiced slavery. "History, both sacred and profane," announced Grotius-minded James Henry Hammond, was on the side of the South.[67]

The only problem with Grotius was that he forgot to mention that slavery had been the norm throughout all of human history, modern as well as ancient. Thus, William Harper began his *Memoir on Slavery* (1837) with these words: "The institution of domestic slavery exists over far the greater portion of the inhabited earth, . . . [especially] in all those portions of it which had made any advances toward civilization. We might safely conclude then that it is deeply founded in the nature of man."[68] Harper's sentiments were commonplace in Southern thought.

The warm embrace of Grotius and Pufendorf was part of a larger movement of Southern thought in an ever more conservative direction. Nathaniel Beverly Tucker, son of St. George Tucker, reversed his father's politics when he proclaimed that history and custom were far more reliable standards of right than deductive reasoning from "first principles."[69] The younger Tucker did not stand alone. William Harper, among others, added his voice to the Southern repudiation of moralistic, judgmental abolitionists: "They do not speak of what exists, but of what ought to exist," he sighed.[70] It was from Grotius and Pufendorf that the Southerners learned their lessons in conflating "is" and "ought."

Grotius was the hero of many Southerners because he allowed them to seize the moral high ground even as they rationalized slavery. How could they fail to avail themselves of the sentence in which he seemed to suggest that slave labor was preferable to so-called free labor? In the world of the slave, wrote Grotius, "the lasting obligation to labor is repaid with a lasting certainty of support, which often those do not have who work for hire by the day."[71] Every Southerner who wanted to stay within the social contract tradition and yet hold fast to the "peculiar institution" could find consolation and vindication in the pages of Grotius and Pufendorf.

From Grotius and Pufendorf the Southerners could also learn how to replace radical claims of rights with far more convenient conservative claims of duties. Southerners followed the lead of Pufendorf, who had issued a handbook emphasizing duties and relegating rights to a secondary status. "No human being can be contented," wrote Harper, "who does not perform the duties of his station"—the free man his, the wife hers, the slaves theirs.[72] William Gilmore Simms sounded the same theme by quoting Coleridge: "I know of no right except such as flows from righteousness. . . . It must flow out of a duty."[73]

Rights had disappeared into duties in Pufendorf, an outcome the Southerners relished.[74] Under attack from the North, they turned to a language of moral stewardship, speaking incessantly of their moral duties and professing to spare no efforts in their endeavors to fulfill the obligation to mold themselves into caring, attentive, dutiful masters, as concerned for the well-being of their slaves as the Northern capitalists were unconcerned for their brutalized workers.

William Gilmore Simms scoffed at the notion of inalienable rights for anyone, black or white. Free white males must learn to accept their responsibilities, and there was no better place to begin than with a frank acknowledgment that civilized life demands an alienation of many of our rights. "Do we not alienate them every day" for the sake of the greater good? "All our rights, whether from nature or society . . . result from the performance of our duties. Unless we perform our duties, we have no rights; or they are alienable."[75] Fellow South Carolinian William Harper made the same point of stressing "the good and safety of society"; our claims as social beings "are no matter of natural right, but to be settled by convention."[76] Quite possibly the arguments of Simms and Harper were cribbed from Pufendorf, for whom the primary concern was always "the welfare or necessity of the commonwealth."[77]

As time passed and Northern attacks on slavery grew more intense, some Southern thinkers concluded that siding with Grotius and Pufendorf and ignoring Locke no longer sufficed. Nothing less would do, they concluded, than an outspoken and aggressive repudiation of the Lockean contract that was being hurled against them. Other Southern ideologues, daring to take the next step, decided the time had come to reject the social contract outright, whether that of Grotius, Pufendorf, or Locke. In its place they offered a "conservative" ideology that featured a retraction of their Jeffersonian youth and a concerted effort to delete everything revolutionary from the American Revolution. The past had to be rewritten, the social contract expurgated from the historical record.

In one of his several moods, William Gilmore Simms was a passionate naysayer to Locke's theory of the social contract.[78] There was little, if anything, he explained, to be said on behalf of the view that humans had ever lived in a state of nature. Nor should we be too quick to accept Locke's notions of self-ownership and the right to govern oneself: "The right of ruling themselves . . . is assumed to be the test of freedom. . . . But the right to govern themselves requires, first, a capacity for such government." Evidence that most free white males, let alone slaves, had not been up to the task stared us in the face every time we saw that the voters "need to be deceived by indirect and circuitous taxation into the expenditures which are necessary for their own good."[79]

According to Simms, Locke's words about equality in the state of nature were good for nothing but destructive leveling. The ideas of the *Second Treatise,* taken seriously in the North, were rapidly undoing the authority and hierarchy that were essential to social well-being. "We are losing our veneration fast," Simms complained, and even marriage was becoming nothing more than a revocable contract. Abolitionists cited Locke with reverence, but why should Southerners take seriously the ideas espoused in states "which really do not appear to possess a single principle of permanence and stability"? To the slaveholders of the South fell the task of acting as "the great moral conservators . . . of the entire world."[80]

History was our best guide, but it must be read selectively, Simms suggested. Our best reason to remember the founders of the republic was that "they left the condition of the social world precisely as they found it." About their disruptive talk of natural rights, the less said the better. Blame it on "sentimental French philosophy, then so current."[81]

Embattled, frightened, convinced the South had become a permanent minority, John C. Calhoun advanced to an outright break with Locke and possibly with all theories of the social contract. The state of nature "is purely hypothetical. It never did, nor can exist. . . . Instead of being the natural state of man, it is . . . the most opposed to his nature." As for the claim that we are equal by nature, it is "the most false and dangerous of all political errors." Unwilling to abandon the noble quest for liberty, Calhoun insisted it was not for everyone: "Instead of liberty and equality being born with man, . . . they are high prizes to be won." By the end of his life, Calhoun could be seen distancing himself from the American Revolution by praising the British constitution.[82]

Of all Southern thinkers, George Fitzhugh was perhaps the most provocative. Five years after the death of John Taylor, Fitzhugh moved to Caroline County, Virginia. It was there, on Taylor's former turf, that Fitzhugh penned his gleeful reversals of Taylor, of Jeffersonianism, and of all thinking in the social contract tradition. Fitzhugh called upon slave owners to aid him in creating a distinctively "Southern thought, we mean a Southern philosophy, not excuses, apologies, and palliations"; "not a half thought, but a whole thought."[83] How far a Southern intellectual would go during the 1850s to defend slavery cannot be appreciated without a perusal of Fitzhugh's vigorous, uncompromising polemics.

Placing Taylor's writings and Fitzhugh's side by side reveals a set of dramatic contrasts. Whereas Taylor was upset that America might be losing its revolutionary "principles," Fitzhugh was sorry that his country had ever had any. In *Cannibals All!* Fitzhugh wrote that "a 'frequent recurrence to fundamental principles' is at war with the continued existence of all government, and is a doctrine fit to be sported only by the Isms of the North and the Red Republicans of Europe."[84] Locke had been Taylor's implicit hero, but he was Fitzhugh's explicit villain; the *Treatises of Government* were repeatedly singled out in *Sociology for the South* (1854), *Cannibals All!* (1857), and other writings of Fitzhugh as the source of many of the miseries of the modern world.[85]

If Taylor spoke of "the plain honest yeomanry," if he addressed his words to "my fellow labourers" and wrote in the name of "we farmers and mechanics," Fitzhugh, in an antithetical vein, remarked that "farming is the recreation of great men, the proper pursuit of dull men."[86] All of Fitzhugh's emphasis was on the landed elite, a ruling class that should oversee the development of a multifaceted Southern economy, commercial and manufacturing as well as agricultural, which, if successfully completed, would free the South to go its own way.[87] Jeffersonians and Jacksonians, with their praise of laissez-faire and the rights of free labor, stood in the way of his program of state-assisted internal improvements, which was one reason why he denounced them on every possible occasion.

Against the radical Jacksonian slogan "The world is governed too much," Fitzhugh posited his motto "The world is governed too little."[88] Northern "free society" was neither free nor a society; it was oppression and anarchy.[89] A labor agitation was in the making in the United States, as in Europe, and might become uncontrollable after the nation reached the Pacific.[90] Yet we needed not despair, for an escape route from the hideous future that threatened us was readily available: all would be well if the institution of slavery was extended to white workers, who would fare infinitely better under its protections than under the delusional freedom of selling their labor. Benevolent slavery was the solution for overcrowded Europe at the present moment and would be for America later, when all the lands had been settled.[91]

All of us were born the "slaves" of society, to which we owed everything, in spite of our mistaken modern belief in the "Sovereignty of the Individual."[92] The workers would not need to alienate their rights when they entered into slavery because neither they nor anyone else had any. There was nothing to be said on behalf of the Locke-inspired notion that workers have a natural right to the fruits of their labor because no one has a natural right to property: "Property is a mere creature of law and society," a "conventional right," to be handled as circumstances dictate.[93]

It was not too late for the South to save itself—and in so doing it might also save the world. A voracious reader, Fitzhugh learned from European socialist writers how severe the social problem was on their side of the Atlantic. The entire Western world was in danger of going up in flames, and it was up to America to show the way out. But before we could accomplish anything, we must first acknowledge that nothing but harm could come from the theories of Locke and Jefferson. "It is better to err with Pope, who thought 'Whatever is, is right,' than with Jefferson, whose every act and word proves that he held that 'Whatever is, is *wrong*.'"[94]

To convince his audience that he was the conservative he professed to be, Fitzhugh had to argue that his philosophy was an affirmation rather than a denial of the American tradition. So he asked his readers to ignore "the mischievous absurdity of our political axioms and principles" while remembering "the wisdom and conservatism of our political practices." "Our Revolution . . . was the act of a people seeking national independence, not the Utopian scheme of speculative philosophers, seeking to establish human equality"; "it was a salutary reform, not a revolution."[95] It said everything about the founders that they retained "the common law of England and the constitution of England" and never allowed their rhetorical "abstractions" to stand in the way of their common sense.[96]

John Taylor had wrapped his thought in the finery of Jefferson and held that the study of political science did not begin until the American Revolution translated Locke from theory into practice.[97] Fitzhugh, several decades later, deemed Jefferson "the architect of ruin, the inaugurator of anarchy," and believed no book on moral philosophy worth reading unless it was at least four centuries old, written before the advent of modern thinking in the social contract tradition.[98]

Fitzhugh took pride in pursuing Southern thought to what he regarded as its logical conclusion. His fellow Southerners, however, thought he had gone too far, both in his proposal of white slavery and in his iconoclastic assertion that "liberty is an evil which government is intended to correct."[99] As the year 1860 approached, the typical Southern politician resumed the languages of 1765 and 1776; lovely freedom and hideous oppression were the topics of the day, and the call was for "resistance" or "revolution." Jefferson came back into vogue, and the editors of the *Daily Picayune* of New Orleans bowed in reverence at the mention of "our revolutionary fathers."[100]

At the moment before the outbreak of the Civil War, there was no shortage of public figures in the South, Whigs and Democrats, who wanted to make a last-ditch effort to save the Union. When the legislature of Georgia passed a bill calling for a secession convention, the strongest unionists—Benjamin Hill, Herschel Johnson, and Alexander Stephens—duplicated the rhetoric of the nullifiers three decades earlier: "The sovereign people" must do everything within their power to offer "resistance," preferably through recognized institutional channels. Secession and revolution might yet be avoided, argued Stephens, if "the National Democratic men—the conservative men in the Senate"—continued to fight the good fight. Invocations of "the right of resistance" could be heard in Virginia, too, and throughout the South.[101]

The word "conservative" permeated the secession editorials of the South and the conventions held in the various states.[102] What it meant, however, was not the increasingly reactionary ideology of the likes of Hammond, Harper, and Fitzhugh. Rather, in 1860 it implied constitutional "resistance" instead of revolution, a return to something resembling the nonrevolutionary Whiggery of 1765. As Calhoun had done before them, the last-gasp Southern unionists of 1860 demanded that the North reconsider its program of "consolidated Democracy," its despotic predilection for outvoting the South on the basis of rule by the numerical majority.[103]

From the standpoint of the South, the electoral victory in 1860 of the sectional Republican Party marked the demise of hope that "conservative" Northerners would ally themselves with their Southern brethren. After the election of Lincoln, Nashville's *Republican Banner* asked, "What is secession?" "As an abstract principle it is an absurdity. It is simple to claim a constitutional right to rebel against the Constitution. . . . But, *practically*, what is secession? Merely another name for *revolution*, an inherent and inalienable right." Editors of the *Louisville Daily Journal* wrote that "the right of secession is properly denounced, but the President elect seems never to have dreamed of a right of revolution."[104] The time had come for the South to revisit 1776 rather than 1765.

When, in 1860, "we, the People of the State of South Carolina [met] in Convention assembled," there was no more Calhoun; no more talk of resistance, nullification, 1765, or old Whiggery. "Revolution" was the favorable watchword of the day; fond memories of the American Revolution of 1776 and even the French Revolution of 1789 were revisited. For decades conservatives had used the revolution in France as a scarecrow to frighten away advocates of natural rights and the social contract. Now the secession convention of South Carolina could offer the good citizens "no better motto than Danton's, . . . 'To dare! and again to dare! and without end to dare!'"[105]

In the name of the "great principles" of the American Revolution, the Southerners of all the rebellious states exited the Union. "It is the right of the people to alter or abolish a Government," they declared. Meeting in conventions, they reaffirmed their adherence to popular sovereignty. Once assembled, they demanded full recognition of their natural rights and proceeded to draw up a Confederate Constitution. Under the banner of Locke and freedom they entered the field of battle, ready to die to protect the institution of slavery.[106]

The Social Contract in the North

Northern thought paralleled Southern in that a dispute took place above the Mason-Dixon Line pitting strong exponents of Locke's social contract against equally vigorous conservative critics. There was, however, a substantial difference between Northern and Southern juxtapositions of radicals and conservatives. The more a philosophy of conservatism became embedded in Southern culture, the less Locke's voice was heard—until the time came to leave the Union. In the North, by contrast, the rise of a conservative outlook did not entail the demise of Locke. All through the antebellum period, radical Northerners refused to yield ground to conservatives, and, perhaps even more tellingly, conservative Northerners constantly found it necessary, when answering Southern claims, to return to Locke.

The radical voices cannot be missed. Jeffersonians and Jacksonians, upset by the manner in which economic development was proceeding, demanded a return to first principles. Newly emerging corporations, cut off from the people, compromising the freedom of future generations, provoked a radical Lockean counteroffensive that persisted throughout antebellum times. The earth belongs to the living, Jefferson had repeatedly said, and Paine had echoed those sentiments in his highly influential *Rights of Man* (1791–1792). Each generation must arrive at maturity unencumbered, free, and autonomous. Why, then, asked the Ohio Board of Commissioners in 1825, had we created "chartered companies, possessing exclusive privileges" that were beyond the reach of the legislature? "The present generation may in this way not only bind themselves, but their posterity forever."[107]

Faithful Jacksonian David Henshaw expressed similar consternation when in 1837 he looked back in anger at the famous Dartmouth College case of 1819. Thanks to the likes of John Marshall and Daniel Webster, the Supreme Court had ruled that Dartmouth was a private institution and, as such, need not answer to the state legislature. "Can corporations," asked Henshaw, "*the mere creatures of the law, created not for themselves, but for the common good,* claim rights . . . above the reach of the legislative power?!!" To make such a claim, as did Federalists of yore and the Whigs of his own day, was completely unacceptable: "Our institutions abhor private perpetuities and monopolies as much as nature abhors a vacuum." With whom should we side, the living or the dead? "The conservatives cling to the dead; I am for the living."[108]

If some Jacksonian Democrats criticized Whigs with arguments drawn from a radical social contract tradition, it is no less true that other reforming Jacksonians turned the same arguments against the Democratic Party. When a group of New York Democrats bolted from Tammany Hall between 1835 and 1837, they did so in the name of restoring "equal rights." The Loco-Foco or Equal Rights Party demanded what William Leggett called "the separation of bank and state."[109] Not just the Bank of the United States—Jackson's target—but state banks, too, had to be destroyed, in order to avoid the rise of monopolies and the advent of a banking aristocracy. A friendly workers' newspaper saw the battle waged by the Loco-Focos as the "first conflict of our second Revolution." "The Revolution of 1776 was against the monarch and aristocracy of England; this of 1836, is against charters and monopolies."[110] Speaking in their own voice, the Loco-Focos stated that "we hold the present banking system to be a system at war with the first principles of the social compact."[111]

Martin Van Buren was unacceptable to the Loco-Focos, to whom he seemed a mere politician and not a man of principle. Hence they nominated their own man for president in 1836 but did not stop there. In a bold move the Loco-Focos demanded that the voters themselves, rather than the party's inner circle, choose candidates for public office. Down with "monopolistic" and "aristocratic" party nominating committees, up with the sovereign people was their cry. "Are our legislators *directly* responsible to the committee and only *indirectly* to the people?"[112] The sovereign people retained their natural rights.

No theme was more central to the conventions and proceedings of the Loco-Focos than the denial that upon entering civil society, we surrender some of our natural rights. Perhaps the gravest problem, they suggested in 1837, was that what is often granted in words is belied by our everyday experience. "However great may be the extent of our *theoretical* freedom, the *practical* doctrine of our government has been that every poor man's child surrenders, at his birth, all the rights it derives from nature and nature's God."[113]

Advocates of the youthful trades union movement of the 1830s outdid the Loco-Focos in their scathing attacks on the courts.[114] Common-law judges, it was widely believed, were the nemesis of the workers. Forever striking down labor unions as "conspiracies"; sometimes describing the relationship between management and labor as that of master and servant; perpetually granting privileges to corporations; never resisting Blackstone's notion that our natural rights had, in effect, been superseded by legally sanctioned customs and civil rights—the common-law "aristocracy" was the sworn enemy of the "producers."[115] Something had to be done to stop the courts from denying the workers their natural right to the fruits of their labors.

During the 1830s Ely Moore, Seth Luther, Frederick Robinson, and Theophilus Fisk were among the labor leaders and spokespersons who took direct aim at lawyers, judges, and the common law. To Fisk the common law, a relic of "feudal barbarism," should never have been "engrafted upon our republican institutions," because it is "oppressive to the workingmen of our country."[116] To Luther it was the common law that was a "conspiracy," not the workers who organized for a fair wage.[117] Robinson held that "judges are members of a secret Trade Union of lawyers, called the bar, that has always regulated the price of their own labor." The unwritten law, Robinson derisively commented, was whatever the judge

CHAPTER TWO

wished it to be, and the precedents cited were frequently "unjust and wicked."[118] Ely Moore chimed in with the thought that the common law "is directly opposed to the spirit and genius of our free institutions, and ought, therefore, to be abrogated."[119]

Both the Loco-Focos and the labor unions appealed to natural rights against the common law. Had the Equal Rights Party of New York succeeded in enacting its proposed state constitution of 1837, juries would henceforth have decided the most difficult cases not on the basis of precedent but "according to natural right and justice."[120] On behalf of the workers, Ely Moore held that labor unions were "measures of *self-defence* and of *self-preservation* and therefore are not illegal," which was perfectly compatible with Locke's natural right of self-preservation.[121] In general, both Loco-Foco and labor representatives had cause to applaud Locke's claim in the *Second Treatise* that the law of nature was "as intelligible and plain to a rational creature . . . as the positive laws of commonwealths, nay possibly plainer."[122] A simplified code of laws, readily comprehended by anyone, should replace the mysteries of the common law.

The radicalism of the workers, significant as it was, was not as potent as the radicalism of the antislavery movement. For while natural rights doctrines were common to the workers and the antislavery agitators, there was a world of difference in their respective conceptions of the God who enjoined the rights of nature. The deity of the labor movement was the distant and unthreatening God of Jefferson and Paine, a God who resembled that of Matthew Tindal and other earlier English deists. In *Christianity as Old as the Creation* (1730) Tindal had spoken of the "rights which Nature and its Author has given Mankind," rights Jefferson reworded in the Declaration of Independence as "the laws of nature and nature's God."[123] Much more immediate, demanding, emotional, and evocative of a sense of sinfulness was the evangelical, millenarian, and transcendental God of antislavery.

Theodore Parker's work is a good example of what natural rights radicalism sounded like when spoken in a transcendental idiom. "The American idea is freedom, natural rights. Accordingly, the work providentially laid out for us seems this,—to organize the rights of man." Sadly, however, our history was compromised by African slavery, "the national sin." No doubt one reason why Parker cared little for Paine was the absence of a sense of sin in the "natural religion" of the eighteenth century. Americans in general, thought Parker, were in danger of becoming too busy with economic adventures and material betterment to acknowledge their sins or attend to moral betterment. The penchant of Americans for building their houses of wood, "a material that soon wears out," was an "apt emblem" of the "always a-changing" times.[124] One can imagine how disgusted Parker must have felt if he read the words uttered by a character in a novel by Nathaniel Hawthorne: "'I doubt whether even our public edifices—our capitols, state houses, courthouses, city hall, and churches—ought to be built of such permanent materials as stone or brick.'"[125] Another sign of the always a-changing times.

Running throughout Parker's writings was the theme that "in transcendental politics the question of expediency is always subordinated to the question of natural right." The complacent Whiggery of the English, therefore, was unacceptable: "[England's] legislation is [merely] empirical; great ideas do not run through her laws; she loves a precedent better than a principle." Too often in England or Scotland it was "common sense" that triumphed rather than "moral sense." Even Locke must be read with care, his natural rights politics applauded but his epistemology and psychology rejected. "Sensationalism knows nothing of absolute right . . . ; only of historical right." In effect, Parker argued that Locke's *Essay Concerning Human Understanding*, with its skeptical and hedonistic implications, should be ignored for the sake of saving the *Second Treatise*.[126]

The transcendental politician, Parker suggested, was different from the ordinary politician in that he "anticipates" and "transcends" history. Consider the example of 1776: "All human history said, 'That cannot be.' Human nature said, 'It can, must, shall.' The authors of the American Revolution . . . were transcendentalists to that extent."[127] Parker demanded of antebellum Americans that they again be transcendentalists; they must find a way to transcend slavery rather than wait for history to remove this greatest of all evils.

The question transcendentalists, evangelicals, and other antislavery advocates felt obliged to answer was how far they would go to end their complicity in slavery. William Ellery Channing wrote a powerful antislavery treatise in 1835 but stopped short of demanding that the Northern states leave the Union. Tirelessly he spoke in favor of inalienable rights and affirmed that they were "violated by slavery." Just as frequently he denied that any of us parted with a portion of our natural rights upon entering civil society, when all we had done was to adopt "new modes of securing them." Nor might the rights of either whites or blacks be "absorbed in the public good." To speak otherwise was to give aid and comfort to "the logic of despotism."[128]

Channing was as interested in "what is right" as in rights. "Duty must be primary, prominent, most conspicuous, among the objects of human thought and pursuit." Channing was not yet William Lloyd Garrison or Wendell Phillips; he was not willing to follow his logic to the point of ending the Union. But when he exclaimed, "What a grievous wrong is slavery!" conservatives North and South feared that it was just a matter of time until the Union would be shattered by the transcendental, evangelical God who sanctioned inalienable natural rights and abhorred the sin of slavery.[129]

Abolitionist William Lloyd Garrison did not hesitate to burn the Constitution, a document that was the worst of all social contracts, a "covenant with death," an "agreement with hell." Not for him the Union-saving compromises of Daniel Webster; nothing less would do than immediate emancipation or a declaration that the North would separate from the South. "Since the commencement of the nineteenth century, the Spirit of Reform has been developed in a shape, and to an extent, unknown to all preceding ages." Garrison identified with Christ, "the universal Reformer," and with Locke, from whom he learned that "every man has a right to his own body—to the products of his own labor." Fearlessly Garrison followed his thought to its conclusion: Laws currently in force admitting a right of slavery, he declared, were "utterly null and void, being . . . a daring infringement of the law of nature, a base overthrow of the very foundations of the social compact."[130]

When Garrison and the abolitionists spoke their uncompromising language, most Northerners shuddered. A conservative reaction was not long in coming. Public officials and journalists living above the Mason-Dixon Line began to rethink the theory of the social contract.

IN THE 1830s NORTHERNERS WERE PUT TO THE TEST. Both the nullification crisis and the abolitionist agitation had raised grave questions about the viability of the Union. Would the leading spokespersons stay with Locke's contract despite its radical implications, or would they have second thoughts and return to the likes of Pufendorf, or abandon social contract theory altogether?

Nathaniel Chipman, chief justice in the state of Vermont, reissued in 1833 the book on the "principles of government" that he had originally published in 1793. His voice, he acknowledged, was old, but he hoped that his message, a restatement of Locke and the principles of the American Revolution, would continue to be new. Our rulers were merely trustees; we had not relinquished our natural rights and could not if we would. The notion of alienable rights, he explained, came from a time "when government [was] supposed to be finally established, not by a compact between the individuals of the people, but between the people and the rulers." Although Chipman conceded Pufendorf's "great influence" in England, he did so only to underscore the distinctive accomplishments of America.[131] Nathaniel Chipman refused to compromise his and America's "principles" in a bid to please the South.

Other Northerners, on the lookout for ways to flatter defiant Southerners, mitigated their Lockean heritage or ransacked the *Second Treatise* in search of a passage useful to slaveholders. James Kirke Paulding, a Democrat who had traveled in the South, published *Slavery in the United States* in 1836. "The right of self-defence . . . cannot be alienated," he stated in what sounded like a gloss to Locke. His very next sentence, however, reinstated the old claim of alienability: "There are other natural rights which may be voluntarily relinquished." Before long it became evident that Paulding's motivation was to work out a social contract rationale for the South's peculiar institution. Slaves, he concluded, "have forfeited the right to freedom before they set foot on our soil."[132]

Paulding never revealed the source of his intellectual inspiration, but there is a strong possibility that he arrived at his position by promoting Locke's marginalia. Perhaps because of his interests in the Carolinas, Locke had modified his claim that we could not enslave ourselves, suggesting an exception for prisoners taken in a just war who might otherwise be put to death. Southerners such as Thomas Dew were quick to pounce on this opening for slave owners in the *Second Treatise*.[133] Paulding did not say so, but he might have done the same.

What Paulding argued from the perspective of a Northern Democrat, Calvin Colton argued from that of a Northern Whig of the second-party system. A leading journalist for his party, Colton declared that he was "always opposed to slavery, still opposed to it, judging it to be wrong, and desiring it to be abolished."[134] That, however, did not prevent him from publishing *Abolition a Sedition* in 1839, a pamphlet in which he gave vent to his contempt for those abolitionists who were brazenly pursuing their cause in defiance of the Constitution.

CHAPTER TWO

From Colton's perspective, the time had obviously come to tame the rhetoric of the social contract tradition. Life in the state of nature was miserable and best abandoned at the earliest possible moment, Colton advised, no matter that rude natural liberty must be left behind. "The moment a man enters into society, he resigns his liberty, and consents to be *subjected* to the regulations of the community." Order should be our primary concern because without order no one has any rights. As for the doctrine of inalienable natural rights, "there is not a single natural right that can be named, which may not . . . be abridged . . . by the artificial organization of society."[135]

Tom Paine, advocate of universal human rights, had proudly proclaimed himself a citizen of the world. Colton, by contrast, ridiculed the abolitionists because "*they* have no country but the world, and no countrymen but mankind."[136] While Colton did not entirely abandon the social contract tradition, he surely drained it of all meaningful Lockean content. His arguments were so similar to those being made in the South that it is difficult to know which came first—his argument or theirs, who influenced whom. One thing is certain: The examples of Paulding and Colton show that a conservative reaction was afoot above the Mason-Dixon Line.

Colton's brand of conservatism was too proslavery for most "Conscience Whigs" of the North, and too much a denial of the American revolutionary past. The conservative Whigs hungered for a usable past and did not hesitate to invent it if necessary. A typical conservative ploy of such Whig luminaries as John Quincy Adams, Daniel Webster, Edward Everett, Joseph Story, and William Seward was, year in and year out, to deliver speeches at Plymouth commemorating the landing of the Pilgrims. On these occasions the famous rock became an altar upon which the Whigs both worshipped tradition and transformed Locke's social contract into an unlikely emblem of continuity.

Senator Rufus Choate, a fervent Whig, suggested that the history of the Puritans should be written not as it happened but as it should have happened—as an American version of a novel by Sir Walter Scott.[137] Whether other Whigs listened to him is unknown, but they did read into the Puritans many views that took root much later, at the time of the American Revolution. Seward projected upon them an unlikely commitment to a "natural right to religious liberty of conscience"; Webster credited them with the honor of having founded their government upon the consent of the governed.[138] But it was John Quincy Adams who did the most to transform the Puritans into forerunners of the American Revolution.

Adams spoke first and set the tone for all subsequent Whig (mis)readings of New England's past. In Puritan history he discovered "perhaps the only instance, in human history, of that positive, original social compact, which speculative philosophers have imagined as the only legitimate source of government." The origins of European nations, by contrast, were obscure, except for England's "bastard Norman tyrant." Adams and other Whigs were determined to forge a marriage between conservatism and the American revolutionary social contract and were not about to allow the glaring absence in Puritan thought of concepts of natural rights and the state of nature, or the absence in social contract theory of a contract between God and people, to complicate matters.[139] The more they distorted history by reading the social contract back into a remote past, the more they demonstrated their devotion to the ideals of the American Revolution.[140]

New England's Whig conservatives did not limit the applicability of the revolutionary social contract to the past. Supreme Court Justice Joseph Story was a man of conservative convictions, a perfect Whig, ever attentive to forging social links through commerce and the common law, hostile to disruptive abolitionists and secessionists.[141] Yet, because America was built on a revolutionary foundation, he took the position that its citizens should not be discouraged from periodically asking questions of political obligation. "What, indeed, can tend more to exalt and purify the mind, than speculations upon the origin and extent of moral obligations?"[142] Rather than side with English Whigs, who suppressed such questions, Story followed his hero John Marshall, who had enrolled the social contract, consent, and popular sovereignty in his nationalist cause.[143]

The pattern of reasoning that Marshall initiated and Story continued was taken up most famously by Daniel Webster during the nullification crisis. Marshall had contended in *M'Culloch v. Maryland* (1819) that the Constitution was "emphatically and truly a government of the people," not the states. In the same vein Webster in the 1830s denied that the Constitution was a compact of states, arguing, "It is the People's Constitution, the People's Government; made for the People; made by the People; and answerable to the People." Webster, Story, and all the nationalists agreed that the people of the United States were sovereign, always adding that they were "one people."[144]

How American and Lockean the New England Whigs were, how little they resembled Hume, Blackstone, or Burke, is nowhere more evident than in the frank and repeated admission of Webster and his cohort of a right of revolution. Even if the Northern conservatives were tempted to pull back from conceding the legitimacy of a Lockean "appeal to heaven," their conflict with the Southerners forced them frequently to reiterate the radical right of revolution—as a trump card against nullification and secession. One Northern conservative after another stepped forth to assert that only if the Southerners were willing to take the final step of declaring revolution could they leave the Union. A constitutional right to disobey the Constitution was an absurdity.

Webster was typical. In answer to Senator Robert Hayne of South Carolina, the senator from Massachusetts said, "We who oppose the Carolina doctrine, do not deny that the People may, if they choose, throw off any government, when it becomes oppressive and intolerable." He did insist, however, that "the right of a State to annul a law of Congress cannot be maintained, but . . . upon the ground of revolution." In answer to Calhoun he argued that "secession as a revolutionary right is intelligible. . . . But as a practical right, existing under the Constitution, . . . it seems to be nothing but a plain absurdity." Webster's meaning was clear even if he was unwilling to state it bluntly: Unless South Carolina wished to go to war, it could neither nullify nor secede.[145]

A revolution was, of course, exactly what the conservatives of the North wanted to avoid. Their gamble was that by raising the stakes so high, they could bluff the South into folding. So the last thing Webster, Story, and their kind desired was to be faced with the threat of revolution on their own Northern soil, as happened in the Dorr Rebellion of the early 1840s. Rhode Island needed a substantial overhaul of the politically regressive Charter of 1636, which still served as the state constitution. When the legislature would not budge, Thomas Dorr called for a "People's Constitution." Events spun out of control, and martial law was declared.

Conservatives, in this situation, found themselves caught between their disdain for the Dorrites and their admission of a right of revolution. Some conservatives panicked and, temporarily at least, abandoned the American revolutionary tradition.[146] The greatest names, however, sought a way to say no to the Dorrites without withdrawing their many earlier statements in favor of the right of revolution. "I believe no harm can come from the Rhode Island agitation of 1841, but rather good," Webster declared before the Supreme Court. He did insist, however, that we "must look elsewhere than out of doors, and to public meetings, irregular and unauthorized, for the decision of such a question as this." No one should object that basic principles of government were being discussed because "harm can never come from their discussion, especially when such discussion is addressed to reason and not to passion." As always, Webster sang the praises of popular sovereignty but insisted that the people must act through their representatives, not directly. The American Revolution—American history in general—had been "marked by a peculiar conservatism." The people, though sovereign, had understood that they must restrain themselves, and now so must the good citizens of Rhode Island.[147]

Faithful conservative Daniel Webster moderated but did not renounce "revolution principles." The conservatives of the North, no less than its radicals, continued to abide by the philosophy of natural rights, popular sovereignty, and the social contract.

NORTHERN WHIGS WERE ABLE TO ANSWER the South but unable to strike a decisive intellectual blow. They had no trouble repudiating the old federalism of the South, the claim that the Constitution was merely an alliance of states; on this issue they even received the backing of President Andrew Jackson, who would only go so far, no farther, on states' rights.[148] But every time the Whigs appealed to the sovereign people of the entire nation, the Southerners effectively countered by calling upon the people of the various states. Both sides had their cases for whether America had been one people or thirteen in 1776 and whether "we, the people" in 1787 had been the people of the states or of America at large. Who signed the social contract? was the question, and it would not be answered until words gave way to guns.[149]

Prior to the Civil War, when the battle was still one of words, Whigs turned to the future for vindication. At Plymouth Rock, John Quincy Adams spoke not only of "veneration for our forefathers" but also of "love of our posterity." Edward Everett's address "The History of Liberty" took for its theme the belief that America was charged with a providential mission to be an exemplar to the world of the wonders that follow in the wake of ever-expanding liberty. He closed his speech by speaking of the link between the generations: "Let us resolve that our children shall have cause to bless the memory of their fathers, as we have cause to bless the memory of ours." William Seward's address "The Destiny of America" offered variations on the standard Whig theme that American freedom was inspiring Europe and South America to shake off the yoke of authoritarian regimes.[150]

Richard Hildreth was one Whig who could not abide the proud claims that America was spreading freedom abroad when he saw that his fellow citizens were quite willing to continue tolerating slavery at home. In 1840 he left the party, complaining that the United States was as much an "experiment of despotism" as an experiment of democracy and freedom. As he saw it, America was a "strange compound of liberty and despotism."[151]

Many other Whigs agreed with Hildreth, and they, too, eventually left the Whig Party to assume membership in the newly formed Republican Party. There the most dedicated of them, most famously Abraham Lincoln, could continue to seek for ways to limit and to choke slavery. In search of inspiration, they turned to the Declaration of Independence and incessantly quoted its ringing phrases about freedom and equality (chapter 5). The words the slaveholder Thomas Jefferson had borrowed from Locke became the promise that America might one day atone for its sins and redeem its providential promise.

THREE

■

The Right to Land
in the Land of Rights

From Thomas Jefferson in the late-eighteenth century to Henry George in the waning years of the nineteenth, American reformers incessantly addressed the question of land and proclaimed a natural right to the soil. Land on the other side of the mountain, land yet unsettled, the irrepressible dream of westward movement, encouraged Americans throughout the course of the nineteenth century to renew the revolutionary themes of natural rights and the social contract. "In the beginning all the World was America," wrote Locke, who recognized that talk about land in the state of nature was neither abstract nor metaphorical when applied to the New World.[1] Because of the continuing availability of land in nineteenth-century America, Locke's writings lived on in the United States, well beyond their European expiration date.

Every time Americans invoked the natural right to land, they found themselves in the odd situation of employing a universalistic political rhetoric while asserting the particularistic notion of "American exceptionalism." Europe and America were different from one another, they explained; America, rich in land, was all that Europe was not; yet all might not be lost on the other side of the Atlantic if only Europeans would discover how to make the most of what land they had. And so it was that Henry George packed his bags and carried his philosophy to the British Isles, where the question of land reform in Ireland was a burning issue at the close of the nineteenth century. What George offered in his own name to the likes of Herbert Spencer and George Bernard Shaw, and, most of all, to the downtrodden peasantry, was in reality a recapitulation of a century of American pronouncements on the inviolability of the social contract, the need to secure the rights of the next generation, and the natural right to the land.

Prior to Henry George, throughout most of the nineteenth century, Americans generally were less concerned with exporting their ideals to Europe than with preventing European degradation from coming to the United States. Americans of the antebellum period were proud to be exceptional but were fearful that their days of being different might be numbered. From the outset of their history Americans awaited with trepidation the moment when a historian would write an essay on the closing of the frontier. Self-consciously, they strove to defer the day when the conditions of the European working class would be duplicated in America.

For so long as there was open land and a recognized natural right to the soil, there was hope. The West was the American answer to what Europeans called the "social problem." And, for a brief moment after the Civil War, there was even a possibility that land might be used—"forty acres and a mule"—to ease the transition from bondage to freedom for the emancipated slaves. Whatever the problem, the natural right to land was the apparent solution.

Agrarianism and "Revolution Principles"

"Dependence begets subservience and venality, [and] suffocates the germ of virtue," Jefferson wrote in the early 1780s. "While we have land to labor, then, let us never wish to see our citizens occupied at a work-bench." Finishing with a characteristic rhetorical flourish, Jefferson announced that "those who labor in the earth are the chosen people of God."[2]

A youthful James Madison agreed that "the freeholders of the Country would be the safest depositories of Republican liberty," but he was as sober in his outlook as Jefferson was enthusiastic: "In future times," Madison told the members of the Constitutional Convention, "a great majority of the people will not only be without landed, but any other sort of property."[3] Much later, Madison the elder statesman continued to warn that "the people will be formed into the same great classes here as elsewhere."[4]

Those Americans who visited eighteenth-century Europe witnessed the poverty of the working classes at first hand and were perhaps the first to turn their thoughts to possible solutions, which more often than not had to do with land and a renewed application of revolutionary "principles." Thomas Paine is the most obvious example and the most influential.

Born in England, the American revolutionary Tom Paine traveled back to Europe in 1787 and participated in the great French events that began in 1789. During the early years of the revolution in France he issued his celebrated tract, *Rights of Man* (1791–1792), which included novel proposals for treating the problem of poverty. Later on, after the French Revolution had gone off course and, to his amazement, turned bloody, he reflected again on the solution to the social problem, setting forth his revised and embellished views in a pamphlet titled *Agrarian Justice* (1796). As he grappled with the problem of poverty, Paine walked a tightrope. On the one hand, he tried not to frighten his readers with the specter of dangerous radicalism; on the other, he grounded his proposals for reform in the radical principles of the social contract he had originally enunciated in *Common Sense* (1776).

Chapter 5 of the second part of *Rights of Man*, containing the program of social reform, was written during the early days of the French Revolution, a joyous time when Paine could praise the abolition of feudal laws and the promulgation of the Declaration of the Rights of Man and of the Citizen. Nothing was more obvious to Paine than that all would go well for France and for all of humankind as a result of the revolution; yet, even during these happy days, he could not avert his eyes from the plight of the poor. In the most civilized countries, he remarked, the elderly ended their lives in workhouses, the young on the gallows, because they found themselves in "a state of poverty and wretchedness, far below the condition of an Indian. I speak not of one country, but of all. It is so in England, it is so all over Europe."[5]

The modern economy, he continued to believe in 1792 as he had in 1776, could not be the problem: "It is a pacific system, operating to cordialize mankind." Predatory government, serving monarchs and privileged classes through the imposition of heavy taxes on the producers, was the underlying cause of poverty. To eliminate indigence he proposed progressive taxation on landed property, the revenue from which would fund such measures as education for the children of the poor, retirement at sixty followed by continuing support for the aged to their dying day, and public employment whenever jobs were otherwise unavailable, all in the name not of charity but of right.[6]

The outstanding political question of the day, Paine felt, was "not whether this or that party shall be in or not . . . , but whether man shall inherit his rights . . . , whether the fruits of his labors shall be enjoyed by himself, or consumed by the profligacy of governments?"[7] Faced with European conditions, Paine's outlook had undergone a transmutation from a laissez-faire, minimalist government position in 1776 to the advocacy of a welfare state in 1792, but even as he altered his stance, Paine remained steadfast in his adherence to a unifying philosophy of natural rights and social contract.

In the first part of *Rights of Man* (1791) Paine had taken the position, previously articulated by Jefferson, that the social contract must be constantly renewed; the generation entering the world must be as free, autonomous, and in control of its fate as the preceding generation. "Every age and generation must be free to act for itself."[8] A year later, in the second part of his treatise, Paine outlined the welfare proposals that were necessary to provide autonomy for the least favored of the new generation. Only if such measures were enacted would talk about the consent of all members of society have meaning.

When he penned *Agrarian Justice* Paine refused to be discouraged by the miscarriage of the French Revolution after 1792. True, the challenge was perhaps more daunting than he had realized four years earlier: "The contrast of affluence and wretchedness continually meeting and offending the eye, is like dead and living bodies chained together." Something had to be done for the poor before they would have the means to do anything for themselves: "The great mass of the poor, in all countries, are become an hereditary race, and it is next to impossible for them to get out of that state themselves." Where the guns of the French army had failed, his social program grounded in revolutionary principles would succeed if enacted by an enlightened government. "An army of principles," he assured his audience, "will penetrate where an army of soldiers cannot."[9]

In the best tradition of state of nature–social contract theorizing, Paine asserted in *Agrarian Justice* that "it is only by tracing things to their origin, that we can gain rightful ideas of them." Like Jefferson before him, Paine turned to American Indians for hints of life in a state of nature and, again like Jefferson, held that "the life of an Indian is a continual holiday, compared to the poor of Europe."[10] When he wrote *Rights of Man* Paine had been confident that the problem of poverty "lies not in any natural defect in the principles of civilization, but in preventing those principles having a universal operation." A mere four years later, in sharp contrast, he wondered aloud "whether the state that is proudly . . . called civilization has most promoted or injured the general happiness of man." Who can deny that the "most miserable of the human race are to be found in the countries that are called civilized?" Deeply entrenched poverty in the most advanced countries made Paine question in *Agrarian Justice* his long-standing assumption that the path from nature to civilization was one of preordained progress.[11]

The culprit was "landed monopoly." Private property in land "could not exist in the first state of man, that of hunters. It did not exist in the second state, that of shepherds." But it did exist in the third state, that of cultivators, and with momentous consequences—for at the same time that agriculture increased the productivity of the land, it "dispossessed more than half the inhabitants of every nation." Private property in land, passed on by inheritance, allowed the dead to govern the living and denied the new generation its birthright; in the name of natural right, something had to be done to offset this cumulative injustice. The earth belonged not to this or that man but was God's gift to all, "the common property of the human race." "Man did not make the earth"; God did, and in a just world, mindful of natural rights, "the value of the improvement only, and not the earth itself, [would be] individual property."[12]

On the verge, it seems, of a radical demand for wholesale redistribution or abolition of landed property, Paine decided that discretion was the greater part of ideological valor. He stepped back from the brink. Although he served as an advocate for all those "who have been thrown out of their natural inheritance by the introduction of the system of landed property," Paine was adamant that "the fault is not in the present possessors"; he expressed confidence that "the fault can be made to reform itself . . . without diminishing or deranging the property of any of the present possessors." Lest we miss the point, he affirmed that "I care not how affluent some may be, provided that none be miserable in consequence of it." The title he chose was "agrarian justice," not "agrarian law," so that no one would confuse his proposals with those of Tiberius Gracchus.[13] In the end, Paine settled in *Agrarian Justice,* much as he had in *Rights of Man,* for a kind of welfare state funded by ground rents and taxes on land. Revolutionary principles, in his hands, were directed at carrying out reform rather than initiating a social revolution. He called for modest redistribution without daring to utter that inflammatory word.

The legacy of *Agrarian Justice* to subsequent American land reformers probably lay more in Paine's two master conceptions than in his specific proposals. His first fundamental claim, repeated endlessly by his epigoni, was that although "the common right of all [to the land] became confounded into the cultivated right of the individual," the right of all to the original commons will nevertheless continue "so long as the earth endures."[14] The right to use of the land—or, in Paine's resolution, to an equivalent payment from a common fund—never ended, even when all the land is taken. Landowners owed something to the landless, who had been unjustly deprived of their heritage.

Paine's second master contention was also momentous. As never before, he advanced beyond the apparent individualism of his thought to a new recognition of how strongly society shapes and molds our being and unhesitatingly spelled out the consequences of his revised outlook for ownership. "Personal property is the *effect of Society;* and it is as impossible for an individual to acquire personal property without the aid of Society, as it is for him to make land originally." Therefore the individual who owns property "owes, on every principle of justice, . . . a part of that accumulation back from whence the whole came."[15] Before the close of the eighteenth century, Paine had already formulated the notion of a "debt to society" that would prove critical, especially in Europe, to later justifications of a welfare state.[16]

Tom Paine's pamphlets always sold exceptionally well and always provoked deeply divided responses. Many Americans never forgave him for the militant anti-Christian deism of *The Age of Reason* (1795), a brief book written to denounce "the obscene stories, the voluptuous debaucheries, the cruel and tortuous executions, the unrelenting vindictiveness, with which more than half the Bible is filled."[17] Paine revivals, nevertheless, have been a commonplace of American history, none more remarkable than that of the 1820s and 1830s. Beginning in 1825 and continuing each year thereafter, a dinner was held in New York City to commemorate his birthday; soon other major cities copied the initiative of the New Yorkers. Behind the festivities stood a significant new development: the birth of a working-class political movement. A stay-maker by trade, Paine identified with and became a hero to the artisans and laborers of England and America.[18]

No one in the workers' movement felt more deeply indebted and akin to Paine than Thomas Skidmore. Both men were autodidacts, both laborers, and Skidmore in 1829 had every reason to believe that Paine, were he alive, would have heartily approved of the substantial role he played that year in calling into being the Working Men's Party of New York. When Skidmore published *The Rights of Man to Property!* (also in 1829), he tellingly adapted his title from Paine's *Rights of Man.*

And yet Skidmore was, in certain respects, Paine's most severe critic. Not for Skidmore the gap Paine had opened between radical revolutionary principles and modest proposals for action. Whether for better or for worse, Skidmore set forth an unflinching attack upon landed property, upon private property in general, and called for a state constitutional convention to enact a general program of redistribution. In the name of the restoration of natural rights, Skidmore demanded what amounted to nothing less than a social revolution.

All of Skidmore's efforts were devoted to securing "the true Social Contract," grounded in "the true principles of government." To honor those principles, he was convinced, he had to criticize and fulfill Paine. "Mr. Paine charged Mr. Burke with not going back far enough into antiquity, in search of principles. . . . I now make a similar charge against Mr. Paine." If we conducted proper researches into principles, Skidmore asserted, we should discover that "in every government, the laws of property, have no reference, or very little, to original principles." "The truth is, *all* governments in the world, have begun wrong." Still not done, Skidmore, near the end of his text, summarized his position with these uncompromising words: "Such is the language of nature; such is the language of right; and such are the principles which will justify any people in pulling down any government which denies, even to a *single* individual of the human race, his possession . . . of this inalienable right of nature." Skidmore would not repeat Paine's mistake, "that of attempting to erect an equal government upon a foundation where inequality had already found an existence."[19]

The contrasting positions Paine and Skidmore took on the Agrarian Law of the Romans typify their differences. Fearing that his enemies would paint him as a dangerous rabble-rouser, Paine went out of his way to show that his proposals bore no resemblance to the legislation that had divided the Roman republic along class lines, inviting the outbreak of civil war between rich and poor. Skidmore, by contrast, did not shy away from the language of class conflict when discussing ancient Rome or modern America. Whereas Jeffersonians and Jacksonians had settled for denouncing metaphorical "aristocrats" who disdained the "people," or, at most, contrasted producers with nonproducers, Skidmore envisioned a world menacingly "divided into two distinct classes, proprietors and non-proprietors; those who own the world, and those who own no part of it."

The reason the Agrarian Law had failed, Skidmore contended, was that the Romans, having no printing press, no commerce or manufacturing, no genuinely representative political institutions, were not prepared for it. Of all that was lacking in antiquity, the most fatal missing ingredient, however, was awareness of the theory of the social contract. For the Romans to have a just agrarian law "required that they should have ascended to first principles: that they should have explored, philosophically, the primitive condition of man, and there have made themselves acquainted with the origin and fountain of all right."[20] The Americans, beneficiaries of progress, suffered from none of the ancient disabilities.

Despite his disagreements with the argument of *Rights of Man*, Skidmore was deeply indebted to Paine's book. On the question of the generations Skidmore could not second Paine too often, particularly his predecessor's theme that "it is the living, and not the dead, that are to be accommodated."[21] Throughout his own book Skidmore borrowed Paine's language to denounce last wills and testaments as the unnatural and illegitimate triumph of the rights-less dead over the rights of the living. The larger moral was clear: It was "manifestly absurd" to believe that the first generation, in signing the social contract, would have drawn up equal allotments for itself while sanctioning inequality for its successors and equally absurd to think that later generations would have consented to such an unjust arrangement. As Skidmore saw it, Paine taken to his logical conclusion was Skidmore, who called for the property of the deceased to be returned to a common pool and redistributed, as needed, to maintain the equality of the generations.[22]

Not surprisingly, Skidmore's peers in the working-class movement shunned him to save themselves and their cause from the charge of radicalism run amok. Ely Moore, perhaps the most widely recognized labor leader in New York and the nation, assured his fellow members of the House of Representatives, after being elected to Congress on the Democratic ticket in 1834, that workingmen wanted nothing to do with the idea of equality of possessions. Stephen Simpson, leading spokesperson of the Philadelphia Working Men's Party, and that party's congressional candidate in 1830, described himself as an "anti-agrarian." Seth Luther, another major figure of the labor movement, wasted no time before offering a public endorsement of private property.[23]

George Henry Evans's response to Skidmore was multilayered. Throughout most of 1829 the two men seemingly had everything in common: Both were founders that year of the Working Men's Party of New York, and Evans was so enamored of Skidmore's program that on the masthead of his newspaper, the *Working Man's Advocate,* he ran the Skidmore-inspired slogan "All children are entitled to equal education; all adults to equal property; and all mankind, to equal privileges." But by the third issue of the paper, November 14, 1829, Evans had deleted the words about property. On second thought, Evans, the future land reformer and godfather-to-be of the Homestead Act, had decided that to side with Skidmore was to discredit the workers' movement.[24]

At the same time that he distanced himself from Skidmore, Evans continued throughout his career to toast Paine's *Agrarian Justice.* In 1846 he raised his glass in honor of "Agrarian Justice: The proper basis of a Republic; the means of intelligence and progress for a universal brotherhood." His toast of 1850 was dedicated to "the author of *Common Sense* . . . : His *Rights of Man* effective artillery for tearing down rotten despotisms; his *Agrarian Justice* excellent material for building up democratic and social republics."[25]

The genius of Evans's "new agrarianism" of the 1840s was that it was unthreatening and popular, yet retained much of the old radicalism. "Vote Yourself a Farm" became his irresistible slogan after he turned from organizing workers into a political party to his new strategy of encouraging them to move West, where seemingly unoccupied public lands beckoned and a new life awaited them. Unlike Skidmore, who raised the explosive issues of confiscation and redistribution of all property, Evans and his National Reform movement concentrated upon distributing land that belonged to no one—or, rather, to everyone.

Despite his quest for respectability and political success, Evans never abandoned his "revolution principles." On the contrary, he insisted that Skidmore's fault was that he had inadvertently undermined the principles of the Revolution. Looking back from 1842, Evans criticized Skidmore's "grand error [in 1829], that men, on entering into society could surrender their natural right to the soil, on condition that every citizen, on coming of age, should receive an equal amount of property." Skidmore was wrong "in supposing that one generation might barter away a natural right of future generations for something which might not be approved as a substitute." On revolutionary principles, "the men of every generation have the same 'original right of soil' that any generation ever had; a right which cannot be affected by any act of any generation that has preceded them," no matter how well intended.[26]

Evans never went as far as Skidmore, for whom all property of every variety was for use rather than individual ownership. Determined to follow "true principles," Evans did, however, insist that the land always belonged to everyone, never to the particular persons to whom it had been lent for a generation. In 1841 he wrote "that the use of the LAND is the equal natural right of all the citizens of this and all future generations, and therefore that the land should not be a matter of traffic, gift or will. In other words, that the land is not transferable like the products of a man's labor. From which it will be inferred that I consider the institution of property in land to be [a] great error." The same sentiments can be found in his *Working Man's Advocate,* 1844: "We hold that men have a right to live on land to till it for a subsistence, but they have no right in nature to *sell* or *give* an exclusive privilege to it to another; . . . it belongs equally to the human family."[27]

Paine, Skidmore, and Evans forged an alliance between practical proposals and theoretical principles. The practical meaning of their agrarianism was protection of American workers from reduction to the European conditions of exploitative wage labor and poverty. The theoretical meaning of their agrarianism, which I shall now explore more fully, was that land reformers had rededicated themselves to revolutionary principles derived from philosophies of the social contract.

Philosophers and Agrarians

Lurking beneath the surface of American nineteenth-century discussions of land reform were the grand European texts of the seventeenth century, wherein the leading minds had articulated different versions of the theory of the social contract. Scratch the writings of Paine, Skidmore, and Evans, and one encounters Grotius, Pufendorf, and Locke, creatively adapted to American conditions.

Grotius comes first, both chronologically and conceptually, and he has far more significance for land reformers than one might anticipate. On first glance there is, of course, every reason to anticipate that the American land reformers would toss their copies of Grotius into the bonfire of the vanities. To them, philosophies of natural law and natural rights were a means to judge and condemn what existed and to demand significant social reform. To Grotius, by contrast, natural law was the pillar of the established order, the source sanctifying whatever legal contracts had been agreed to, yet it had no voice of its own except when the civil laws were silent. Whatever is, is right, so long as it is legally sanctioned, might have been his motto.[28]

It was Grotius's remark that the land had been given by God to all humans in common that attracted the attention of agrarian reformers. Not everything on the face of the earth was meant to be held as private property, said Grotius—certainly not the sea, which would ever belong to everyone and therefore to no one. So he wrote in *The Free Sea* (1609), in defense of Dutch claims to the right of unfettered access to lucrative markets in the East Indies. Later, in *The Law of War and Peace* (1625), he repeated the argument that "the sea . . . cannot be subject to private ownership," while adding the important new claim that once upon a time the land, also, had not been held as private property. Speaking of the primitive and simple times of yesteryear, he remarked that "the enjoyment of this universal right [to land] then served the purpose of private ownership." This "community of property arising from extreme simplicity, may be seen [today] among certain tribes in America, which have lived for many generations in such a condition without inconvenience."[29]

Over the centuries private ownership of property had arisen. "This happened not by a mere act of will . . . but rather by a kind of agreement, either expressed . . . or implied, as by occupation. . . . All agreed, whatever each one had taken possession of should be his property."[30] What had been done could not be undone without inducing an outbreak of the disorder and chaos that Grotius had dedicated his work to eradicating from civilized societies. Arrangements centuries in the making were right and just because they had been agreed upon, no matter that some persons had been left behind either during the original occupation of the commons or at a later date.

For Grotius the original community of property was past and gone, and it was unthinkable that anyone should appeal to those prehistorical days to justify schemes of forcible redistribution of property. Nevertheless, he did admit that the original commons had some bearing in his own day upon the plight of the poor: "In direst need the primitive right of user revives, as if community of ownership had remained." Obviously no one would have agreed to the original contract if the consequence might have been starvation: "We must consider what the intention was of those who first introduced individual ownership; and we are forced to believe that it was their intention to depart as little as possible from natural equity." Hence, he concluded, sometimes there is justification for extremely necessitous persons to seize upon and make temporary use of property belonging to others.[31]

Pufendorf counts in the story of American agrarians only to illustrate what they could not accept. Prominent in American thought during the years preceding independence (chapter 1), sometimes invoked during antebellum times (chapter 2), he was irrelevant to the land reformers of the nineteenth century by virtue of his rejection of Grotius's never-quite-defunct original commons. To Pufendorf's mind, the notion that the poor could under extreme circumstances avail themselves of the possessions of others was a formula fatally destructive of established property rights. If there had been an original commons granted by God to man, it belonged not to everyone but not yet to anyone and had absolutely no contemporary significance. By a "covenant either tacit or express" the land had been taken possession of in ages past, and present property arrangements were protected by the web of contracts which designated mine and thine.[32]

Pufendorf was not unwilling to do something for the poor in cases of dire necessity, but his program was along lines that American land reformers categorically rejected.[33] The absolute monarchy of Pufendorf's aspirations had expansive powers to serve the public good by regulating the economy. Controlling wages and prices, exercising eminent domain, overseeing guilds, and sponsoring trading companies were among the economic functions his government might discharge. Taking care of the poor could be added to the list, but as a matter of serving the public good rather than honoring natural rights.[34]

At the opposite end of the spectrum, then, was Tom Paine, who insisted in both *Rights of Man* and *Agrarian Justice* that his programs for the poor were grounded in long-overdue recognition of their natural rights. Paine was equally insistent that government would actually shrink in size as a result of his reforms, which would eliminate the pensions and subsidies enjoyed by the privileged social orders. Never did Paine completely disabuse himself of the notion, expressed in *Common Sense*, that "government even in its best state is but a necessary evil."[35] And what was true of Paine was no less true of the land reformers who followed in his footsteps: All pleaded their cases in terms of natural rights, not charity, and all believed their schemes would reduce the size and power of government to insignificance.

Even Skidmore, the most radical of the reformers, was convinced that after his proposals for redistribution were enacted by a state constitutional convention, the government of New York would be greatly simplified and its powers curtailed. Like Paine before him and agrarians afterward, he took it for granted that minimal government was good government. "I take it to be a truth not to be controverted, that each individual knows better how to apply his own industry, his own facilities, advantages, opportunities, property, etc. than government can possibly do."[36]

Henry George, too, in his grand end-of-the-century synthesis of the agrarian tradition, announced that "whatever savors of regulation and restriction is in itself bad." Not the least of the virtues of his program of land reform was "the great simplicity which would become possible in government." Indeed, "society would thus approach the ideal of Jeffersonian democracy, the promised land of Herbert Spencer, the abolition of government."[37] Pufendorf, the defender of expansive and paternalistic government, the denier of the original commons, was obviously odd man out in the world of the agrarians.

No one will be surprised to learn that John Locke, not Grotius, and certainly not Pufendorf, was the intellectual godfather of the agrarian reform movement in America. God's original grant of the land to humankind as a common possession was affirmed in *Two Treatises of Government*, as it had been in Grotius's writings. But in Locke's work, unlike Grotius's, our original God-given natural rights were never alienated, never decisively overridden by subsequent civil law, and could always be cited by reformers in justification of their call for change. Grotius and Pufendorf within the social contract tradition, and Filmer its critic, had decided what ought to be on the basis of what had been and was. Locke was the welcome exception: Arguments from history had "no great force," he insisted; natural law, he added, was "plainer" than the laws of the commonwealth. On these matters the American land reformers were in complete agreement with him.[38]

In a number of other important ways Locke offered the American agrarians much of what they desired. Their vision was of a producers' republic, not a rural arcadia, so they nodded approvingly upon reading in Locke, "Labour makes the far greatest part of the value of things"; "Tis Labour then which puts the greatest part of value upon land."[39] Locke's economic views were forward-looking, unlike Pufendorf's, which made Locke perfect for America, where the agrarians were enamored of the scientific agriculture of Jefferson. From Paine onward, American land reformers stressed not visions of idyllic, bucolic life, and not the land per se, but the value added by progressive, inventive labor.

To say that the American agrarians were the devoted offspring of Locke is true but not the entire truth because they subjected the *Second Treatise* to vigorous revisionism. A passage in George Henry Evans's *Working Man's Advocate*, 1844, illustrated both their agreements and their disagreements with Locke. "Man has no right to sell or destroy his own life," wrote the editor, whose words echoed Locke's claim that we never have the right to destroy ourselves or sell ourselves into slavery. But whereas Locke believed that land was justly removed from the original commons and transformed into private property, Evans and his coterie held that this amounted to permitting man to destroy his livelihood, as if "he has a right to destroy his life." Only by keeping landed property common, argued Evans, could Locke's natural rights be sustained. Both use-rights of land and ownership of the product of one's labor must be safeguarded at all costs, but we would be guilty of denying the next generation their natural rights if ownership of the land itself were permitted.[40]

How strongly the land reformers defined themselves not only with but also against Locke is nowhere more evident than in Skidmore's formulations. Precisely because he was uncompromising, Skidmore is an excellent source for unearthing exactly what the land reformers found wanting in Locke. A more systematic thinker than Evans and most agrarians, Skidmore responded not to the *Second Treatise* alone but also to Locke in relation to other writers; in Skidmore one finds a striking recapitulation and update of the most famous debates of seventeenth-century social contract theorists with one another and with the critics of the social contract. The ghosts of Locke, Grotius, Filmer, and possibly even Rousseau flitter across the pages of *The Rights of Man to Property!*

Presumably Skidmore understood that it was Filmer whom Locke was answering—Filmer, the archenemy of the social contract, who had mischievously inquired how universal consent to the privatization of property could possibly be secured: "Certainly it is a rare felicity," wrote Filmer in a taunting tone, "that all men in the world at one instant of time should agree together in one mind to change the natural community of things into private dominion." Had not Grotius and the social contractualists presupposed that nothing less than unanimity would suffice? inquired Filmer. "For if but one man in the world had dissented, the alteration had been unjust. . . . And then it will be lawful for every man, when he please, to dissolve all government, and destroy all property."[41] In short, the theory of the social contract was unworkable and anarchical.

"I shall endeavor," Locke wrote in response to Filmer, "to show how men might come to have a property in several parts of that which God gave to mankind in common, and that *without any express compact of all commoners*."[42] Within Locke's world there clearly was no problem with presupposing, in the first place, that self-owning, rational individuals would unanimously agree to a contract protecting their lives and liberties. As for the far more difficult problem, the question of how the original commons could ever be unevenly but consensually divided, labor was the solution. Universal agreement was not required; it was enough that each person in mixing his labor with a parcel of land made it his own, an extension of his person. By "the labour of his body and the work of his hands," he "excludes the common right of other men"; and since some persons labor more than others, they deserve more.[43] Locke had discovered an ingenious way to undo the damage Filmer had inflicted on philosophies of consent.

Skidmore's decisive move was to reject Locke's argument that labor could be substituted for unanimous consent. Quite possibly the citation to Jean Jacques Rousseau in his opening pages was more than a literary nicety, for Rousseau had stated in advance the case that Skidmore would make against Locke's position: "In vain the rich might say, I earned this field by my labor," argued Rousseau in the *Discourse on Inequality;* "Do you not know that a multitude of your brethren die or suffer from need of what you have in excess, and that you needed express and unanimous consent of the human race to appropriate to yourself anything from common subsistence that exceeded your own?"[44]

Albeit his words were less eloquent than Rousseau's, Skidmore set forth precisely the same argument, that neither labor nor anything less than "the consent of all" was acceptable to justify the demise of the original commons. "If we were to allow the principle," Skidmore asserted, "that because a man came into possession, even by rightful means, of the materials of the world . . . , and employed upon them his industry . . . , that *therefore,* the materials as well as the labor employed upon them, were of right his property, . . . it would go to the length of annihilating, *in toto,* the rights of every subsequent generation."[45] What Filmer had argued to destroy the theory of the social contract—his claim that unanimous consent was unthinkable—was reiterated by Skidmore for the opposite purpose of accentuating the radical implications of the philosophies of Grotius and Locke. By right the land was, is, and ever will be common property.

Skidmore's radicalism is less shocking if we recall how much he and the subsequent land reformers owed to the prior writings of English radicals. American revolutionary ideology had a respectable English pedigree in the radical Whiggery of the likes of Price, Priestley, and Paine, and the same was true of the land reformers. England's Thomas Spence, disturbed by the enclosure movement, had preceded and inspired the American land reformers with writings such as *The Real Rights of Man* (1775). Long before the agrarians of America had made their mark, Spence had radicalized Locke by announcing that "the first landholders [were] usurpers" who had wrongly claimed the land "as if they had manufactured it and it had been the work of their hands." That which began as common land must again be held in common; and once the land had been reclaimed, "the power of alienating the least morsel . . . is denied." American agrarianism consisted of glosses to Spence, and some of his formulas, such as the affirmation "that mankind have as equal and just a property in land as they have in liberty, air, or the light and heat of the sun," were destined to be endlessly reiterated in America.[46]

Although Skidmore was assuredly at the extreme end of the spectrum, he was less out of the mainstream of American thought than has sometimes been maintained.[47] As we have seen, it was not only Skidmore but Paine and Evans, too, who maintained that the original commons did not end when we departed from the state of nature to take up residence in the state of civil society. The same idea, we shall find, was hinted at, alluded to, and sometimes explicitly endorsed by a plethora of land reformers in the period leading up to the Homestead Act, and later by Henry George.

The great advantage of the land reformers over Skidmore was that they could pursue their goals by advocating a relatively unthreatening distribution of unoccupied public lands, whereas he preached a utopian doctrine of redistribution of all private property in the state of New York. Land reform was not utopian, definitely not beyond the pale in land-rich America.

Nor was it reactionary. When land reformers spoke of the soil their voices were not nostalgic; they did not quote from Horace or yearn to return to the past, nor did they express dismay that a machine was about to disrupt the tranquility of their idyllic garden.[48] Their objective, rather, was to reap the rewards for all Americans that would inevitably ensue if only their fellow citizens remembered that the terms of the social contract had yet to be fulfilled. Jefferson's words, in effect, were theirs: "I like the dreams of the future better than the history of the Past."[49]

To the Homestead Act

Throughout the antebellum era, land reformers unceasingly proclaimed the natural and inalienable right to the soil. Despite their relatively small numbers, George Henry Evans's National Reformers were emboldened by their awareness that in a period of intense conflict between major political parties and a proliferation of third parties, one party or another might be willing at any given moment to attempt to win an election by taking up their cause of free homesteads. Far from being marginalized, the land reformers distinguished themselves as influential theorizers, image-makers, and politicians.

In the creation of popular symbols the agrarian reformers excelled and proved how politic they could be. A recurring and effective motif in their speeches and writings, borrowed from labor organizers and radical democrats, was the theory-laden metaphor of a banquet. As was so often the case, it was Thomas Skidmore who set the tone: "Those who have gone before us, have been the first to sit down to the table, and to enjoy themselves without interruption from those who came afterwards; . . . they have disposed of the whole dinner, in such a manner, that nine-tenths of the beings that now people this globe, have not wherewith to dine, but upon the terms such as these first monopolisers shall choose to dictate."[50] Frederick Robinson offered his version of the same theme in a speech delivered to the Trades Union of Boston, 1834: "All mankind are one great family, and the Almighty Father of us all has made our common mother earth to produce bountifully. . . . He spreads his great table before us and loads it with abundance. He gives all an equal right to partake, and yet a few gormandizers devour the whole and leave the rest to want."[51]

From the Working Men's Party and the trades unions, the metaphor of the banquet passed naturally to the land reform movement and eventually into the pages of *Progress and Poverty*. "The child of the people, as he grows to manhood in Europe," wrote Henry George, "finds all the best seats at the banquet of life marked 'taken,' and must struggle with his fellows for the crumbs that fall, without one chance in a thousand of forcing or sneaking his way to a seat."[52] Soon, he warned, America may resemble Europe.

The banquet metaphor was successful because it effectively captured the notion that each new generation must be autonomous but never would be if generations dead and gone were permitted to distribute nature's bounty to the few while denying it to the many. The earth belonged to the living— all the living, the working classes included. Jefferson was the hero of both the working-class organizers and their offspring, the National Reformers.

Even more popular than Jefferson, of course, was the Bible. Paine in *The Age of Reason* had tossed out the Old Testament as an obscene and barbaric text; George Henry Evans, more politic than Paine, regularly quoted from Leviticus on the masthead of his newspaper, *The Radical*: "The land shall not be sold forever; for the land is mine; for ye are strangers and sojourners with me."[53] Some land reformers believed Moses had advocated use-rights rather than ownership; all proclaimed Moses' support for the congressional bills leading up to the Homestead Act.

Religious imagery and spiritual justifications came in handy, but the theories behind the new agrarian movement were quite independent of revealed religion. Arguably the single most fully realized theoretical articulation of the outlook of National Reform is John Pickering's *The Working Man's Political Economy* (1847). Beyond the popular imagery, beyond the journalism of Evans, Pickering set forth a mature and fully developed account of the philosophy of National Reform.

Pickering began with a set of assertions that were standard fare in the circles of labor movements: "Men do not accumulate property in proportion to their industry; but the reverse." Farmers, mechanics, and laborers "create all the wealth of the world, not even excepting its capital"; yet the producers are systematically robbed of the fruits of their labors, with the result that "in all civilized countries, as the rich become richer, the poor become poorer."[54]

What stands out in Pickering's account is that he did not stop at sounding the standard alarm that the miserable conditions of the working poor of England might soon find their analogue in America. He went on to warn that by welcoming the writings of William Paley and William Blackstone, Americans had placed themselves in danger of capitulating in advance and in permanence to the systematic social injustice that plagued the Old World.

When Paley delivered his lectures, originally published in 1785, his explicit objective had been to free the texts of Grotius and Pufendorf from "the profusion of classical quotations" with which the authors had burdened the reader.[55] He succeeded so effectively that his might well have been the most popular textbook on moral and political philosophy in America from the 1790s to the Civil War.[56] As for content, Paley's trademark was the utterance of radical-sounding phrases, quickly withdrawn in favor of arguments blessing the status quo. When all was said and done, Pickering complained, Paley was merely "an orthodox author" whose writings sanctioned everything that must be repudiated.[57]

It was characteristic of Paley that he should offer a sympathetic account of the image of the banquet and then quickly retreat to the statement that "the real foundation of our right is, THE LAW OF THE LAND." Also remarkable and indeed notorious was the passage in which "pigeon Paley" spoke of a flock of pigeons, ninety-nine of whom labored to feed one. "Among men, [likewise] you see the ninety-and-nine toiling and scraping together a heap of superfluities for one . . . , while they see the fruits of all their labour spent or spoiled; and if one of the number take or touch a particle of the hoard, the others joining against him, and hanging him for theft." After such a promising beginning, after asserting that "inequality of property, in the degree to which it exists in most countries in Europe, abstractly considered, is an evil," Paley immediately informed his audience that to question private property, society's most sacrosanct institution, was in no one's interest.[58] Charity and poor relief were the most that he was prepared to offer, which led Pickering to this summary of Paley's position: "The rich give up none of their rights, and get all the protection; while the poor give up all their rights, and get none of the protection."[59]

Pickering quoted with warm approval Paley's statement that "the poor have a claim founded in the law of nature, which may be thus explained: All things were originally common."[60] Unfortunately, thought Pickering, the conservative English moralist lacked the courage to draw the conclusion that the land must be returned to the original commons. Paley was unwilling to face up to the truth that Pickering was eager to underscore, namely, that the transformation of the commons into private property was "the primary cause of all the moral and social evils of society." "The fundamental error" of our ancestors, Pickering maintained, was that of "making private property of the elements of nature, which were the free gift of God in common to all mankind."[61]

Blackstone, too, had stated views that, if taken seriously, would have made him the future friend of the National Reformers. "The principal aim of society is to protect individuals in the enjoyment of those absolute rights which were vested in them by the immutable laws of nature," we read in the *Commentaries*.[62] "Now we should like to know," asked Pickering, "if anything can be written more radical than the foregoing sentiments of Mr. Blackstone?"[63] Another of Blackstone's utterances was so much to the liking of the National Reformers that Pickering quoted it and George Henry Evans ran it on the masthead of his newspaper: "There is no foundation in nature or in natural law, why a set of words upon parchment should convey the dominion of land."[64] To all appearances Blackstone had anticipated Paley, who called private property in land "paradoxical and unnatural."[65]

The problem with Blackstone was that, far more indebted to Grotius and Pufendorf than to Locke, he allowed many of our natural rights to be bartered away at the signing of the social contract. "Every man, when he enters society, gives up part of his natural liberty," Blackstone announced from the outset, and then devoted his studies to determining "what degree every man retains of his natural liberty; what he has given up as the price of the benefits of society." "The original of private property is probably founded in nature," he suspected, but long ago human-made laws were rightly recognized as providing "those civil advantages, in exchange for which every individual has resigned a part of his natural liberty."[66]

Pickering would have none of it. Blackstone, admittedly, was "a profound thinker," but the miserable "object and end" of his four volumes was to show "by what means and by what rules man's absolute, natural and unalienable rights might and should be violated." His *Commentaries* "rob [the worker] of his unalienable right in the soil, and plunder him of the labor of his own hands." In the pages of Blackstone, the alienable rights of Pufendorf trump the inalienable rights of Locke.[67]

Pickering insisted that his quarrel was not with the man named William Blackstone: "We battle not with men, but false principles," the false principles of 1688. True principles, of course, were those of 1776. When Pickering turned to his positive message, his references were to popular sovereignty; the Declaration of Independence; and the "restoration" of the "absolute, natural, unalienable rights of all men." Never should Americans settle for anything less than the fulfillment of the demand that flowed inexorably from their revolutionary principles: "A free soil for a free people, and an inalienable homestead for all."[68]

From 1848 to 1860, as old parties broke apart or reconfigured themselves and new ones emerged, the National Reformers were frequently in the position of being courted by parties old and new. Though the new agrarians rarely succeeded in their own right in winning election to office, their slogans and positions had a way of cropping up in the most respectable company.[69]

For a good example of a new party that included land reform in its program, we need look no further than the abolitionist Liberty Party and its presidential nominee in 1848: Gerrit Smith. National Reformers must have thought they heard their own echo when Smith stood up on the floor of Congress and took the stand "that the right to the soil is as natural, absolute, and equal, as the right to the light and the air." In the matter of land reform, as elsewhere, Smith insisted that the nation adhere "to the great and precious principles at its birth."[70] Neither George Henry Evans nor John Pickering could have said it better. Nor could they have been in stronger agreement with his comments on generational autonomy, which in 1854 he applied specifically to the question of land: "They, who compose a generation, are, so far as natural rights are concerned, absolutely entitled to a free and equal start in life; and that equality is not to be disturbed, and that freedom is not to be encumbered, by any arrangements of the preceding generation." Perhaps most strikingly, but entirely in keeping with the beliefs of Evans and Pickering, Smith held that "what a man produces from the soil, he has an absolute right to. . . . But no such right can he have in the soil itself."[71]

Gerrit Smith had a radical temperament, but he knew how to temper his challenging rhetoric and mollify his audience. Donning his radical persona, he held that "arguments drawn from precedents are of doubtful value. An age of progress should rise above precedents—should make precedents for itself." Then, in an effort to reassure apprehensive voters, he suggested that in a country as sparsely populated as America there was no immediate need to redistribute landed property; moreover, for many years to come, the maximum amount of land at anyone's legitimate disposal would remain as high as five hundred acres in America, which he contrasted with overpopulated Ireland, where holdings should not exceed thirty or forty acres.[72]

Support for a Homestead Bill was not unusual within the ranks of the Democratic Party, some of whose members moved on from denouncing the "Bank monopoly" to the next step of rejecting the "land monopoly."[73] The speeches in Congress of Andrew Johnson, loyal Jacksonian and future president, are a case in point. Although a practical politician, Johnson did not shy away from high-sounding language about the "great first principles which lie at the foundation of all things." Moses and natural law philosophy, he said, had shown him the way to the Homestead Act, and so had President Jackson, from whose annual speech to Congress, 1832, Johnson quoted at length.[74] Many another advocate of land reform would likewise cite Jackson's speech of December 4, 1832.

In his speech President Jackson, ever attentive to the West and opposed to the policies of Henry Clay, argued vigorously that "our true policy [should be] that the public lands shall cease as soon as possible to be a source of revenue, and that they shall be sold to settlers in limited parcels at a price barely sufficient to reimburse to the United States the expense of the present system." His goal was "to afford to every American citizen of enterprise the opportunity of securing an independent household." Andrew Johnson quoted Jackson's statements that "independent farmers are everywhere the . . . true friends of liberty" and that "it is their labor alone which gives real value to the lands." He did not quote but would certainly have approved of Jackson's grounding of his claims in concern for "human rights" and a duty to be "guided by a lofty spirit of devotion to the great principles on which our institutions are founded."[75]

Andrew Johnson "wished to be distinctly understood that he was no agrarian, no leveler. . . . His system was to elevate, not to pull down." Land reform in America would save the nation from the upheavals of Europe. On the Continent the passing of the soil into the hands of the few had given rise to calls for "the overthrow of monarchies, revolutions in aristocracies, and the crumbling down of rotten and corrupt dynasties." Because of the denial of "original" principles, "revolution begins [in Europe], and those principles are partially or entirely restored." In America, by contrast, revolution was unnecessary because the original principles of the Revolution had been misplaced but not abandoned and were ever available to anyone who remembered the words of "the immortal Jefferson" and applied them to land reform.[76]

The advent of the Free Soil Party in 1848, dedicated to keeping slavery out of the territories, opened another door of opportunity for the proponents of free homesteads. "Let the soil of our extensive domains be kept free," read the platform of 1848, "for the hardy pioneers of our own land, and the oppressed and banished seeking homes of comfort and fields of enterprise in the New World." By 1852 the rhetoric had undergone a significant upgrade: In the name of fundamental principles and natural rights, the party demanded that land be granted, free of cost, to landless settlers. "All men," stated the 1852 platform, "have a natural right to a portion of the soil; . . . the right of all men to the soil is as sacred as the right to life itself."[77]

George Washington Julian was a Free Soil delegate in 1848, the vice-presidential candidate of the renamed Free Democrats in 1852, and a member of Congress whose speech of January 29, 1851, in favor of a homestead bill, is a perfect compendium of familiar sayings. He, too, quoted Andrew Jackson's speech, castigated land monopoly, and warned that America must not become Ireland. "The bill under consideration . . . abandons the idea of holding the public domain as a source of revenue; it abandons, at the same time, the policy of frittering [it] away by grants to the States . . . ; and it makes it free, in limited portions, to actual settlers, on condition of occupancy and improvement." The policy he advocated, he told his fellow congressmen, "is the doctrine of nature, confirmed by the teachings of the Bible. In the first peopling of the earth, it was as free to all its inhabitants as the sunlight and the air." "I am no believer in the doctrines of Agrarianism, or Socialism," he informed his nervous auditors. "The friends of land reform . . . advocate no *leveling* policy." They do, however, insist that "the right to life . . . carries necessarily with it the right to the *means* of living, including not only the elements of light, air, fire, and water, but *land* also." To which he added, "I advocate the freedom of the public domain, in the first place, on the broad ground of natural right. I go back to first principles."[78]

The Whig Party was possibly the least receptive to homestead bills. Henry Clay wanted revenues from the lands to fund internal improvements, and Whigs in general worried that frontiersmen were likely to be immune to calls for moral uplift, temperance, and self-control. John Quincy Adams expressed a recurrent Whig fear when he remarked that "the thirst of a tiger for blood is the fittest emblem of the rapacity with which members of the new States fly at public lands."[79] Nevertheless, it was a Whig, Horace Greeley, who coined the famous phrase "Go West, young man."

Greeley was, by his own account, the devotee of a "genial Conservatism," an "enlightened Conservatism." He explained that his support of land reform was grounded in his mission to act as "a mediator, an interpreter, a reconciler, between Conservatism and Radicalism." It must be said, however, that the more Greeley took up the cause of land reform, the more his Whiggery temporarily faded into the background. Ordinarily Whigs spoke with disdain, if at all, about Tom Paine, but when Greeley wrote about land reform, he found himself embracing the great radical of times past. "The Rights of Man—his natural, unchanging, inalienable, Rights *as* Man—have fitly become, in our day, the theme of general and earnest discussion," wrote Greeley. It was to Paine's credit, contended Greeley, that he had brought to the modern world the enlightenment missing "in Homer, Plato, or Cicero—in Magna Charta" or the constitutions of limited monarchies.[80]

Greeley's newfound respect for Paine had much to do with his worry about the plight of American workers, whose labor had become "a commodity—a marketable product, like cheese or chocolate." As never before, the problem of the urban underclass gripped America and required immediate action. "The base of our Social Edifice is not Justice, but Power—the right of the strongest." Land monopoly was the chief problem of Great Britain, Ireland, and, increasingly, America. Land reform was the solution, "the natural and sure basis of all Social and Industrial Melioration." Greeley filled his pages with talk of "the right to Labor, and to receive the rewards of Labor . . . , where the right to the Soil, originally free and common of all, has been granted away to a part." The right to labor would be honored and all problems resolved, if the poor of the cities were granted the lands in the public domain.[81]

In historical hindsight, it is clear why Greeley, precisely because he was a Whig, should vigorously promote the Homestead Act. The perennial theme of the Whigs had been the harmonious interdependence, the so-called holy alliance, of the two major social classes: capitalists and laborers.[82] A strategy for bridging the gap between the Whigs and the National Reformers, and also between capitalists and laborers, had been available from the moment Evans penned his brochure "Vote Yourself a Farm." In it Evans affirmed that if the proposals of the National Reformers were enacted, "the antagonism of capital and labor would forever cease."[83] Even Calvin Colton, a cautious Whig, held that "as a last resort the American laborer can at any time go to the back woods."[84] Whigs began as the enemies but ended as the friends of the land reform movement.

Ultimately, it was the newly formed Republican Party that played the decisive role in passing the Homestead Act of 1862, signed by President Abraham Lincoln. Needing votes from the Northwest, the Republicans had included in their platform of 1860 a call for free homesteads for settlers.[85] Among the luminaries joining the Republican Party were Horace Greeley from the Whigs and George W. Julian from the Free Soil Party. From the Democrats there was Congressman Galusha Grow, who had lectured his colleagues on "Man's Right to the Soil" and decided to switch parties as a result of Democratic President Buchanan's veto of the Homestead Bill of 1858.[86]

On the face of it, the legislation of 1862 was a victory for the cause that had been vigorously championed by George Henry Evans and the National Reform Association. In truth, however, the Homestead Act passed by the Republicans was fatally flawed. Instead of preserving the public domain for the landless, Congress lavished public land on railroads, permitted speculators to accumulate large tracts, and undercut the residence requirement. The goals of the land reformers were betrayed from above.

There was also, arguably, a betrayal from below. Land hunger pertains to the least-favored members of society no less than to the richest of plutocrats. Those ordinary persons who settled on the Western preserve quite predictably wanted to pass their newly acquired property on to their children. Allowing the land to return to the commons at the end of each generation was an idea whose time had not come—and might never come.

Land reform suffered defeat, yet again, immediately following the Civil War, when the proposals of Thaddeus Stevens and George Julian to redistribute plantation lands to freed slaves were ignored by the Republican Party leadership and the voters.[87] Years would pass before another movement of land reform, that of Henry George, gained momentum.

Henry George in America and Europe

Henry George was noteworthy for both his writings and his travels. His publications near the close of the nineteenth century were a restatement of the utterances of previous American land reformers, a distillation of their wisdom, and a higher synthesis of their reflections. His trips to Ireland, Scotland, and England may be seen in retrospect as the completion of an intellectual cycle. Circa 1800, such British authors as Thomas Spence and William Ogilvie had served as the original inspiration of American land reformers; circa 1900, Henry George did his best to revitalize land reform in the British Isles by espousing there much the same natural rights philosophy as that of his worthy but unsuccessful British forerunners.[88] What began in Britain and Ireland returned to Britain and Ireland in the suitcases of Henry George.

The immediate backdrop to Henry George's most important book, *Progress and Poverty* (1879), was the depression of 1873. The long-term backdrop was the failure of the Homestead Act (1862) and his recognition that "the public domain is almost gone," that "our advance has reached the Pacific." Both the disappointing past and the threatening future, then, gave him good reasons to set forth a systematic critique of the present. Taking up a theme common to all his predecessors in the land reform movement, George addressed the overriding problem of modern times: the juxtaposition of the extreme riches of the nonproducers and the extreme poverty of the producers. "All the increased wealth which modern progress brings goes but . . . to make sharper the contrast between the House of Have and the House of Want"—between the idle, glutted few and the starving, laboring many.[89]

Among the intellectual riches George may have inherited from the National Reformers, not the least was a knack for attacking conservative readings of the social contract. David Hume thought he had struck a telling blow against Locke by pointing out that "almost all the governments, which exist at present, or of which there remains any record in [hi]story, have been founded originally, either on usurpation or conquest, or both, without any pretence of a fair consent, or voluntary subjection of the people."[90] Whether George specifically recognized Hume as the enemy is unclear; what is clear is that he transformed Hume's style of "realism" into a radical critique of reality. Landed property, George admitted, "nowhere springs from contract; . . . it has everywhere had its birth in war and conquest." But in George's retelling of Hume's tale, the proper moral to be drawn from a realistic account of history was that all established land holdings were "robbery" and must give way to a social contract founded on justice.[91]

Nor did George yield anything to Grotius, Pufendorf, and their notion that the sovereign people have the right to alienate their natural rights. "Though the sovereign people of the State of New York consent to the landed possessions of the Astors, the puniest infant that comes wailing into the world in the squalidest room of the most miserable tenement house, becomes at that moment seized of an equal right with the millionaires. And it is robbed if the right is denied."[92] So George argued in *Progress and Poverty,* basing his position, in part at least, on what he had written in his earlier book, *Our Land and Land Policy* (1871): "Every man born into this world has a natural right to as much land as is necessary to his own uses. . . . To deny this is to deny the right of man to himself."[93]

Solidarity with previous land reformers on all matters concerning the social contract was George's single most important but not his only affinity with the likes of Evans and Pickering. Antebellum land reformers had come to believe that educational reform, by itself, was not the answer, and George agreed that "our common schools will be in vain" unless "we come back to first principles."[94] They had said the fate of Indians was not half as bad as that of workers, and Henry George agreed that "there are in the heart of our civilization large classes with whom the veriest savage could not afford to exchange." They were full of optimism for the historical mission of the public land, its calling to save the immigrant workers; he, too, thought that unfenced land "has been the transmuting force which has turned the thriftless, unambitious European peasant into the self-reliant Western farmer." They had reassured wary voters that their proposals signified not the arousal but the definitive demise of class antagonism, and Henry George similarly held that "the antagonism of interests is not between labor and capital, as is popularly believed, but is in reality between labor and capital on one side and landownership on the other."[95] To Henry George no less than to previous land reformers, David Ricardo had shown the way in spite of himself when he cast landlords in the role of parasites and capitalists and workers in the role of producers.

Despite all the affinities of Henry George's work with that of earlier land reformers, it must be admitted that he chose to speak of how little had been said before he arrived on the scene. His emphasis was on how the special circumstances of early America, its surfeit of land, had militated against discussions of the legitimacy of private property in landed holdings. Had the colonists been starved for land, "there can be no doubt that they would have reverted to first principles . . . ; and individual land ownership would have been rejected, just as aristocracy and monarchy were rejected." The seemingly endless expanse of unsettled territory across an immense continent "prevented any question of the justice and policy of private property in land from arising."[96] The founders had fallen short in their application of "revolution principles," and the self-educated Henry George did not clearly indicate that their deficiency had come under critical scrutiny in antebellum America. The names of Evans and Pickering do not appear in the index of *Progress and Poverty*.

Possibly George did not begin by reading the reflections of the leaders of the National Reform movement, which would explain why it took him some time to catch up to their positions. In *Our Land and Land Policy* he advocated a natural right to the land that was compatible with the multiplication and even-handed distribution of privately owned plots. Eight years later, in *Progress and Poverty*, he announced his conviction, thereafter constantly reaffirmed, that the inevitable and deleterious effect of the subdivision of land "is to prevent the adoption or even advocacy of more thorough-going measures, and to strengthen the existing unjust system by interesting a larger number in its maintenance." The mature Henry George affirmed that "private property in land is a usurpation, a creation of force and fraud." Even the best distribution among the living cheated the generations to come. As Evans and Pickering had before him, Henry George concluded that "we must substitute for the individual ownership of land a common ownership." Improvements to the land were properly owned by individuals; not so the land itself.[97]

George uncompromisingly insisted that "private property in land has no warrant in justice, but stands condemned as the denial of natural right." He was, however, willing to compromise on the method of enforcement. Rather than confiscate the land, he would confiscate the rent by a single tax that would replace all others; henceforth, rent would be paid to the public, not to private landholders. The result would be to transform society, root and branch, for the better. Were America to adopt his proposal, the march of progress would resume, the threat of corruption and decay recede, and civilization would rise to "yet nobler heights."[98]

Paine, it will be recalled, had spoken of a debt the landholder owes to society, that is, to the collective mores and institutions without which there would be no property. Along the same lines, George noted that rent "is due to nothing that the land owners have done. It represents a value created by the whole community . . . [and] necessarily belongs to the whole community."[99] It was not the landlord but New York City that raised the value of the land.

Despite its excessive length, *Progress and Poverty* was a runaway best seller, by some accounts one of the ten most popular nonfiction books in the history of the United States.[100] Henry George was the recipient of delirious applause in America, and when he visited England, Scotland, and Ireland he discovered that his reputation preceded him because his message was timely on both sides of the Atlantic.

OMINOUS REFERENCES TO IRELAND WERE STANDARD FARE in the speeches and writings of America's antebellum land reformers.[101] Henry George repeated those warnings in *Progress and Poverty*, and two years later he devoted an entire book to *The Irish Land Question*. Before, during, and after his trips to Europe, he placed Ireland at or near the top of his concerns, always warning that "the Irish land system, which is so much talked of as though it were some peculiarly atrocious system, is essentially the same land system which prevails in all civilized countries— . . . the same system which all over the civilized world men are accustomed to consider natural and just."[102]

The timing of George's trip to Ireland was fortunate, coming as it did in the wake of a prolonged Anglo-Irish public debate about the best way to respond to the Fenian Brotherhood, formed in 1858 to cast off the British yoke by any and all means. No doubt Henry George knew that Liberal Prime Minister William Gladstone had been an advocate of land reform in Ireland. He also knew that the great liberal intellectuals John Stuart Mill and Herbert Spencer had supported land reform. If, in *Progress and Poverty*, he had spoken critically of Mill and Spencer, that was because they had made the mistake of thinking the landowners must be compensated for being stripped of their titles of ownership.[103]

Still, to George's mind, there was no denying that British liberals were his potential allies. Mill, in language familiar to American land reformers, had written in his essays on Ireland that each man is entitled to "the fruits of his own labor." Even more strikingly, he had spoken of land as "a thing which no man made, which exists in limited quantity, which was the original inheritance of all mankind," and which, if appropriated as private property, "when there is not enough left for all, is . . . an usurpation on the rights of other people."[104] Spencer, too, in his *Social Statics*, had suggested that land should not be held as private property: "Our civilization is only partial. It may by and by be perceived that Equity utters dictates to which we have not yet listened; and men may then learn that to deprive others of their rights to the use of the earth is to commit a crime inferior only in wickedness to the crime of taking away their lives or personal liberties."[105]

To all appearances Henry George was in fundamental agreement with the British liberals, but appearances can be deceiving. The English public figures he truly resembled were not those of the late nineteenth century but the earlier followers of Thomas Spence, who from the late eighteenth through the middle of the nineteenth century had taken as their motto the words "the land is the people's farm." The pronouncements of Spence and his followers paralleled those of the National Reformers in every respect: the same stress on natural rights, the same attribution of all social evils to land monopoly, the same claim that the cure for the ills of labor was public ownership of land.[106]

Very different was Gladstone, a liberal to the core, but one who prepared for Irish reform by immersing himself in Edmund Burke's speeches on that topic.[107] Not very different from Gladstone was Mill, who by the 1860s was self-consciously striving to offer his readers something "which in virtue of its superior comprehensiveness might be adopted by either Liberal or Conservative."[108] Neither Gladstone nor Mill had any sympathy for the radicals of yesteryear; both had affinities with Burke.

When Mill penned his essay "England and Ireland" in 1868, his focus was primarily on restoring the health of the ailing British empire.[109] The parallel with Burke in 1783 and 1791 is remarkable. As a response to the loss of the American colonies in 1783, Burke turned his attention to India in an attempt to avoid further blunders leading to new imperial disasters. On the floor of Parliament, he outlined a plan for a better imperial government that would respect Indian mores, refrain from heavy-handed interventions, and rule justly. No longer would the East India Company be permitted to abuse the natives and treat them with disrespect.[110] In 1791 Burke turned his attention from India to Canada and demanded that both the English and the French populations be permitted to adhere to their respective mores, as opposed to Charles James Fox's policy of forced amalgamation.[111]

Similarly, Mill in 1868 beseeched the public to remember how well England had learned to govern India and asked that Ireland be treated the same way. "India is now governed . . . with a full perception and recognition of its differences from England." The time had come for Englishmen to understand what was distinctively Irish about Ireland, much as they had already learned to understand what was Indian about India. Unlike England, Ireland is "wholly agricultural" and consequently "bears more resemblance to almost any other country in Europe than she does to Great Britain."[112] Some measure of agrarian reform was necessary for the ultra-agrarian people of Ireland.

With the advantage of historical hindsight we can see that there was, however, considerably less than met the eye in Mill's comments about restoring the land to the peasants. The least amount of redistribution

England could get by with in Ireland was all he advocated—just enough to shore up the empire, nothing more. The modesty of Mill's proposals is not especially surprising if we remind ourselves that he had no use for philosophies of natural rights and social contracts. His proposals were dictated by pragmatic, utilitarian considerations, not by principles of right.

Henry George had far less in common with Mill than he imagined. The distance that separated the two land reformers, Mill and George, was the glaring gap that separated Burke from such radicalized Lockeans as Spence, Paine, or Evans. Henry George held fast to natural rights and the social contract, whereas Mill, had he still been alive, might have shared George Bernard Shaw's perplexity over Henry George's pious references to "Liberty, Justice, Truth, Natural Law, and other strange eighteenth-century superstitions."[113]

Herbert Spencer did not believe in colonialism but did believe in natural rights and argued at length against Jeremy Bentham's verdict that natural and imprescriptible rights were "nonsense upon stilts."[114] Henry George and Herbert Spencer held conspicuously overlapping positions on natural rights and the landed commons, so the American was shocked when his would-be English counterpart sharply repudiated the proposals presented in *Progress and Poverty* for ending private ownership of landed property. Despite his earlier comments in *Social Statics* (1850), Spencer now adamantly rejected "the movement for land-nationalization . . . pressed by Mr. George" on the grounds that it was "a scheme going more than half-way to State-socialism."[115]

To Henry George, an outspoken enemy of state socialism, the only plausible conclusion was that the once great Spencer was guilty of "intellectual prostitution" and had become "as a philosopher ridiculous, as a man contemptible."[116] To Spencer, however, there was no inconsistency because his earlier comments were about a state of society to which humanity had yet to evolve.[117] Under existing conditions, the confiscation of private lands would be unjust and would surely foster the growth of overly mighty government.

Only one thing is certain about Henry George's fate in Britain and Ireland: The English pundits distanced themselves from him as much as the common people in his audiences cheered him. In Europe he was but half successful.

To the tale of henry george, america, and europe there are three noteworthy endings, and thus there are three stories waiting to be told, each throwing light on the larger theme of the social contract in America.

The first story is one of Henry George as the fulfillment of a long-standing American reform movement. In this scenario George inherits and updates the efforts of Paine, Evans, Pickering, and the many other figures who had renewed the social contract by applying its "revolution principles" to land reform. If America were to remain exceptional, if it were to protect its workers from degenerating into European conditions, it would need self-consciously to will its exceptionalism, and there was no better form of willing than that of the social contract. Each generation must consent but can do so only if measures are taken that permit young men and women to assume control of their lives. Land reform is the most effective solution, the least costly, and, Spencer notwithstanding, the least intrusive.

The second story is that of Henry George and Herbert Spencer, which begins with Spencer's dismissal of George's effort to proselytize in Europe and culminates in Spencer's 1882 visit to America. On tour in the United States, Spencer struck up a friendship with Andrew Carnegie; by the time he departed, the philosophy of natural law and natural rights, formerly the weapon of the workers, had been transformed into the dogma of the survival of the fittest.[118] Thanks to the combined efforts of Carnegie and Spencer, natural law switched allegiances and henceforth served the robber barons and capitalists.

The third story is a continuation of Shaw's sympathy for some of George's proposals, combined with his amusement that anyone could still phrase his thoughts in the outmoded language of natural rights. Many American Progressives responded to Henry George in similar fashion, and some made the mistake of thinking that Spencer's conservative version of natural law and rights was what characterized the entire intellectual tradition.

Henry George's thought was a fulfillment of a major strand of antebellum reflections on natural rights and the social contract. Was it also a postbellum finale, a final gasp before going quietly into the night? To this issue we shall return (chapter 6) when it is time to raise the question, "The End of the Social Contract?"

■

FOUR

Burke in America?

Upon returning to Europe from America, Thomas Paine confronted Edmund Burke at the outset of the French Revolution in a debate that proved to be a dramatic and explosive showdown between radical and conservative Whig ideologies. Did acolytes of Burke eventually arise in America to challenge Paine and the radical Whigs in the New World, much as Paine, Mary Wollstonecraft, and other radical Whigs had earlier challenged Burke in the Old World? Did the day ever arrive when conservative Whiggery could relish its American "moment"? Is American history a tale not of one but of two Whiggeries? These questions are vital for our purposes because the discovery of Burke at or near the center of American discourse would likely signify a serious curtailment of the social contract tradition in the United States, whereas evidence of his marginality might well offer noteworthy further proof of the predominance of the theory of the social contract on this side of the Atlantic.

Scholars have forcefully demonstrated that radical Whiggery was central to the American Revolution, and my own findings indicate that left-wing Whiggery vigorously reasserted itself time and again in later periods (chapters 1–3). The presence of radical Whiggery is not, then, in doubt; the same cannot be said, however, for right-wing Whiggery. For when it comes to Burke in America, scholars are in deep disagreement. On the one hand, there is the famous claim of Louis Hartz in *The Liberal Tradition in Amer-*

ica (1955) that Burke was never successfully employed by publicists in the United States. On the other, there are the assertions of various historians writing a generation after Hartz, particularly those studying the Whigs of the second-party system, who aver that Burke's thought was common currency in America.[1]

The strength of Hartz is that when he denied the existence in America of a Burkean tradition, he drew upon comparative analysis to make his point. The weakness of Hartz is that his finding nevertheless bears earmarks of an almost a priori judgment rather than a sustained historical analysis. Deeply indebted to Karl Mannheim's *Ideology and Utopia* (1929), Hartz staunchly defended the proposition that European conservatism, being the ideology of the aristocracy, could not possibly have taken root in middle-class and therefore liberal America. Unfortunately but not surprisingly, Hartz went out of his way to avoid finding Burke in the American setting.

The strength of post-Hartzian students of Whig political culture is that they cite actual allusions to and quotations from Burke in the speeches and journalism of American public figures. The weakness of these scholars is that their citations are frequently to this or that particular item in Burke but do not, as promised, add up to unmistakable proof of an overall commitment to Burkean thought. Another problem is that too often the claims of Burkean influence are based more on arguments by analogy than on genuine evidence: Something in the writings of various American figures of historical importance reminds these researchers of Burke, which leads them to conclude, before carefully weighing the evidence, that all such public figures must have been Burkeans.[2]

"Burke in America?" is a question that still awaits its answer. To make a contribution to deciding the matter, we must march with all deliberate speed across the American historical landscape in search of Edmund Burke.

In the Beginning: The Revolution and the Founding

Around the year 1776 there probably was no member of Parliament who spoke more knowledgeably about America or more appreciatively of the character of its people than Edmund Burke. Nor could many parliamentarians come close to matching Burke's record of eloquent speeches strongly critical of the government's colonial policy. So sympathetic to the colonists were Burke's pronouncements that the American Tory Jonathan Boucher, after taking flight to England, lashed out at the great Irish orator and bitterly accused him of complicity in the crime of revolution.[3] And yet, come the year 1776, the newly independent Americans never gave a second thought to Burke. Their decisive rhetorical shift from "the rights of Englishmen" to "the rights of man," and from the inherited constitution to constitutions willed into being by the sovereign people, had rendered him irrelevant and invisible.

Although Burke faded quickly from the American scene after 1776, he did matter somewhat to the colonists in the years leading up to the final rupture, especially when he provided them with rationales for conclusions they had already drawn. A good example is the case of Burke's stand on the government's treatment of the radical Whig John Wilkes, who was denied his seat in Parliament, forbidden to publish his "subversive" opinions, and driven into exile for several years. To the colonists Wilkes was a man after their own hearts, a London favorite tormented as they were by an untrustworthy and perhaps treacherous ministry; hence all British Americans sat up and took notice when Boston's Sons of Liberty engaged Wilkes in an ongoing correspondence.

Our man on the spot in London, Benjamin Franklin, might dismiss Wilkes as a figure "of bad personal character, not worth a farthing." No matter to the Americans, for on their side of the ocean Wilkes's personal failings were willfully overlooked so that he could be touted as the advocate of the "inflexible principles" already cherished by the colonists. Before the Revolution the Americans were very much *British* Americans, and in consequence they were eager to embrace anyone in the mother country willing to join them in fighting the good fight of resistance to overblown authority. To have an ally in England who was a conspicuous public figure, entitled by the votes of the public to a seat in Parliament but denied his rightful place, constituted proof of the respectability of American pleas against the rulers of England. Small wonder, then, that from 1768 to 1770 Wilkes was the English political actor most admired in America.[4]

Burke could not help but endear himself to the Americans when he rose on the floor of Parliament in 1770 and spoke against the government's repression of Wilkes. "Resistance to power has shut the door of the House of Commons to one man," said Burke of Wilkes, "obsequiousness and servility, to none." Nobody, added Burke, should take seriously the charge that Wilkes was a threat to the nation and had to be silenced. "I will not believe, what no other living man believes, that Mr. Wilkes was punished for the indecency of his publications." How can that be true "when I see, that, for years together, full as impious, and perhaps more dangerous writings to religion, and virtue, and order, have not been punished?" No, Wilkes was brought to heel for one reason, and one reason only: "This gentleman, by setting himself strongly in opposition to the court cabal, had become an object of their persecution."[5]

Americans could also derive deep satisfaction from the portrait Burke drew of them in his justly famous speech of 1775 on conciliation with the colonies. "I think I know America," Burke boasted two years later, "for I have spared no pains to understand it."[6] His speech of 1775 leaves no doubt that Burke was, indeed, exceptionally well educated in American affairs and capable of unusual empathy with the Americans. During the late 1750s and early 1760s a youthful Burke had worked on a detailed history of the colonization of America, perhaps with the assistance of his cousin William. As of 1771, Edmund Burke held the position of agent in Great Britain for the colony of New York. All of Burke's cumulative wisdom about America bore fruit in his speech of 1775.

At the center of Burke's oration is his account of the *"temper and character"* of the colonists, or what in the parlance of our age might be called his reading of American political culture. The colonists, Burke explained, were English, English to the core, proudly English, English in their reasons and even more so in their passions. Unlike other parliamentarians, Burke regarded the Americans not as incomplete Englishmen but rather as Englishmen of a different and distinctive stripe. No doubt the governors of the home country had cause to complain that the colonists "augur misgovernment at a distance, and snuff the approach of tyranny in every tainted breeze." But if Americans were exceptionally irritable, it was because they were "so spirited," so infected with the English appetite for liberty. "In the character of the Americans a love of freedom is the predominating feature.... This fierce spirit of liberty is stronger in the English colonies, probably, than in any other people of the earth." What, after all, was the American obsession with taxation, if not the expression of a pronounced English trait? "The great contests for freedom in [English history] were from the earliest times chiefly upon the question of taxing."[7]

America, it seemed, borrowed from England precisely those cultural resources that were likely to make its people chafe at even the most mild and well-meant bit. When the Continental Congress met to deliberate on the future of the colonies, noted Burke, "the greater number of the deputies . . . were lawyers." Well versed in Blackstone, adept at litigation, Americans were highly skilled at articulating their grievances, real and imagined, and in seeking redress. Their religion, even more than their legal education, made it unlikely that Americans would submit docilely to Parliament. "The people are Protestants, and of that kind which is most adverse to all implicit submission of mind and opinion," Burke remarked. Then, with New England in mind, he uttered this memorable insight: "All Protestantism . . . is a sort of dissent. But the religion most prevalent in our northern colonies is a refinement on the principle of resistance: it is the dissidence of dissent, and the protestantism of the Protestant religion."[8]

Perhaps even more pleasing to the Americans than seeing themselves through Burke's flattering mirror were the remedies he proposed for saving them from a war for independence. In his speeches on taxation in 1774 and on conciliation in 1775, Burke advocated major concessions to meet the demands of the colonists. Against Lord Mansfield, Thomas Whately, Francis Godolphin Osborne, and anyone else who argued that the Americans were "virtually represented" in Parliament, Burke argued that the colonists must be allowed to return to their old habit of conducting their own affairs. Taxes were for them to levy as they saw fit, not for Parliament to impose from afar, although the mother country would continue to oversee trade. "My idea of an empire . . . ," he told his fellow parliamentarians, was one in which "the subordinate parts have many local privileges and immunities."[9]

If much in the speeches on taxation and conciliation was music to colonial ears, there were other passages in the same texts that explain why the Americans would soon lose interest in Burke. They were increasingly on the lookout for first "principles" of political obligation—a quest that would lead them to seek ways to translate the social contract from theory into practice. By contrast, Burke's strategy was to deflate all issues of dangerous principle into unthreatening distinctions between able and clumsy governance, and heated discussions of ends into calm conversations about means. "I am not here going into distinctions of rights," he explained on April 19, 1774; "I do not enter into these metaphysical distinctions; I hate the very sound of them. Leave the Americans where they antiently stood, and these distinctions, born of our unhappy contest, will die along with it."[10]

On the surface Burke and the Americans were in agreement, but just beneath there lurked a world of difference. When Burke's Rockingham

Whigs took up the American cause, they did so not on America's terms but on theirs, which were the vindication of the rights of Parliament, threatened since 1760 by George III. They believed that parliamentary sovereignty must be upheld, and Burke fully shared their view, even if he deemed it foolish to speak in such terms to the colonists. The American talk about natural rights made no impression on him or them; the "distinctions of rights" that he would politely omit from discussion were those concerning the undoubted right of Parliament to tax the colonies.

As good old Whigs, Burke and his cohort longed for a return to the reigns of Georges I and II (1714–1760), when Parliament ruled while the king stood aside as a passive onlooker. George III's insistence upon governing by exercising "influence" over Parliament outraged the Whigs, who were thereafter ever on the lookout for governmental scandals to denounce.[11] If Burke spoke in favor of Wilkes, he did so mainly to condemn the ministerial toadies who were enforcing the arbitrary royal will. More useful than the case of Wilkes, of course, were the events leading up to the American rebellion because examples of governmental incompetence and malfeasance abounded in the dealings of George and his ministers with the colonies.

There were occasions when the Rockingham Whigs won popularity in America, as, for instance, when they opposed the Massachusetts Government Act of 1774, which stripped the lower house of its long-standing power to choose the upper and transferred that authority to the executive. Nevertheless, unmistakable signs existed at an early date that the Whigs would eventually disappoint the Americans. Initially the Marquess of Rockingham saw nothing wrong in the Stamp Act, and when the Virginians responded by passing a hostile resolution, the Rockingham Whigs called the countermeasure "a daring attack on the constitution of this country."[12] Although the same Whigs helped repeal the Stamp Act in March 1766, they immediately agreed to the Declaratory Act, which proclaimed Parliament in principle supreme over the home-grown American governments "in all cases whatsoever." "I have in all seasons adhered to the system of 1766," said Burke in 1774, by which he affirmed his continuing conviction that Parliament was unquestionably supreme in theory but should discreetly refrain in practice from flaunting its supremacy when dealing with a willful colonial people.[13]

Burke spoke in the present tense in 1777 when he uttered the words "I know America." He should have spoken in the past tense, for the America of his mind was the British America of prerevolutionary times. He *had known* America—he knew its past. He no longer knew it—he did not know its present. Throughout the conflict he remained oblivious to the ideology of natural rights, popular sovereignty, and social contract that the Americans employed to justify their break with England. The reason why he did not denounce the American revolutionary ideology was that he refused to acknowledge its existence.[14] Other Europeans might look with astonishment at the Americans as they willed their new constitutions into being in 1776 and thereafter; not Edmund Burke, who never had anything to say on the subject. As of 1776 Burke did not know the Americans, and they had lost their reasons for knowing him.

DID BURKE STAGE A COMEBACK IN 1787 OR AT ANY TIME during the era of the Founding? His speeches on such topics as political representation, frequency of elections, and the use of "influence" to govern the legislature could have been used by both sides, each for its own purposes, in the American debate about the new federal constitution. On the face of it, both the Federalists and the Antifederalists might have turned to Burke: the former to sing his praises, the latter to denounce him. In truth, however, Burke's influence during the Founding was minimal at best and grew but little during the early years of the new federal government.

Whereas the Federalists could have taken comfort in, the Antifederalists might have been offended by the view of government that Burke enunciated in 1774: "Parliament is not a *congress* of ambassadors from different and hostile interests, which interests each must maintain, as agent and as advocate, against other agents and advocates; but Parliament is a *deliberate* assembly of *one* nation . . . , where not local purposes, not local prejudices, ought to guide but the general good."[15] A more perfect "federalist" sentiment is difficult to imagine, yet the Federalists could not embrace Burke without committing political suicide. They were well aware that the Antifederalists were ever ready to charge the promoters of the new constitution with the crime of seeking to institutionalize in 1787 the very British-style government that the Americans had repudiated in 1776. In a secret speech to the Constitutional Convention, Alexander Hamilton endorsed the English model, "influence" and all, as "the best in the world," but with the subsequent publication of the *Federalist* essays he had to sing a very different tune.[16] Even if he wanted to cite Burke, or any other British writer, he could not do so in public and on the record.

A fundamental theme in the essays of the Antifederalists was that our legislative representatives must simply record the wishes of their constituents and refrain from voting their own views.[17] The position Madison staked out in the *Federalist*, that representatives should "refine and enlarge the public views," directly contradicted the Antifederalists.[18] Here, it would seem, was a perfect opportunity for the Antifederalists to unmask their Federalist opponents as closet Anglophiles, a task they could easily have accomplished by citing Burke's 1774 address to the electors of Bristol. In this famous speech Burke informed his constituency that, as a dedicated public servant, as a statesman and not a groveling politician, he would consult them but vote his conscience.[19] The door was wide open for the Antifederalists to smear Madison (and Hamilton) as disciples of a member of Parliament. Their failure to do so reveals how thoroughly Burke had disappeared from American consciousness after 1776.

"Where annual elections end, tyranny begins." This radical Whig formula was one the Federalists wanted to forget, but they met with stiff resistance from the Antifederalists: Frequent elections and rotation in office, in the Antifederalist view, were essential to keeping the governors from exploiting the governed. On this issue, too, Burke's speeches could have been of considerable interest to the Americans. Time and again Burke rejected proposals for triennial rather than septennial elections, at first in a temperate tone, but by the early 1780s he had worked himself into such a frenzy that his audience might have concluded that the English Constitution itself would crumble if elections were held every three years.[20] Once again the Antifederalists missed a golden opportunity to paint their foes as British lackeys. They could not hurl Burke's name as an epithet at the Federalists because they were unfamiliar with his speeches. Not until he published his *Reflections on the Revolution in France* (1789–1790), the treatise that won him instant international fame, would Burke begin to make an impression on the post-1776 Americans.

When James Wilson delivered his *Lectures on Law* in the early 1790s, he devoted several telling pages to Burke's recent polemical essay on French events. Although Wilson had clashed with Paine's followers over the Pennsylvania state constitution of 1790, his disagreement with them did not redound to the benefit of Burke. Paine's preference for the unicameral legislature and weak executive of the 1776 constitution, Wilson's for the bicameralism and strong governor of 1790, was an argument over *forms* of government, not over *principles*, on which the two men were in harmony. Wilson believed as fervently as Paine in the principles of the Revolution and took Burke to task for belittling the social contract.

Wilson began by asking whether Burke believed men capable of self-government. "To this question, Mr. Burke, in the spirit of his late creed, has answered in the negative." The consequences of Burke's stand, Wilson explained, were deplorable: "This negative answer has been, from time immemorial, the stronghold of tyranny." Next he criticized Burke's stand on rights. For the circumscribed rights of Englishmen that Burke endorsed, Wilson substituted natural rights and categorically rejected Burke's claim that we surrender some of our rights when we establish government: Upon entering into civil society, Wilson asserted, "man's natural liberty, instead of being abridged, [should be] increased and secured." Finally, Wilson rejected Burke's apparent view that one generation can decide on constitutional arrangements for all succeeding generations. Had not the English changed the line of succession in 1688?[21]

Wilson's assertion of generational autonomy might not be as sharply articulated as Paine's in *Rights of Man* (1791–1792). In Pennsylvania the followers of Paine might think Wilson far too conservative, but there is no denying that Wilson welcomed Burke to American soil solely for the purpose of administering an uncompromising attack on the man who would go down in history as Mr. Conservative. The great Federalist James Wilson rejected Burke and vigorously reasserted the social contract.

Wilson wrote when the Federalists, occupying virtually all the highest public offices, exuded self-confidence and looked forward to the future with keen anticipation. Within a few years they would feel threatened by the growth of an opposing Jeffersonian movement and would find themselves on the downward slide to oblivion by 1816 or thereabouts. Faced with Jeffersonians who proudly rallied to the banner of Paine's *Rights of Man*, the Federalists might have responded by lauding Burke's *Reflections*. The stage was set for an American version of the Paine-Burke debate—but the curtain never went up on this play. Nineteen editions of *Rights of Man* appeared in America between 1791 and 1793, and only two editions of *Reflections*.

As Americans split into two parties in the 1790s, they did so by speaking for and against Paine while ignoring Burke. Beginning in 1793, voluntary associations formed in many states, from Maine to Georgia, to celebrate the French Revolution. At the meetings of these Democratic-Republican Societies, countless toasts were made to Tom Paine and *Rights of Man*, but no one bothered to curse Burke.[22] Whenever Old Federalists held counter-meetings, Paine was denounced as a "loathsome reptile" or something worse, but apparently no glasses were raised in honor of Edmund Burke.[23]

Years later, in 1814, a Federalist called Burke "the Fisher Ames of Europe."[24] Had Ames been still alive, he would likely have refused the intended compliment. "I will not be a Tom Paine on the federal side," he had told an acquaintance; that is, he would not play the role of counterrevolutionary ideologue.[25] What he would do, instead, was change his stand on the legitimacy of political parties. In 1799 Ames wrote that "of all the causes of seduction from virtue, perhaps none is so powerful as the fellowship of party." By 1803, in an about-face, he had become convinced that the advent of a Federalist party, offsetting the Jeffersonian party, might yet restore America to its senses.[26]

Ames might have justified his conversion to party politics by citing Burke's noteworthy 1770 call for the Rockingham Whigs to form a principled party.[27] The absence of Burke in this instance is not surprising, however, considering that Burke appears nowhere in Ames's writings. Whether Burke was "the Fisher Ames" of Europe is far from certain; what is clear is that Ames was not the Burke of America.

One expression from *Reflections on the Revolution in France* did make the rounds during the Federalist-Jeffersonian conflict: "the swinish multitude." Just after Jefferson's election the Federalist Lewis Ogden wrote, "I think it will be truly laughable to see the *swinish multitude* (as Mr. Burke observes) . . . swilling whiskey to seditious toasts."[28] Federalist John Sylvester John Gardiner also took to demeaning the rank and file voters as a "swinish multitude." For their part, the devotees of the emerging Jeffersonian party gleefully cited the words "swinish multitude" as a way of exposing the vanity of the Federalists, arch-Jeffersonian journalist Philip Freneau going so far as to designate himself "ONE OF THE SWINISH MULTITUDE."[29]

Noah Webster, spying the trap into which his fellow Federalists were in danger of falling, dedicated himself when writing his dictionary to honoring the usages of ordinary Americans. The Federalists would have to speak the English of Americans, not the English of Englishmen, if they wanted to win elections.[30] Burke's insults to the many, Burke's diction in general, could not be spoken in America.

What, in summation, has our journey through the periods of the Revolution, the founding of the Constitution, and the founding of the early republic revealed? That there is a significant record of thoughtful commentaries by Burke on America cannot be denied. But that he ever played a role of consequence in American thought and debates is very much in doubt. The story of Burke *on* America is rich; the story of Burke *in* America is not.

Chronicles of the Adams Family

No one can deny that Burke figured occasionally in the letters and formal writings of the remarkable Adams family. In 1791, writing under the pseudonym "Publicola," John Quincy Adams entered directly into the Burke-Paine debate. In 1800, at the time of his father's bid for reelection, he translated into English Friedrich Gentz's explicitly Burkean tract, *The French and American Revolutions Compared*. While John Adams said far less than his son, he did sprinkle his correspondence with occasional comments on Burke and more-than-occasional hits at Paine. There is no question that Burke visited America under the auspices of the Adams family; what needs to be investigated is whether they invited him to stay.

John Adams could vent his spleen as well as any man, and he frequently did so at the expense of Paine. "What a poor, ignorant, malicious, short sighted, crapulous mass is Tom Pain's *Common Sense*," wrote Adams in 1819. According to the entries in his diary, Adams had thought the same as early as 1776 and responded at the time with *Thoughts on Government* to Paine's call for a government "without any restraint or even any attempt at an equilibrium or counter poise." Paine the proponent of a unicameral legislature was "a star of disaster," a "disastrous meteor," "a mongrel between pig and puppy, begotten by a wild boar on a bitch wolf." To Adams it was a cruel satire on his age that Paine for thirty years had exerted perhaps more influence in America than anyone else. "Call it then the Age of Paine," moaned Adams, who probably had in mind the original spelling of his adversary's name: Pain.[31]

Adams's disgust with Paine did not, however, translate into admiration of Burke. In 1809 the senior Adams told his friend Benjamin Rush that Burke had "uttered and published very absurd notions on the principles of government."[32] When Adams came across the expression "swinish multitude" in the *Reflections*, he called Burke the "impudent libeler of your species!" and complained bitterly that anyone could ever have confused his own remarks on the regretful but inevitable rise of political elites with Burke's enthusiastic championing of the aristocracy.[33]

Such scattered and unsystematic comments as we have from Adams on Burke's *Reflections on the Revolution in France* are uniformly unflattering. Burke was wrong, Adams explained, to claim that the French possessed the makings of a proper constitution in the Estates-General. As for Burke's oft-quoted remarks on the unchivalrous treatment of the queen during the early days of the French Revolution, Adams offered a verdict that was as much an insult as a compliment: "In his description there is more of the orator than of the philosopher."[34] One can well imagine how annoyed Burke would have been, for Tom Paine and Mary Wollstonecraft had cited the same passage on Marie Antoinette as proof of Burke's emotional instability and penchant for rhetorical excess.[35]

The closest Adams ever came to admitting a line of influence was to suggest offhandedly on one occasion that, if it existed, it ran from him to Burke rather than the other way around. He had taken nothing from Burke, but Burke might have taken something from him.[36]

What made it impossible to consort with Burke was Adams's unflinching commitment to the natural rights and social contract "principles" of the American Revolution. Ironically, it was his painstaking effort in 1786–1787 and 1790 to find a "form" of government that could uphold those "principles" that led to the repeated charge that he had abandoned his principles. "John Adams is a man of paradoxical heresies," thought Tom Paine. "He wrote a book entitled *A Defence of the American Constitutions*, and the principles of it are an attack upon them."[37] Jefferson, too, was troubled by Adams's *Defence* and *Discourses on Davila* and praised Paine's *Rights of Man*, expressing satisfaction that "something is at length to be publicly said against the political heresies which have sprung up" in America.[38] Earlier in 1787 and later in 1814, John Stevens and John Taylor published works accusing Adams of betraying American "principles."[39]

Unfortunately, Adams's investigation of the rise of European aristocracies was so overburdened with information that his argument was easily lost, and his critics took him to be advocating precisely what he wished to avoid. His quest, in truth, was for a form of government that could offset the consequences of what a later age would call the iron law of oligarchy. Upholding popular sovereignty is a demanding and uphill task requiring institutional arrangements rendering the elites as harmless as possible.

"Thirteen governments founded on the natural authority of the people alone, without a pretense of miracle or mystery . . . are a great point gained in favor of the rights of mankind," Adams stated in the *Defence*.[40]

Read with patience, his bloated multivolume study published in 1786–1787 reveals exactly the principles that had characterized the writings of his revolutionary youth. What had changed was that he had lost his earlier confidence in the future. America had to begin preparing for the unfortunate day when it would suffer the problems of Europe. "There is no special providence for Americans, and their nature is the same as others."[41] The citizens of America could learn much from the political history of Europe, Adams believed, but he never suggested they could learn anything from Burke's principled English avoidance of principles.

John Quincy Adams published his 1791 "Publicola" letters on Burke's *Reflections* and Paine's *Rights of Man* as a response to Jefferson's remark about "the political heresies which have sprung up among us." Because most of his critical remarks were directed to Paine, the younger Adams was careful to alert his readers not to jump to a false conclusion: "It is not my intention to defend the principles of Mr. Burke." Adams junior approved neither Burke's "continued invective upon almost all the proceedings of the National Assembly" nor Paine's "applause, as undistinguishing as is the censure of Mr. Burke." If Adams focused on Paine, he did so because the two men were in agreement on principles, Paine's mistake being that of "inferring questionable deductions from unquestionable principles."[42]

Determined to cool revolutionary ardor, young Adams appealed not to Burke but from Paine's radicalized Locke to Locke's own more temperate doctrine. Quoting from the *Second Treatise of Government,* John Quincy embraced both Locke's "rights of man to life, liberty, and property" and his "appeal to heaven" when revolution is the only answer to tyranny. What Adams could not accept was that "Mr. Pain seems to think it as easy for a nation to change its government as for a man to change his coat." Locke had insisted that overturning the regime was a last regrettable resort, and the younger Adams upheld the same view a century later.[43]

John Quincy Adams made clear that the Americans were justified in their rebellion and that their written constitution was superior to England's unwritten one, but he also believed the governments of the various American states acted wisely when they adopted the common law even though it "cannot be produced in a visible form."[44] The new, open, and democratic society of America could benefit from the ballast provided by the common law's universe of precedents. In his earlier as in his later years John Quincy Adams disdained the belief of Jefferson that each generation should redo the Constitution.

John Quincy Adams opposed Paine's call for an uprising in England, if necessary, to replace its phony constitution with a real one based on the sovereignty of the people. His disagreement did not, however, move him in the direction of Burke. Far from it; young Adams acknowledged that Paine was correct in principle but thought his proposal completely wrong-headed in practice. "The principal and most dangerous abuses in the English government arise less from the defects inherent in the Constitution than from the state of society—the universal venality and corruption which pervades all classes of men in that kingdom, and which a change of government could not reform." Moreover, the fanatical Gordon anti-Catholic riots of 1780 suggested that an uprising from below would likely be as unenlightened in England as similar episodes had been right and proper in the American colonies.[45] Natural rights were universally true but, sadly, only selectively applicable at the present time. To John Quincy Adams, it was reform that England needed, not risky revolution.

The elder Adams had complained that he was condemned to be one of the most misunderstood persons in America. Perhaps his was a family curse because the son's fate was no better. Among other things, John Quincy was accused, long after he had become a National Republican and then a Whig, of being a reactionary Federalist and/or a Burkean who abhorred the ideals of the American Revolution. Nothing could have been more untrue. When he rejected the Federalists, John Quincy Adams did so by writing a scathing critique of them under the title *American Principles: A Review of the Works of Fisher Ames* (1809). Throughout his account Adams condemned the reactionary New England Federalists on the grounds that "they have renounced the principles of their better days." In the strongest possible terms Adams repudiated their "anti-republican prejudices" and their apparent call for insurrection. He detected "the last flutterings of a nervous system in ruins" in those Federalists who were contemptuous of the people who refused to vote for them. Rejecting the Federalists and reaffirming his allegiance to the ideals of the Revolution were for John Quincy Adams one and the same act.[46]

Possibly the greatest wrong inflicted upon John Quincy Adams came from Theodore Lyman Jr. in the *Boston Jackson Republican*, August 20, 1828. "The leading trait in the opinions of Mr. Adams is a distrust of the qualifications of the people, in matters of government. His opinions were formed in the school of Burke, who adopted it as a leading principle, that government is, in sound theory, if not in actual origin, a *compact*, in which the people and the government are respectively the contracting parties. Our government, on the other hand, derives entirely from the people."[47] In fact, Lyman was entirely right in what he said about Burke and about America but entirely wrong about Adams.

It is true that Burke in *An Appeal from the New to the Old Whigs* (1791) derived political authority from Pufendorf's notion of a contract between government and governed that severely limited the people, as opposed to Locke's position that the government, being the mere trustee of the people, has no rights of its own to assert against the people. It is also true that, to Burke, the *"original contract"* was for all practical purposes a permanent alienation of sovereignty on the part of "the people," who existed solely within an already constituted civil society, never within a state of nature, where they would be only "vague, loose individuals." All this was true of Burke but false of John Quincy Adams.[48]

The Lockean credentials of Adams are impeccable because ever present. As we have seen, it was to Locke's warnings against rushing into revolutions that the Adams of the "Publicola" letters turned when he did his best to rein in Paine. Years later, on the frontispiece of *American Principles,* there appeared a quotation from Locke. In his most mature writings, Adams continued to cite Locke, as when in 1839 and again in 1842 he remarked with pride that America had transformed Locke from theory into practice.[49] To which we may add that Adams's philosophical treatment of "the family" is a self-conscious, explicit repetition of Locke's response to Robert Filmer's authoritarian teaching.[50] Ever loyal to Locke's political philosophy, Adams consistently followed his master, who in the *Second Treatise* retained the contract of association, the social contract, but deleted Pufendorf's contract of submission between rulers and ruled. To Adams no less than to Locke, the people were and ever would be sovereign, while the public officials remained their servants, never their masters.

The great concern of John Quincy Adams was to do everything he could to make American public life worthy of a nation that would soon be a major power. To that end, and out of personal conviction, he devoted speech after speech to the ideals of natural rights, the sovereignty of the people, and the social contract. On July 4, 1831, he told his audience what had made the American Revolution memorable: "In the history of the world, this was the first example of a self-constituted nation proclaiming to the rest of mankind the principles upon which it was associated, and deriving those principles from the laws of nature." Sounding much like Paine in

Rights of Man, he went on to note that the Americans of 1776 had been accused of dealing in abstractions, but, he explained, it was precisely "those abstractions [upon which] hinged the justice of their cause. Without them, our revolution would have been but successful rebellion."[51]

Invited to speak on the fiftieth anniversary of the inauguration of George Washington, Adams once again celebrated "this mighty revolution, not only in the affairs of our own country, but in the principles of government [of] civilized man." Americans had wisely moved beyond the rights of Englishmen to "the imprescriptible rights of man and the transcendent sovereignty of the people." "In the history of the human race this had never been done before."[52] Three years later, in 1842, Adams delivered a speech titled *The Social Compact, Exemplified in the Constitution of the Commonwealth of Massachusetts.* "The philosophical examination of the foundations of civil society, of human governments, and of the rights and duties of men, is among the consequences of the Protestant Reformation," he remarked in a historical vein. Passing in review the writings of political theorists of the seventeenth century, Adams rejected Hobbes on the grounds that his theory "extinguishes all the rights of man, and makes force the cornerstone of all human government." Filmer, if anything, was even worse because Sir Robert "did not perceive that, by the laws of nature and of God, every individual human being is born with *rights.*" Sidney and Locke were the heroes of the speech, and the heroes of American history as told by John Quincy Adams.[53]

Late in life Adams received an invitation to lay the cornerstone of the Cincinnati astronomical laboratory. The speech he delivered on that occasion reveals that he never grew tired of professing the tenets of Lockean contract theory. Once again, he congratulated his countrymen for taking their stand in favor of "the fundamental principles" of "inalienable rights" and "the natural equality of mankind," then proceeded to draw a vivid contrast between England and America. "Government had by the people of England been declared to be founded on a compact between the sovereign and the people. . . . It was asserted that by entering into the social compact man surrendered *all* his rights." One may summarize Adams's view by suggesting that England was the land of Grotius, Pufendorf, Burke, and mitigated rights; America the land of Locke and rights triumphant.[54]

On only one issue did Adams's outlook duplicate Burke's, and that was the fear of both men that a democratic society might destroy the links of sentiment and obligation between the generations. "Democracy has no forefathers, it looks to no posterity. It is swallowed up in the present and thinks of nothing but itself," wrote a worried Adams in 1831.[55] What bothered him was the Jeffersonian, Painite, and Jacksonian incantation "The earth belongs to the living." One can well imagine how horrified John Quincy would have been had he lived to read Jacksonian Nathaniel Hawthorne's depiction of the Puritan forefathers in *The Scarlet Letter* (1850): overwhelmed by guilt, crushed by the past, estranged from nature.[56] Taking the opposite position was Adams, who wanted the living not to indulge themselves but to respect the dead and prepare the way for the next generation.[57] On the face of it, Adams was in agreement with Burke's famous dictum that society is indeed a contract, "a partnership not only between those who are living, but between those who are living, those who are dead, and those who are to be born."[58]

Yet even in this instance the difference between the two men was fundamental. Where Burke's primary emphasis was on the past and tradition, Adams's was on the future and progress. The present generation, in the view of Adams, had moved beyond the previous generation and would itself be outstripped by the next generation. One guarantee of progress came from the scientific discoveries that he lauded at the Cincinnati astronomical laboratory. Another guarantee of temporal advance came from forces beyond and above history: "Progressive improvement in the condition of man is apparently the purpose of a superintending Providence."[59] His father might think "there is no special Providence for Americans"; John Quincy thought otherwise.

When Burke uttered the words "society is indeed a contract," he spoke metaphorically and quickly made clear that society was precisely the opposite of a voluntary agreement. John Quincy Adams, in direct contrast, took the contract seriously and insisted that the point of American history was, or should be, to fulfill the promise of natural rights and the social contract. History for Adams was teleological; it was headed toward a better future, whence it followed that apologies for the present were not to be condoned.

Just after the election of Jefferson in 1800, the most rabid Federalists tried to recruit John Quincy Adams as a contributor to their Anglophile journal, the *Port Folio*. Insofar as he responded, he did so strictly by trying to upgrade American literature so that his countrymen would no longer suffer from a sense of inferiority vis-à-vis England.[60] Near the end of his life he was still laboring to create a distinctive American political and literary character, free of British influence.[61] About the last thing he desired was for anyone to think of him as a sympathizer with the outlook of Burke. Rather, he was tenaciously American and consistently one of the greatest champions of the "American principles" of the social contract.

Burke as Yankee and as Cavalier

History is a record of what was, of what happened—and sometimes a reflection on what might have been but did not happen. If ever the time was ripe for the Americanization of Burke, the era in question was antebellum America. Throughout the nation, but especially in the North, the many Jacksonian toasts to Paine gave the Whigs ample incentive to turn to Burke: A Burke-Paine debate, sponsored by the second-party system, might have been played out on American soil. For their part, Southerners found a flattering portrait of themselves in Burke's speech on conciliation, and when, in a self-protective mode, they increasingly turned to conservative argumentation in the years leading up to the Civil War, Burke might have been a useful ally. Both conservative Northerners and Southerners, moreover, reacting against abolitionism and labor radicalism, resorted to pinning the Jacobin label on the agitators—and Burke, of course, provided a rich source of epithets against the French revolutionaries.

Nevertheless, it is doubtful that Burke was ever successfully naturalized either as Yankee or as Cavalier. When the Southerners seceded they abandoned conservatism, identifying instead with the revolutionary heritage (chapter 2) and the Declaration of Independence (chapter 5). As for the North, its story can be told, in shorthand, by pointing to the youthful Daniel Webster's *Appeal to the Old Whigs of New Hampshire* (1805).[62] Although the title was borrowed from Burke's *Appeal from the New to the Old Whigs*, the unintended effect of Webster's performance was to underscore the dramatic difference between England and America. For whereas Burke's appeal was from England's new radical Whigs to its old conservative Whigs, Webster's appeal to the old American Whigs could be only to radical Whiggery.

Edward Everett's speeches are an illuminating guide to Burke's place in Whig sensibilities. One of the most intellectually formidable of the Whigs, widely regarded as the golden-tongued Cicero of his age, Everett consistently enriched his speeches with citations gleaned from the entire corpus of Burke's writings. What did this exceptionally well-informed and presumably sympathetic observer make of Edmund Burke?

Within a single paragraph Everett spoke of Burke both as a "great man" and, in a far less complimentary vein, as the conjurer of "splendid paradoxes."[63] Everett was delivering a speech called *The Principle of the American Constitutions* and could admire much about Burke, but not the Anglo-Irishman's aversion to discussions of political principle. Elsewhere he praised Burke for speaking shortly *before* the Revolution in favor of "the rights of America," but in his speech on political principles he rejected Burke's *Appeal from the New to the Old Whigs*, penned long *after* independence.[64] In this speech of 1791 Burke finally broke his silence about the American Revolution only to disappoint Everett by explicitly denying that the event had had anything to do with aspirations to expand human freedom. Ministerial misconduct and its adverse consequences were all that Burke ever saw in the Revolution in America.[65]

Everett always believed, in contradistinction to Burke, that "a mighty issue of political right was at issue between the two hemispheres." For in no European government "was the truth admitted, that the only just foundation of all government is the will of the people."[66] "Without disparaging foreign governments, we may be allowed to prefer our own, . . . to seek to maintain them on their original foundations and on their true principles."[67]

Our English heritage should be cherished, but "I am not . . . the panegyrist of England," Everett explained.[68] America was different from Europe and potentially far superior, for it had it in its power to be the practical fulfillment of the noblest speculations of the philosophers.[69] It was all to the good that many Americans were not of English descent because their mixed heritage permitted them to assert their own distinctive nationality, founded on the ideals of the Revolution. Other nations might eventually follow the Americans, thought Everett, if only his countrymen continued to abide by their professed principles.[70]

Everett was well aware that his outlook was at loggerheads with Burke's, and he did not shy away from criticizing the Englishman he most admired. Burke was all too English when he wasted his gifts on an effort "to prove that the people of England have not a right to appoint and remove their rulers; and that, if they ever had the right, they deliberately renounced it, at the glorious revolution of 1688, for themselves and their posterity forever." So far as Everett was concerned, the Whig notion of an "original contract" shared with Tory divine right the assumption that all government was based upon "the right of the strongest."[71] Despite his many quotations from Burke, Edward Everett was emphatically not a Burkean.

Our chances of discovering a Yankee Burke may improve if we turn to the likes of Joseph Tracy, Hubbard Winslow, and Rufus Choate, three figures disenchanted with the Whig faith in a progressive future. "The great [American] experiment is but begun, and . . . its final result is . . . highly problematical," wrote Winslow, in a confession of doubt that might have been uttered by either Tracy or Choate.[72] In a conservative mood, each of the three turned to Burke—how meaningfully remains to be seen.

Tracy and Winslow were Congregational clergymen whose religious devotion deepened in proportion to their increasing fear of the social world surrounding them. Writing in the 1830s, they abhorred the new abolitionist movement; in Tracy's case there were, in addition, painful recent memories of calls for an equal division of property at a New York state constitutional convention. New England clergymen in 1795 had led the way to repudiation of the French Revolution, and now, in the 1830s, their descendants shouted "Jacobin!" at home-grown American radicals.[73] Inevitably, Burke, the master of anti-French invective, wended his way into their radical-bashing sermons.

Winslow's Burke was an "illustrious scholar and statesman" whose "writings should be in the hands of all American citizens." As an antidote to radicals eager to "sweep away, with one great burning blast, all the collected wisdom and experience of the ages," he exhumed Burke's most dire warnings of the consequences of wanton innovation.[74] Tracy's Burke was much the same. Afraid that radicals would encourage women to forget their place, or ruin marriage outright, Tracy highlighted a passage in Burke rebuking the French for pronouncing marriage "no better than a common, civil contract." Tracy nodded with firm approval when Burke expatiated upon "the horrible consequences of taking one half of the species wholly out of the guardianship and protection of the other."[75] Existing abolitionists and potential feminists were radicals, as evil as French radicals, and they threatened to destroy America.

On a closer inspection, however, there is less Burke than meets the eye in the sermons of these two Congregational ministers. Rather than disciples of an English Whig, Tracy and Winslow were embittered, disillusioned, but devoted American Whigs, devoid of Everett's confidence in the future, yet ever faithful to Whiggery and its standard solution to all social problems: the cultivation of moral character. If for them, unlike most American Whigs, history was not on their side, then they would respond by struggling all the more mightily to shape, mold, and educate the citizenry. By means of public art and excellent schools, Winslow would restore to all Americans, rich and poor, the fading mores of the fathers of the republic.[76] Before moving forward, Americans needed to retrieve the virtues of their past—an argument he could have made without referring a single time to Edmund Burke.

Rufus Choate, Yankee senator, has been deemed "an enthusiastic disciple of Edmund Burke."[77] Certainly no one familiar with his speeches can be unaware of his many allusions to Burke, all favorable. We also know that Choate called himself a "conservative" and advocated "conservatism" as an answer to the grave problems bedeviling antebellum America.[78] Ultimately, however, what his case perhaps best illustrates is that in America a dedication to the mores of the legal profession often preempted the development of Burkean political philosophy.

More than anything else, it was Choate's speech of 1845 on "the position and functions of the American bar" that defined his political position. Unwilling to discard the ideology of the Revolution, he urged lawyers to minimize its radical potential. "Because we are lawyers, we are statesmen. We are by profession statesmen," charged with the duty to inscribe "this vast truth of conservatism on the public mind, so that no [abolitionist] demagogue denies it." Specifically, the task of lawyers was "to interpret these constitutions, to administer and maintain them, this is the office of our . . . profession."[79]

Natural rights, the right of the people to a new constitution, the right of revolution—all these Choate conceded in theory but asked the lawyers and judges to nullify in practice. Against Locke and Rousseau, Choate insisted that the state was something more than a contract, more than "an encampment of tents on the great prairie." Even if law and the state were once a matter of human will, they should now be treated as if they were fixed and quasi-religious institutions. The common law was "not of one age, but of all ages of the past." In one of his few undeniably Burkean turns of phrase, Choate proclaimed that "there is a deep *presumption* in favor of that which has endured so long." Above all, we should leave "the Constitution and the Union exactly as they are" until at last they are worshipped at the same throne as the common law.[80]

The final act of Choate's career was a sad tale of a decision that would doom him to be the forgotten man of American history. First and foremost a unionist, Choate had condemned the abolitionists in the earlier years of his career, and toward the end he would pour the same invective upon his many fellow Whigs who joined the new sectional Republican Party. Overnight he lost his Whig confidence in historical progress and in his fury poured out vituperation against the very Declaration of Independence that the Republicans took as their defining emblem (chapter 5). The Civil War buried Choate and tossed him into historical oblivion. His death was also the demise of Burke as Yankee.

DESPITE A LATE START COMPARED TO the numerous and best-selling editions of Paine, publications of Burke's writings slowly but surely multiplied in America, reaching sixteen editions of the collected works by the outbreak of the Civil War. One work in particular attracted the attention of Americans: the *Speech on Conciliation*. Delivered just two months before the outbreak of war at Lexington and Concord, Burke's speech had no significant immediate effect in the colonies. Later, during the antebellum age, Americans had time to reflect after the fact on Burke's great address.

Northerners only occasionally commented on the speech, usually to praise Burke for appreciating the interconnections among religion, politics, and liberty in the New England colonies or to express gratitude for his refusal to condemn the unruly Americans. Southerners simply could not cite the speech too often; thousands of references to it appeared in the speeches and journalism of spokespersons for the embattled slave states.[81] The reason why Southern spokespersons found Burke's speech irresistible was that it propped up their self-images and offered them a line of defense against Northern attacks on the peculiar institution of slavery.

After offering his appraisal of the political culture of the North, Burke turned his attention to the South. In the colonies of the American Cavaliers Burke spied a circumstance making "the spirit of liberty still more high and haughty than in those of the northward. It is that in Virginia and the Carolinas they have a vast multitude of slaves. Where this is the case in any part of the world, those who are free are by far the most proud and jealous of their freedom. Freedom is to them not only an enjoyment, but a kind of rank and privilege. . . . In such a people, the haughtiness of domination combines with the spirit of freedom, fortifies it, and renders it invincible."[82]

Robert Hayne, Thomas Roderick Dew, William Harper, and George Fitzhugh were among the Southern luminaries who turned Burke's speech into what he would never have sanctioned: an apology for slavery. While debating Daniel Webster in 1830, South Carolina Senator Robert Hayne soon found himself defending the "character" of Southerners. "Ardent love of country, exalted virtue, and a pure and holy devotion to liberty," he assured his audience, were the most pronounced and unmistakable features of the people of the Southern states. Making such nobility possible was the institution of slavery, and anyone who thought otherwise, he suggested, should consult Burke's famous speech on conciliation.[83] Dew of Virginia wrote in response to the heated legislative debate over emancipation following Nat Turner's rebellion. One of his trump cards was a long quotation from Burke on the splendors of freedom in a slave society.[84] Prominent proslavery polemicist Harper warmly recommended the speeches of Burke, not least the speech on conciliation.[85] What Hayne, Dew, and Harper said in the early to mid-1830s, George Fitzhugh was still saying in the late 1850s. Never one to overlook an argument defending the South, Fitzhugh, too, cited Burke.[86]

It is worth considering the possibility that the many tributes to Burke's speech on conciliation had something to do with what he permitted Southerners to avoid. Their embarrassing situation was that of embracing the social contract during the Revolution, then criticizing it in antebellum times, and, finally, invoking it again when they seceded (chapter 2). Burke's speech offered them a respite from their difficulties. His aversion to principles was perhaps as much to their liking as was his praise of their devotion to freedom. Every time they cited his speech, they could serve their ends without siding for or against the social contract—and without siding for or against Burke's larger political philosophy.

Burke's speech did more than help Southerners avoid Locke, even as they professed their ardent love of freedom. His words also encouraged them to discover an enticing doctrine of reaction in Aristotle. While writing about the South in his speech on conciliation, Burke briefly noted that "ancient commonwealths" based on slave labor had been the wonder of classical times. Nothing more was necessary for Harper, Dew, Fitzhugh, and James Henry Hammond to agree that they were modern Greeks and Romans, or for them to recommend Aristotle's *Politics* to all educated Southerners. Their view was that slavery had been the "cornerstone" of the old republican edifice, that it was likewise the cornerstone of the new, and that it should therefore be protected at all costs. "Our citizens, like those of Rome and Athens, are a privileged class," wrote Fitzhugh.[87] Harper agreed and rallied his fellow Southerners to their civic duty: "Resembling the ancients in our institutions, we should resemble them in their public spirit."[88]

The reactionary appeal of a return to the classics was not limited to the states below the Mason-Dixon Line. To the North, Hubbard Winslow had similarly saluted Burke, only to leave him behind when issuing a call for citizens to return to the good old republican virtues of the fathers. "Only the same virtues which originated and established our republic, can perpetuate and prosper it. . . . Let our children then be early and faithfully taught the true republican doctrine."[89]

Northerners and Southerners in search of a conservative dogma did their best to forget the natural rights republic of the Revolution and Founding. The more complete their self-induced amnesia, the more they could fill the resulting void with misleading images of a classical America in the recent, eighteenth-century past. Burke remained in the background as ultraconservatives North and South rode off on a quest to recapture an American past that had never existed.[90] His day never came, either to be Yankee or Cavalier.

Woodrow Wilson and Edmund Burke

If Burke failed to make his mark in antebellum America, where his prospects were at their most promising, we should not be surprised to discover that he was insignificant during the Gilded Age and throughout the succeeding Progressive Era. There was, however, one noteworthy exception: Burke thrived in the prolific publications of scholar and public figure Woodrow Wilson.

Among other things Wilson was a Southerner whose historical works include approving citations of Burke's thoughts on the happy conjunction of slavery and freedom in the antebellum South.[91] Every claim made by proslavery writers before the Civil War was repeated as matter-of-fact truth in the histories written by Wilson—the analogy with classical republics; the claims that domestic slaves were treated "with affection and indulgence," that only absentee masters were ever guilty of misconduct, that *Uncle Tom's Cabin* was a book to be scorned.[92] In the first instance, then, Wilson loved Burke insofar as the speech on conciliation vindicated his deep-seated racism.

Time would tell that Wilson's encounter with the speech of 1775 was only the beginning of his love affair with Edmund Burke. It was typical of Wilson that he credited Burke with offering the world "the best political thought of the English race."[93] Such statements, of course, were not new in America. What is novel is that, unlike antebellum writers, Wilson gave depth to his praise by displaying an impressive command of Burke's works and biography. Wilson's many references to Burke's speeches always had a point beyond rhetorical window dressing, and the essay he wrote on Burke's life and works in 1896 under the title *The Interpreter of English Liberty* still bears reading for its insightful commentary.

The essay of 1896 was an exercise in intense Anglophilia, combined with a novel if muted recognition of the ambivalence of Burke's early pronouncements. On the side of conventional wisdom we hear Wilson proclaim that "from first to last Burke's thought is conservative." In much the same vein is the comment that "there is no page of abstract reasoning to be found in Burke." The responses of Burke to the four crises of his career—the American war for independence, the question of parliamentary reform, the government of India, and the French Revolution—were all made of one evolutionary cloth. "The history of England is a continuous thesis against revolution," Wilson assured his readers, and Burke was perhaps the greatest exponent of this English thesis.[94]

Novel in Wilson's essay was his reluctant concession that Burke's credentials as a hard-bitten conservative were not always beyond reproach. As a young man Burke had written *A Vindication of Natural Society* (1756), which sounded for all the world like the work of a radical Whig—like Tom Paine, in fact, but decades before Paine. Eventually Burke added a preface explaining that he was parodying Bolingbroke's *Vindication of Natural Religion*. "The design," explained Burke in the second edition, "was to show that . . . the same engines which were employed for the destruction of religion, might be employed with equal success for the subversion of government."[95] Maybe so, but Wilson was correct to note that Burke's radical Lockean treatise was so convincing that it fooled "some very grave critics." After submitting Burke's treatise to a careful examination, Wilson concluded that "the book is not, indeed, a parody"—and then hastened to add that although Burke had agreed with all the particular criticisms of society, he had not meant the overall thesis to be taken seriously.[96]

Some of Wilson's observations on Burke's life were undoubtedly unsettling to a conservative readership. Rather than seeking a respectable career in the law, Burke sought fame and fortune in the dubious social netherworld of journalism, Wilson observed. His was a "roving mind"; he was a "high-minded adventurer" who lived with "Bohemian" friends. Near the end of his essay Wilson remarked, reassuringly, that "the radical features of Burke's mind were literary," not overtly political.[97] Wilson could not quite bring himself to take the final step of admitting that the youthful Burke had come very close to being the kind of unattached intellectual that the later member of Parliament would charge with fomenting the French Revolution.

Wilson could be reasonably forthright about Burke's possible youthful indiscretions because he knew they were of no consequence. For that matter, neither were the actions of Burke's maturity of any immediate consequence, considering that members of Parliament taunted him and walked out on his speeches. "His great authority is over us rather than over the men of his own day," Wilson pointed out, quite accurately.[98] The curtain went up for Burke after his death, particularly in the nineteenth century, a period when both the Tories revamped as Conservatives and the Whigs recast as Liberals claimed his legacy. The Burke with whom Wilson identified was the Burke of the Liberals William Gladstone, Walter Bagehot, and Henry Maine, the reigning deities of politics, political literature, and historical studies, respectively.

Like Burke and the later English Liberals, Wilson applauded 1688, condemned 1789, and in works such as *The State* (1889) went so far as to suggest that "from the dim morning of history . . . the law of coherence and continuity in political development has suffered no serious breach."[99] Less dogmatically and far more effectively, he called upon Bagehot's *The English Constitution* (1867) to learn how to study American political institutions. Behind "the literary theory" of separation of powers, Bagehot had detected the reality of cabinet government. Employing the same tactic, Wilson in *Congressional Government* (1885) spied—behind the misleading rhetoric of checks and balances—the reality of government by congressional committees.

For our purposes it is important to stress that not least among the items Wilson borrowed from the English Liberals was their Burkean animus against natural rights and the social contract. When Gladstone referred to the franchise as a "right," his fellow Liberals gasped in disbelief, even those who intended to vote with him. How, they inquired, could their leader speak in a language that echoed the old talk about natural rights, now discredited in England as French, revolutionary, and destructive?[100]

Henry Maine in *Ancient Law* (1861) had taken direct aim at the social contract and derided it as ahistorical nonsense because the pattern of human development, properly understood, had not been from contract to society but from early societies based on "status" to modern societies awash in contracts—but not the social contract.[101] Wilson dutifully followed suit. His book *The State* features a section called "Contract Versus Status" arguing that the social contract "simply has no historical foundation. Status was the basis of primitive society: the individual counted for nothing."[102]

Elsewhere Wilson parroted the English Liberals by forgetting Locke and discarding the social contract theory on the grounds that it was the theory of the French Revolution. "No state can ever be conducted on its principles," he wrote in his essay on Burke, "for it holds that government is a matter of contract and deliberate arrangement, whereas in fact it is an institute of habit."[103] Although there were no Jacobins to denounce in America, Wilson uncritically regurgitated the old baseless Federalist depictions of Thomas Jefferson as a fellow traveler. Jefferson, he wrote in *A History of the American People,* was "touched at every point of touch by the speculations which were the principles of the revolution over sea."[104] He made the same misleading charge in *Division and Reunion, 1829–1889,* and in his essay "A Calendar of Great Americans."[105]

Perhaps the most striking story to be told about Wilson's intellectual life is that of how he began by referring to "the rights of man" in sarcastic tones and ended by embracing the rights of man; and, in a parallel movement, of how he evolved from vilifying Jefferson to seizing his mantle.[106] Political events help us understand this apparent reversal, especially Wilson's decision to join forces with the Progressives and, still later, his response to world affairs in World War I. But we should not overlook the extent to which Wilson's transformation was a step-by-step internal development rather than simply a sudden rebirth under external pressure.

A good place to begin an examination of Wilson's evolution is with a recognition that his conservatism always had a critical edge when applied to America. Bagehot's work praised the government of England at great length, occasionally underscoring its excellence by making comparisons with the deficient American system. Wilson's *Congressional Government* made Bagehot's criticism of America its focus and in the margins contrasted it with England's excellent cabinet government. What Wilson did was to develop systematically Bagehot's belief that responsible government in England promoted educational debates in Parliament, unlike America, where whispers in congressional committees stifled public life.[107] Long before he became a Progressive, Wilson was a critic and reformer.

Wilson might have entitled his book on congressional government *The American Constitution,* in imitation of Bagehot's *The English Constitution.* "We of the present generation are in the first season of free, outspoken, unrestrained constitutional criticism," he announced in the opening pages.[108] In truth, Wilson was being far too modest: It took great courage to criticize the American Constitution in 1885, not least because Americans knew that prominent Englishmen such as Gladstone had reversed Bagehot and were now heaping praise on the American Constitution.

"Kin Beyond Sea" was the title of an article that Gladstone published in the *North American Review* in 1878. In it he remarked that "as the British Constitution is the most subtle organism which has proceeded from the womb and the long gestation of progressive history, so the American Constitution is . . . the most wonderful work ever struck off at a given time by the brain and purpose of man." For generations to come Americans in want of English validation cited Gladstone's words.[109]

More surprising than Gladstone's diplomatic comments to an American audience was Henry Maine's praise of the American Constitution in his *Popular Government* (1885). Maine's reversal of Bagehot is striking because they were both conservative, antidemocratic liberals, yet Maine belatedly turned away in fear from cabinet government and looked to the American system for salvation. It was the third reform bill of 1884 that frightened him, much as Bagehot had been scared out of his wits by the passage of the second reform bill (1867), immediately following the publication of his famous book. In the introduction to the second edition Bagehot sounded the alarm felt by many British liberals. "I am exceedingly afraid of the ignorant multitude of the new constituencies," wrote Bagehot in 1872; "what I fear is that both of our political parties will bid for the support of the working men."[110] Passage of the third reform bill found Maine embracing the American system that Bagehot had disdained in *The English Constitution* and abjuring the British model that Bagehot had championed. Were not the American checks and balances more likely than the British fusion of powers to thwart the will of the unwashed populace?[111]

It is to Wilson's credit that he was not a blind disciple of his cherished English liberals. Though he shared their conservative liberalism, he never granted anything to their antidemocratic views. On the contrary, he chided Bagehot because "he has no sympathy with the voiceless body of the people. . . . He would have the mass served, and served with devotion," but would never permit them "to serve themselves."[112] Wilson wanted nothing to do with the repugnance felt by Bagehot and other "literary men" for democracy.[113] The lesson of American history must be heeded. "The war for independence had been a democratic upheaval, and its processes had seriously discredited all government which was not directly of the people."[114] Wilson was always a democrat (lower- and uppercase), and his faith in democracy made it that much easier for him to enter a Democratic version of the Progressive movement.

Wilson's New Freedom speeches of 1912 contain what might be called a Burkean rationale for his shift of position. "I am forced to be a progressive," he announced in a campaign speech, "if for no other reason, because we have not kept up with our changes of conditions, either in the economic field or in the political field."[115] Did not his position in 1912 follow directly, he might have asked, from the words he had uttered in 1889: "The method of political development is conservative adaptation, shaping old habits into new ones, modifying old means to accomplish new ends"?[116] The new Wilson came to the fore as the preserver of all that was worthwhile in the old America. "If I did not believe that to be progressive was to preserve the essentials of our institutions, I for one could not be a progressive."[117]

Wilson had motive, then, to be a progressive, and the rise of the modern presidency afforded him the means. The Spanish-American War had taught Wilson that the leadership he thought essential but absent from congressional government could come from the executive office for which he was now campaigning.[118] All that was wanting was a program, and that, too, could be provided by the New Freedom program of saving America from the corporate plutocrats.

Everything British in Wilson's makeup disappeared during the campaign of 1912, replaced in part at least by the old American faith in popular sovereignty and rights. "Every society is renewed from the bottom," he proclaimed during the campaign. "The people of the United States understand their own interests better than any [representatives]"; hence, progressives were duty-bound to "bring the government back to the people."[119] As a Democratic progressive, Woodrow Wilson learned to sing the praises of the very Jefferson he had previously chided; had Jefferson been alive in 1912, Wilson expressed confidence that he would have been an advocate of the New Freedom.[120] Last but far from least, the new Wilson strongly endorsed the doctrine of rights: "What I am interested in is having the government of the United States more concerned about human rights than about property rights."[121]

Burke may have helped ease Woodrow Wilson into the Progressive movement, but the movement eased Burke out of Wilson's speeches. World War I had much the same effect on Wilson. Beginning with Gladstone's notion of the self-determination of nations, Wilson quickly moved on to declare that "we are champions of the rights of mankind."[122] Again and again he returned to his theme: "We are fighting for what we believe to be the rights of mankind."[123] The devoted Burkean had evolved to the point of speaking with the voice of Tom Paine.

The French Disconnection

Burke could not fare well in America because throughout so much of its history it has been the land of the social contract—whether in full vigor throughout the passionate political struggles of the antebellum era or, in later times, as a default language from which Woodrow Wilson could not escape. Burke has, however, scored one noteworthy recent victory with the republication in the 1950s of his disciple Friedrich Gentz's *The French and American Revolutions Compared*. Anyone swayed by Gentz is likely to think the French Revolution a revolution, the American Revolution a non-revolution. From the Cold Warriors of the 1950s to our own day, Americans influenced by Gentz have omitted revolutionary principles from their accounts of the American Revolution.

Burke himself never offered a fully developed comparison of the American and French revolutions. That was because the former British colonies were of little interest to him after their departure, his focus shifting in the years following 1776 to finding a better way to administer the Indian part of England's empire. And when the French Revolution occurred, all his emphasis was on denying the radical Whig Richard Price's likening of 1789 to 1688. Burke never addressed the American Revolution except in passing, and not until Gentz was there a systematic "Burkean" comparison of 1776 with 1789.

Burke's scattered comments about revolutionary America contain a few germs of Gentz's later work, especially insofar as Burke completely missed in 1777, and then denied in 1791, the existence of the radical ideology of the Americans. Burke's *Address to the British Colonists in North America* was a final effort, in 1777, to persuade the Americans to reconsider independence. He conceded that England's employment of foreign mercenaries had been a mistake, but he warned the colonists that life outside the protections of English empire was likely to be difficult. To his mind there was still hope because the Americans were concerned about the preservation of their "privileges and liberties"—their English liberty.[124] Burke either had not read or did not comprehend the radical words of the Declaration of Independence. In another speech delivered in 1777, Burke took comfort in finding that "for a long time, even amidst the desolations of war, . . . the American leaders seem to have had the greatest difficulty in bringing up their people to a declaration of total independence."[125]

In 1791 Burke turned, belatedly and briefly, to the American Revolution to answer new Whig critics who charged him with inconsistency in saying no to the French Revolution after having said yes to the American. Burke explained that his conversations with Benjamin Franklin had led him to conclude that the Americans "were purely on the defensive in that rebellion." He considered the Americans "as standing at that time . . . in the same relation to England as England did to King James the Second in 1688. He believed that they had taken up arms from one motive only: that is, our attempting to tax them without their consent."[126] With these brief comments, spoken in the third person, Burke began the work that Gentz would complete in his pamphlet of 1800.

The point of *The French and American Revolutions Compared* is to persuade the reader that "every parallel between these two revolutions will serve much more to display the *contrast* than the *resemblance* between them." Unlike the French, the Americans sought "only to preserve, not to erect a new building"; "it never occurred to them . . . to *reform,* even their own country, much less the whole world." The French did, the Americans did not proselytize. Also in contrast to the French, the Americans fought a war of independence rather than a civil war. In general, "the American revolution was . . . merely a *defensive revolution;* the French . . . *an offensive revolution.*"[127] All told, 1776 was the replay of English glory in 1688 rather than the precursor of French damnation in 1789.

To transform 1776 and 1789 into thesis and antithesis, Gentz had to omit from his account of America the confiscation of Loyalist property, the tar and feathers borne by officials who attempted to enforce the Stamp Act, the proud American assertions of a *novus ordo seclorum,* and the universalistic ideals that the American revolutionaries and their descendants repeatedly invited Europeans to adopt. Until 1795, a full year after the Terror, even the Federalists were enthralled by the thought that the French were vindicating in Europe the earlier revolution in America.[128]

Gentz realized that the greatest obstacle to his objective of disconnecting the two revolutions was the undeniable kinship of the Declaration of Independence with the Declaration of the Rights of Man and of the Citizen. "True it is, that the declaration of independence . . . is preceded by an introduction, in which the *natural* and *unalienable* rights of mankind are considered the foundation of all government. . . . It is likewise true, that most of the constitutions of the United States, are preceded by those idle *declarations of rights,* from which so much misery has at a later period been derived upon France." The best Gentz could do to save his argument was to assure us "that they allowed to these speculative ideas no visible influence upon their practical measures and resolves." Scrambling to shore up his sagging argument, Gentz changed the topic and drew "a contrast between the wild, extravagant, rhapsodical declamation of a Paine, and the mild, moderate, and considerate tone . . . of a Washington."[129]

There is little to indicate that Gentz's essay had significant influence in America when it was published in 1800, nor that it received much attention in later American history. The reason for this neglect is not obscure. Many Americans have been quite willing to make the mistake of denying that the principles of their revolution had anything in common with France's; they have often been willing to forget that the notions of popular sovereignty, natural rights, and the right of the people to will a new constitution into being belong to both revolutions (chapter 5). They have frequently had recourse to "Jacobin" as a curse word. But what Americans have only rarely accepted in the disconnection of America and France has been the outright denial of their own social contract tradition, their own political principles.[130]

Only occasionally did they go that far, but the 1950s was one of those occasions. The new edition of Gentz, introduced by conservative pundit Russell Kirk, was a hit because of the Cold War. Gentz had feared *"eine Total-Revolution,"* as had Burke in his final work, the almost obsessive *Letters on a Regicide Peace* (1795–1797). American conservatives of the 1950s and Cold War liberals overlapped in their fear of "totalitarianism." In the climate of opinion of the day, the French and Bolshevik revolutions became interchangeable, and the American was deliberately denied its status as a revolution.

Burke had always lost throughout American history, for no matter where he turned, the social contract tradition blocked his way and marginalized him. It is ironic, then, that Burke and his counterrevolutionary follower Friedrich Gentz, the champions of tradition, have in recent times had some success in persuading Americans to lose sight of their tradition. They have invited Americans to forget that theirs has been the land of the social contract, and not a few American commentators have gladly accepted the invitation.

FIVE

■

Declarations of Independence

The Declaration of Independence may well be the single most important text in American history, despite its arguable irrelevance in 1776 and its present-day immersion in embalming fluid. Originally the Declaration was merely a document that added a rhetorical gloss to what the Second Continental Congress had agreed upon two days earlier—that America was independent—hence John Adams's reasonable expectation that "the second day of July, 1776, will be the most memorable epocha in the history of America."[1] Today we no longer hear solemn readings of the Declaration on its anniversary, nor do we witness anything that resembles the great orations of the past celebrating it on the fourth of July. Nevertheless, it is undeniable that between its unremarkable beginning and its barely noticed finale, the Declaration cast a long shadow over public life and kept alive the theory of the social contract and its critics.

The 1960s witnessed both one of the most glorious moments in the history of the Declaration and also its subsequent disappearance from political life. Martin Luther King Jr.'s remarkable "I Have a Dream" speech of 1963 drew upon the Declaration for its inspired language, but the nationalization of the Bill of Rights in the same decade had the unintended effect of escorting the Declaration off the stage. Appeals beyond the Constitution to secure basic rights—appeals made in the name of the Declaration's vocabulary of the social contract—vanished into the past.

Any account of the place of the Declaration in American history must situate Martin Luther King's speech inside the larger story of the many disadvantaged groups that have relentlessly pursued their dream of full inclusion in American citizenship by availing themselves of the preamble's language of natural rights, consent, equality, and self-government.[2] The complete story of the Declaration cannot stop there, however, but must incorporate the voices of the skeptics and naysayers—those who denied its social contract premises outright, or restricted its coverage, or interpreted it according to the words following the preamble.

Was the Declaration a defense of revolution, a platform soliciting reforms, a statement of America's position in the world of nations, or a legal brief drafted to condemn royal misconduct? Each possibility has received strong support from one or another set of passionate advocates, and each interpretation has profound political consequences. Over the course of American history, to interpret the Declaration has been to define the past of the country and to set its goals for the future.

Declarations in 1689, 1776, 1789

There are good reasons why we should initially study the Declaration of Independence not by itself but in relationship to the English Declaration of Rights preceding it and the French Declaration of the Rights of Man and of the Citizen succeeding it. Our own contemporary understanding of the American Declaration stands to benefit thereby, which is in itself sufficient reason to engage in a brief comparative examination. Another reason for a comparative overview is that throughout their history Americans have often waged ideological warfare by placing their Declaration alongside the English or French Declarations. In choosing which comparison to make, the English or the French, Americans have frequently been preoccupied with the underlying issue of whether to accentuate or suppress the standing of the Declaration of Independence in the social contract tradition.

The Declaration of Independence consists, arguably, of three parts. The first is a preamble written in the high and abstract language of the political philosophy of the social contract; the second is an indictment drawn up against the king; the third is a declaration of independence from Great Britain. One explanation of why the Declaration has meant so many different things to different persons is that commentators both today and yesterday have had a way of writing about one of its three components while saying little about the other two.

The first and second parts of the Declaration have invited comparison with England and sometimes with France; not so the final part, the quest for admission to the international community. England in 1689 and France in 1789 had long been members of the world of nation-states, unlike America in 1776, which needed a Declaration of Independence to join the international club. At the end of the Declaration of Independence, Jefferson repeated the words Richard Henry Lee had uttered on June 7 at the Continental Congress, "that these United Colonies are, and of right ought to be, free and independent States," to which Jefferson added that henceforth the ex-colonies claimed "full power to levy war, conclude peace, contract alliances, establish commerce, and to do all other acts and things which independent states may of right do."

In August 1775 King George had denounced the colonists as rebels; on April 6, 1776, Congress had opened American ports to all comers. So by July 1776 the Americans needed France as an ally but could not hope for help from abroad until they announced their independence. Much of the original significance of the Declaration pertained, then, to the legal context of "the law of nature and of nations," soon to be known as "international law." The social contract had nothing to do with this aspect of the Declaration, at least not immediately, although, as we shall see, antebellum Americans wanting to downplay the Lockean preamble sometimes did so by calling attention to the document's primary purpose of declaring American independence. To the present day, the third part of the Declaration is sometimes cited to diminish the first, especially by students of international law.[3]

The second part of the Declaration, the legal brief drawn up against the king, has likewise been and continues to be utilized to demote the preamble. Some scholars have deemed this second section proof that the American Declaration is little more than a reheated 1689, in which case Locke and the theory of the social contract do not matter. Historians of the common law, in particular, have been quick to seize upon the Declaration's item-by-item indictment to argue that the American document was in truth just one more moment in the long history of English Whiggery. Recently one legal historian has been so eager to deny the Declaration's affiliation with the Lockean social contract that he has asserted, without citing a shred of evidence, that Jefferson believed all rights are alienable. Without realizing it, he has refashioned Thomas Jefferson and the Declaration of Independence in the images of Grotius and Pufendorf.[4]

This much must be granted to those legal scholars who cite the second part of the Declaration to ignore, deflate, or overrule the theoretical language of the preamble: The American Declaration did indeed hail from a line of English petitions, addresses, and declarations dating as far back as the fourteenth century. It is perfectly true that British Americans from 1765 to 1776 made numerous appeals to colonial charters, the common law, "the original contract" (Pufendorf), and the Petition of Right (1628), and they held especially dear the English Declaration of Rights issued in 1689 and the Bill of Rights passed by Parliament a few months later. Perhaps nothing more resembles the American Declaration's list of the misdeeds of George III than the complaints lodged by the English against James II in the Bill of Rights.[5]

Legal historians are perfectly right to place the American Declaration against the backdrop of the English Declaration and to note the continuities. The problem comes when they absorb 1776 into 1689 instead of completing their analysis by using 1689 to underscore how far the Americans had moved beyond their English starting point. If there is one key difference that marks the distinctiveness of the American performance, it is the bold theoretical language of the preamble, for which there is no English counterpart. The English abjured, the Americans embraced, the language of Locke's social contract.

The English Declaration of Rights consisted of a series of compromises between Whigs and Tories.[6] It was essential, therefore, to silence the social contract, abhorred by the Tories, or to speak its language obliquely through the conservative voices of Grotius and Pufendorf. In the settlement of 1689 the members of Parliament designated the past as the one and only standard of all that was right and righteous. Every innovation of the Convention Parliament was misleadingly and deliberately passed off as another instance of what was old, established, venerable, or embedded in the common law. Perhaps, it was said, Parliament had to restore some provisions that the monarch had suspended, but there was no admission of anything new under the sun. Such was the standard account of the Glorious Revolution, handed down from generation to generation and passed from one side of the Atlantic to the other.

The preamble of the American Declaration diverged significantly from the English Declaration on such vital matters as rights, consent, and sovereignty. Unlike the document of 1689, which spoke of historically sanctioned rights, the rights of Englishmen, "ancient rights and liberties," the contrasting Declaration of Independence spoke of "unalienable rights," natural rights, the rights of all humans. The issue of consent was skirted in the English Declaration but faced head on by Jefferson and the American signers, who held that governments "deriv[e] their just powers from the consent of the governed." Probably the kind of consent the members of the Convention Parliament had in mind was similar to that announced in the Petition of Right, "common consent in parliament."[7] The underlying difference was that whereas the English affirmed the sovereignty of Parliament, the Americans posited the sovereignty of the people.[8]

Above all, what separated the Americans from their English predecessors were conflicting positions on the social contract. Throughout their debates, the members of the Convention Parliament would go no further than to side with Pufendorf's notion of an original contract agreed upon once and forever; and even this modest doctrine did not survive the editorial revisions of the Declaration of Rights. Only later, in the works of writers such as Burke, was the harmless notion of an original contract read back into 1688–1689.[9] The preamble of the Declaration of Independence, by contrast, enshrined a full-blown version of Locke's theory. Rather than taking government for granted, as had the English in 1689, Jefferson's text saw it as something willed into being by the sovereign people to protect their inalienable natural rights. In the event that the government fails to discharge its duty, the people, who have contracted with one another but not with the government, may remove their rulers and change the political system. What the people giveth, they may taketh away. The contract is ongoing, not signed once and forever.

Ever fearful of a return to the bad old days of the Puritan Revolution, the parliamentarians of 1689 pretended the king had "abdicated." Not for them the popular sovereignty, natural rights, and social contract of the Levellers. If the Americans had anything in common with the English Whigs, their ties were to the likes of Richard Price, Tom Paine, and the radical Whigs of the late eighteenth century, who were marginal actors in England.[10] The right of revolution that frightened the parliamentary Whigs, but not all the radicals, was a central tenet of the American Declaration of Independence.

Jefferson, the author of the Declaration, knew how to sanction the right of revolution without going too far. He did not take the position Price and

Paine embraced, their idea that the people could remake the government whenever they pleased; instead, the Jefferson of the Declaration insisted that "governments long established should not be changed for light and transient causes." On this occasion he agreed, in effect, with Locke rather than with Locke's radical heirs. "Appeals to heaven," Locke had contended, should only be made if "a long train of abuses" proved that the rulers had entered into a deliberate "design" to rob the people of their freedom.[11] Jefferson's so-called common-law indictment of the tyrannical actions of King George III was in reality central to building his Lockean case for revolution.

The French Declaration of 1789 has played a role in the history of the United States insofar as it has sometimes encouraged Americans to trumpet, at other times to constrain the revolutionary principles they adapted from Locke. Directly inspired by the American Declaration, the French version proclaimed that "men are born and remain free and equal in rights." Exactly as Jefferson had, the French championed "the natural, inalienable, and sacred rights of man." If for Jefferson these were self-evident truths, for the French they were "incontestable principles." A young and insecure American people, struggling to become a nation, could not help but conclude that the French Revolution was a vindication of the American. Throughout the nineteenth century, especially during the antebellum era, many Americans—Jeffersonians and Jacksonians most conspicuously—hoped for the advent of a sister republic in Europe and cheered each time the French overthrew a government in the name of the ideals enshrined in the Declaration of Rights.[12]

Other Americans, although they may have initially cheered the French Revolution, learned to denounce it. Southerners, for instance, had become extremely worried when slave uprisings broke out in Haiti, so when the abolitionist movement took hold at a later date, the slave owners did their best to pin the label of "Jacobin" upon the likes of Wendell Phillips and William Lloyd Garrison. Under such circumstances the Declaration of Rights could not fare well for long in Southern opinion, and the possibility arose that as the French Declaration declined in prestige in the Southern states, so might the kindred American Declaration.[13]

Throughout American history conservative forces have every now and then been tempted to cut the Declaration of Independence down to size by likening it to the Declaration of Rights of the dreaded French. But more frequently, the conservatives have praised the American Declaration while flirting with the idea of interpreting it as a mere update of the unthreatening English Declaration. Either way, the Declaration of Independence has suffered a calculated demotion.

Wanting to shed the "Jacobin" label maliciously conferred upon them by conservatives, America's reformers have chosen to forget the links between the American and French Declarations. Even less, however, have they been willing to understand the Declaration of Independence as a mere reprise of 1689. Reformers have treated the Declaration of Independence as a singular and exceptional text, unlike any other in the history of America or Europe, a model of what the United States might be and an invitation for Europe to follow. They have held dear the phrases of the preamble of the Declaration of Independence—the words about freedom, equality, consent, natural rights, and the social contract.

The Declaration as Inclusion

Much of the history of reform in America is the history of the Declaration of Independence, and much of the history of the Declaration is the history of reform. Not every chapter of this history has been entirely admirable, of course; the "Anti Masonic Declaration of Independence" of 1830, for instance, was without question based upon serious misunderstanding of the Freemasons.[14] Yet the grounds on which the Masons were condemned—that they were a secretive and exclusionary organization—were typical of the politics of reform. Until quite recently, groups suffering the ill effects of exclusion or public figures speaking on behalf of the excluded have inevitably appealed to the Declaration when staking their claims to full citizenship for all Americans. Slaves and former slaves, abolitionists, workers, women, immigrants, land reformers, single-taxers, Populists, and Debsian socialists—all have appealed to their fellow citizens in the name of the Declaration of Independence.[15]

The Missouri controversy of 1819 to 1821 is an especially important moment in the history of the Declaration because it marked the first time that members of the House of Representatives and the Senate confronted a major issue by drawing upon its preamble. Representative James Tallmadge of New York ignited the controversy when he proposed an antislavery amendment to a bill then pending for admission of Missouri to the Union. Throughout January and February of 1820, antislavery representatives and senators called upon the words "all men are created equal" to oppose an expansion of slavery.

The view toward which the antislavery members of Congress were groping in 1820 was that, in the absence of decisive guidance from the Constitution, the way to decide the newly arisen question of slavery was to revisit the Declaration. Charles Rich, a representative from Vermont, suggested that "the legality of [slavery] must be determined by reference to the laws of nature and natural rights, and not to the Constitution"; the Declaration, he concluded, provided the proper standard. Representative Timothy Fuller of Massachusetts, exploiting the constitutional provision that all states must have republican governments, argued the necessity of turning to the Declaration for "a definition of republican government."[16] His contention may have been strained, but his intention was clear: to put the Declaration first.[17]

Quite possibly the most important speech of 1821 dealing with the Declaration was that of John Quincy Adams. At a moment when the first significant murmurs of sectional discontent were still audible, Adams stepped forth and delivered an address not in the tones of a New Englander but in those of an American nationalist, the secretary of state, speaking in Washington, D.C., on the fourth of July. Before ending his performance Adams read the text of the Declaration to his audience—the entire text, but it was the preamble that preoccupied his comments on July 4, 1821, and for many years thereafter.

In his opening comments Adams destroyed the notion that 1776 was a mere continuation of English constitutional history. "The people of Britain, through long ages of civil war, had extorted from their tyrants not *acknowledgements,* but *grants,* of rights.*" It was to the discredit of the English, said Adams, that "instead of solving civil society into its first elements in search of their rights, they . . . claimed their rights but as donations from their kings." The great accomplishment of the Americans, in comparison with their English forebears, was that they "proclaimed the first principles of which civil society is founded," nowhere better than in their justly celebrated Declaration of Independence.[18]

Adams conceded that the Declaration was originally only an "occasional state paper," an "exposition to the world of the causes which had compelled the people of a small portion of the British empire to cast off [their] allegiance." The beginning, however, should matter far less than the meaning of the document for the present day, for all peoples, and for all ages to come. "The interest, which in this paper has survived the occasion upon which it was issued; that interest which is of every age and every clime; the interest which quickens with the lapse of years, . . . is in the principles which it proclaims." The glorious preamble set forth "the only *legitimate* foundation of civil government. . . . It swept away all the rubbish of accumulated centuries of servitude. It announced in practical form the transcendent truth of the unalienable sovereignty of the people. It proved that the social compact was no figment of the imagination."[19]

Eighteen years later, in a speech delivered on April 30, 1839, Adams continued to highlight the Declaration of Independence, even though his ostensible topic was "the jubilee of the Constitution." For all the undeniable greatness of the Constitution, "the omission of a clear and explicit Declaration of Rights was a great defect," a shortcoming that "has been imperfectly remedied by the ten Articles of amendment [the Bill of Rights]." A Declaration of Rights "would have prevented many delicate and dangerous questions of conflicting jurisdiction which have arisen, and may yet arise between the general and the separate state governments. The rights reserved by the people would have been exclusively their rights, and they would have been protected from the encroachments not only of the general government, but of the disunited states."[20]

More than ever, therefore, Americans needed to rally to the saving grace of the Declaration of Independence because the challenges facing them were far graver in 1839 than in 1821. Threats of nullification and secession had been added to the political agenda during the intervening years, and the possibility was undeniable that white Southerners would continue forever to exclude slaves from citizenship by excluding themselves and their section from the Union. To fill the void left by failure to issue a Declaration of Rights in 1787, Americans should return to the preamble of the Declaration of 1776.

Not the people of "each colony" but "the whole people" had declared their independence in 1776, Adams insisted. "Each colony was already bound in union with all the rest; a union formed de facto, by the spontaneous revolutionary movement of the whole people, and organized by the meeting of the first Congress in 1774." The right of a state to secede from the Union is "disowned by the principles of the Declaration of Independence." It was to the Declaration that we must appeal to overrule "the grossly immoral and dishonest doctrine of despotic state sovereignty." "The Declaration of Independence and the Constitution of the United States are parts of one consistent whole, founded upon one and the same theory of government, . . . expounded in the writings of Locke."[21]

John Quincy Adams was exceptional by virtue of his family name and his superb education but quite typical of American reform in his reading of the social contract and the Declaration. Like him, other antebellum reformers paid far less attention to the state of nature or the hypothetical past and far more to the possible future, a time when the promise of the Declaration's preamble would at last be fulfilled. For them the words "all men are created equal" did not refer to the state of nature but served as a battle cry for remaking society to include the excluded. History was teleological, providential; its purposes, far from mysterious, could be appreciated and promoted by anyone who read the Declaration.

The antislavery movement is surely a case in point. When, finally, the North sent an army to battle the slave owners of the South, Wendell Phillips announced that "the war is one of opinions: it is Civilization against Barbarism: it is Freedom against slavery. The cannon-shot at Fort Sumter was the yell of pirates against the Declaration of Independence."[22] Although Phillips may have been more radical than most opponents of slavery, his vision of American history as a contest between slavery and the Declaration had a long pedigree.

Many abolitionists sought to fend off the accusations habitually lodged against them, the incessant charges that they were anarchists or Jacobins, by saying they were merely reminding their fellow citizens of what the founders had in mind when they had signed the Declaration. In *Despotism in America* (1854) Richard Hildreth wrote that "the general intent of the framers of the constitution is clearly and comprehensively expressed in its preamble." When the colonists set forth their Declaration in 1776, "it was a solemn pledge on the part of all the states, and a tacit condition of the Union, that slavery should be done away with as soon as possible."[23]

Gerrit Smith, abolitionist and congressman, used the Declaration to deny claims that the Constitution must surely have sanctioned slavery, given that slaveholders had signed it. "They who argue thus confound the slaveholders of that day with the slaveholders of this. They forget that the slaveholders of that day breathed the spirit of the Declaration of Independence. . . . They forget that the slaveholders of that day were impatient to emancipate their slaves." Throughout his career Smith held that "the Declaration of Independence is the very soul of every legitimate American Constitution—the Constitution of Constitutions—the Law of Laws."[24]

George Julian, another abolitionist and congressman, was determined to keep slavery out of the western territories. To bolster his cause he infused his speeches of the 1850s with allusions to the degradation of the Southerners, who had gone so far as to dismiss the Declaration as "humbug," "sophisms," and "self-evident lies"—treating it, in sum, as a "political abomination." In the name of the "fathers," including the Southern "fathers," who "could not avoid seeing that slavery was practically at war with the Declaration of Independence," Julian insisted upon an end to the expansion of slavery. "We mean to stand by the Constitution as they understood it. . . . We simply demand a return of the government to its early policy in relation to slavery." Returning to the fathers and recurring to "first principles" were one and the same, each a matter of reclaiming the Declaration.[25]

Theodore Parker was well aware that Southerners were spinning out hideous versions of a historically affirmed social contract in which blacks had alienated their natural rights to whites. In response, he frankly admitted that "human history could not justify the Declaration of Independence." Yet he refused to abandon hope because "the great political idea of America [is] the idea of the Declaration." First principles and natural rights, human rights, the rights of man, rights "not inherited from past generations, . . . but rights that are derived straightway from God" were the building blocks of America, its hope for the future, no matter that the Southerners had forgotten their views of 1776.[26] For the transcendentalist Theodore Parker, as for many another abolitionist, the Declaration was to the Constitution as Jesus was to the Bible.[27]

William Lloyd Garrison agreed that the Declaration should be proudly displayed next to the New Testament; he urged abolitionists to "plant [them]selves upon the Declaration of our Independence and the truths of Divine Revelation, as upon the Everlasting Rock." To his mind the ultimate irony was that every July 4 Americans recited the record of English misdeeds, when these were nothing "in comparison with the wrongs which our slaves endure." Waiting for the future, one step at a time, to end the sin of slavery was unacceptable. Nothing less would suffice than "immediate emancipation," which Garrison demanded in the name of the Declaration's "self-evident truths."[28] On the fourth of July he burned a copy of the Constitution because it permitted slavery, while holding high a copy of the Declaration for all to admire.

Sometimes black Americans, usually ex-slaves, spoke for themselves instead of waiting for white abolitionists to make the case against slavery. David Walker, son of a free black woman, expressed his horror of slavery in an appeal of 1829 "to the colored citizens." Throughout his pamphlet, he struggled to come to terms with Jefferson, the figure who most tormented him. Mocking the Jefferson of the *Notes on Virginia* who had advanced his "suspicion" that blacks were inherently inferior, Walker decided to "advance my suspicion of them, [the whites], whether they are *as good by nature* as we are or not."[29] The Jefferson he appreciated, predictably, was the man of July 4, 1776: "See your Declaration, Americans!!! Do you understand your own language?"[30]

Free persons of color, suffering daily in Northern states from humiliating "black laws," feared the time might never come when they would be accorded full citizenship. In 1830 some forty black delegates from eight states assembled "to devise and pursue all legal means for the speedy elevation of ourselves and brethren to the scale and standing of men." Of no interest, they announced, were the schemes of colonizers to send them—blacks "born and nurtured on this soil"—to the now foreign climes of Africa. Neither, however, could they stay. Having begun their "address to the free people of color of these United States" with a recitation of the relevant words of the Declaration, they ended by endorsing the idea of moving to British Canada. Only by excluding themselves from America would they ever attain the inclusion promised by the Declaration of Independence.[31]

Without question the most famous speech made by an ex-slave was Frederick Douglass's "What to the Slave Is the Fourth of July?" The immediate occasion was the Fugitive Slave Law; the larger cause was that of slavery itself. Douglass delivered his great oration on the fifth rather than the fourth of July, 1852, to underscore the failure of America to include blacks in the Declaration. "I am not included within the pale of this glorious anniversary! . . . This Fourth [of] July is *yours,* not *mine. You* may rejoice, *I* must mourn." White Americans, he bitterly complained, "hurl anathemas at the crowned headed tyrants of Russia and Austria. . . . You are all on fire for France or for Ireland; but as cold as an iceburg at the thought of liberty for the enslaved of America.—You discourse eloquently on the dignity of labor; yet, you sustain a system which, in its very essence, casts a stigma upon labor." He took heart, however, in the thought that the Constitution does not mention slavery and invited all Americans, not only the lawyers, to interpret the document of 1787. The Declaration, the Constitution properly understood, and the progressive tendencies of the age emboldened Frederick Douglass to hope that time would show slaves and ex-slaves the way to the promised land.[32]

Reformers who supported one cause frequently gravitated to another, taking a copy of the Declaration with them. Mainly it was female veterans of the abolitionist movement—and Frederick Douglass—who met on the morning of July 19, 1848, at Seneca Falls, New York, to launch the women's movement. Elizabeth Cady Stanton hit upon the strategy of issuing an updated version of the 1776 document, renamed the Declaration of Sentiments. Where the original text had listed the king's tyrannical actions against the colonies, the women listed men's wrongdoings against women—most notably, perhaps, the complaint that "he has never permitted her to exercise her inalienable right to the elective franchise." The preamble they left untouched except for one bold, decisive interpolation: "We hold these truths to be self-evident: that all men *and women* are created equal." Three generations of women would draw moral and political sustenance from the declaration of 1848.[33]

Before being captured by slaveholders, the Democratic Party sometimes made effective use of the Declaration. Andrew Jackson regarded himself as Jefferson reborn, so it is not surprising that his followers hailed each of his most noteworthy political victories—such as his undoing of the Bank of the United States, the advent of the Independent Treasury, and passage of the Walker Tariff—as a second Declaration of Independence.[34] As for the theme of inclusion, the Democratic Party made its most important use of the Declaration on behalf of immigrants. From 1840 to 1856, every four years, one plank of their national campaign platform read: "Resolved, That the liberal principles embodied by Jefferson in the Declaration of Independence . . . which makes ours . . . the asylum of the oppressed of every nation, have ever been cardinal principles . . . ; and every attempt to abridge the present privilege of becoming citizens . . . ought to be resisted with the same spirit which swept the alien and sedition laws from our statute-book."[35]

For a labor movement struggling to be born, the fourth of July was a godsend. As far back as 1794, the workers of New York paraded through the streets on the fourth to celebrate American independence—and their own.[36] Before long, speakers for the newly emerging union movement learned how to avail themselves of the persuasive powers of the Declaration, citing the preamble on seemingly every possible occasion. When Stephen Simpson published *The Working Man's Manual* in Philadelphia in 1831 he quite characteristically began by asserting that, although the truths of the preamble might not have been self-evident prior to 1776, they became so the moment they were uttered.[37] Similarly, Frederick Robinson, delivering a fourth of July speech to the trades union of Boston in 1834, explained that the Declaration was far more than a pronouncement of independence from England; it also marked "the commencement of a new era in the social and economic condition of the people."[38]

Robinson's comment was characteristic of a larger pattern: One of the leading themes of labor leaders was that the Declaration was about social freedom no less than political freedom. On the fourth of July 1843 Ely Moore called upon the mechanics and working men of New York "to reassert the principles of the Declaration of Independence." Hardly a radical, Moore nevertheless spelled out the meaning for American society of the Declaration's assertion of revolutionary principle: "The social revolution which is quietly but steadily working its way through the masses of society, derives its origin and its stimulus from that salutary and philosophical principle."[39] Along the same lines, Seth Luther looked beyond the mill workers of New England to "the condition of the producing classes in Europe and America" and voiced the hope that the Declaration "will some day emancipate the world."[40]

Although addresses to workers were interchangeable in message, they varied considerably in their intellectual presentation. Seth Luther liked to begin his informal and unassuming talks with a quotation from the Declaration accompanied by a disclaimer about his skills as an orator. "A practical mechanic," he was no Edward Everett, no American Cicero; "he *could not,* if he *would,* amuse you with well turned and polished periods," he said of himself to his plain-spoken audience.[41] At the opposite end of the spectrum was Ely Moore's formal and philosophical address of 1847 to the New York Typographical Society. Not until he was well into his speech did Moore mention the Declaration and its preamble, only after treating his audience to a lengthy discourse on "civil government, . . . its origin, the object of its creation, and the principles on which it should be founded and administered." Moore assumed his working-class audience would be pleased to learn how the Declaration fit into the larger history of social contract theory.[42]

Possibly nothing better epitomizes the standpoint of the politicized laborers than the alternative Declaration of Independence issued in 1829 by the newly formed Working Men's Party of New York. In place of the list of colonial grievances against the king, there was an item-by-item account of the wrongs suffered by "we, the working class of society." Throughout the document the workers inserted themselves into the text, much as the women would do for themselves in 1848. The time had come, wrote George Henry Evans, author of this alternative Declaration, "for one class of a community to assert their natural and unalienable rights in opposition to other classes."[43]

Evans took the Declaration with him when he moved on, a few years later, to advance the cause for which he is best known: land reform. In 1842 Evans remained as certain as he had been in 1829 that the struggle of American workers was "hardly second in importance to the revolution which separated these states from Great Britain."[44] He filled the pages of his newspapers with reprints of the Declaration, quotations from the preamble, and commentaries on the text.[45] One of his typical utterances, written in conjunction with his colleague John Windt, read: "We would say to [the governing authorities], no longer withhold from men their rights 'to life, liberty, and the pursuit of happiness,' the very foundation of which is the right to the soil. Undo what you have done contrary to that first great principle of your Declaration of Independence."[46]

Another great moment for the Declaration came with the Republican Party, Lincoln, and the Civil War. Charles Sumner spoke not only for himself but for many members of the recently formed Republican Party when, in his eulogy of Lincoln, he held that the task of the Declaration was to prove the providential design behind America's second great war. The objective of the first war had been independence; "the second will have failed unless it performs all the original promises of that Declaration which our fathers took upon their lips when they became a nation." Sumner did not doubt that George Washington, the leader of the first war, had been a good man and a statesman; unfortunately, "in the ample record of what he wrote or said there is no word of adhesion to the great ideas of the Declaration." Far different was Lincoln; "the topic," noted Sumner with satisfaction, "to which the future President returned with the most frequency . . . was the practical significance of the Declaration of Independence in announcing the Liberty and Equality of all men."[47]

It was characteristic of Lincoln that at the time of the Kansas-Nebraska Act (1854), he repeatedly quoted the Declaration to oppose the expansion of slavery into the western territories. "No man is good enough to govern another man, *without the other's consent*. I say this is the leading principle—the sheet anchor of American republicanism. Our Declaration of Independence [makes this clear]." Lincoln's constant theme throughout the

1850s was that exclusion was incompatible with the Declaration and must therefore be condemned. "I am not a Know-Nothing," he announced in 1855. "As a nation, we began by declaring that '*all men are created equal.*' We now practically read it 'all men are created equal, *except Negroes.*' When the Know-Nothings get control, it will read 'all men are created equal, except Negroes, *and foreigners, and Catholics.*'"[48]

Lincoln was ever on the lookout for ways to stave off demotions of the Declaration and to promote its grandeur. When Southerners attempted to play down the preamble by reminding citizens that the Declaration was really only an announcement that America had joined the club of nations, Lincoln was quick to respond: "The assertion that 'all men are created equal' was of no practical use in effecting our separation from Great Britain; and it was placed in the Declaration, not for that, but for future use." The language of human rights, Lincoln understood, was for all times and all people: "I had thought the Declaration contemplated the progressive improvement in the condition of all men everywhere."[49]

The speeches of Lincoln are a fitting culmination to my sketch of the antebellum uses of the Declaration as a doctrine of inclusion. A man for all seasons, a Whig and a Republican with a Jacksonian appeal to the common man; high-toned but with an earthy touch and a sense of humor; Westerner by birth but Easterner by ideals, Lincoln brought the Declaration back to the people—all the people. Everyone knew the man and the meaning when he rose to utter the memorable words "Four score and seven years ago [1776] our fathers brought forth on this continent a new nation, conceived in liberty, and dedicated to the proposition that all men are created equal."

After the Civil War things were never quite the same for the social contract in America (chapter 6), but the Declaration did reassert itself, now and then, by fits and starts. Some but by no means all of the speeches of the centennial celebrations in 1876 renewed the old themes. "Nowhere . . . in the Declaration of Independence is the word *white* used," one orator remarked. Another speaker reiterated a once familiar faith: "The proposition that all men are created equal is to be still further demonstrated. Human rights are to be vindicated and set free from all that would deny them. . . . We have opened our doors to the oppressed. Are those doors to be closed? No; a thousand times no."[50] Charles Francis Adams, son of John Quincy, dared "express a modest doubt whether the [English King] was in reality such a cruel tyrant as he is painted" in the Declaration. The preamble, he explained, was what mattered—and the deleted passage in which Jefferson eloquently denounced the king for fostering the slave trade.[51]

Generally speaking, Americans of the postbellum period shied away from the antebellum practice of automatically beginning or ending speeches with allusions to the Declaration. By no means, however, did they abandon the great document of 1776. George Washington Plunkitt of Tammany Hall, Henry George, Eugene Debs, Edward Bellamy, Woodrow Wilson the progressive, William Jennings Bryan and the Populists, W. E. B. Du Bois—all, at one time or another, appropriated the Declaration.

What political institution was more interested in the politics of inclusion than the political machine, and what machine was more successful in this regard than Tammany Hall? "Nobody pays any attention to the Fourth of July any longer except Tammany," complained George Washington Plunkitt. "When the Fourth comes, the reformers, with Revolutionary names parted in the middle, run off to Newport or the Adirondacks. . . . How different it is with Tammany! . . . As soon as the man on the platform starts off with 'when in the course of human events,' word goes around that it's the Declaration of Independence, and a mighty roar goes up."[52]

Agrarians of all stripes, Georgists as well as Populists, enlisted the Declaration in their respective causes. Near the close of *Progress and Poverty*, Henry George summarized the significance of his argument: "What is it but the carrying out in letter and spirit of the truth enunciated in the Declaration of Independence—the 'self-evident' truth . . . 'That all men are created equal.'"[53] Lorenzo Lewelling, William Peffer, James H. Davis, and other Populists, having renewed the Jacksonian slogan "Equal rights for all; Privileges for none," proved even more concerned than Henry George to enroll the Declaration in their cause.[54]

It is a great tribute to the Declaration that public figures seemingly unlikely to embrace it felt obliged to kneel at its shrine. As a socialist and student of Marxian thought, Eugene Debs might have denounced or ignored the Declaration; instead, he chose to speak of inalienable rights to "life, liberty, and the pursuit of happiness" and called for "the vindication and glorification of American principles . . . , as proclaimed in the Declaration of Independence."[55] Perhaps he knew that throughout the nineteenth century, labor groups had issued a succession of declarations of independence on behalf of disadvantaged workers.[56] Definitely, he knew how to Americanize the socialist message.

Many Americans eased into a non-Marxian socialism or Progressivism through the pages of Edward Bellamy's novel *Looking Backward* (1888). His vision of nationalized industry and cooperative association might have made him an unlikely admirer of Jefferson and the Declaration. Nonetheless, when nine years later he published a sequel under the title *Equality*, Bellamy held that his scheme was based on "the true American constitution—the one written on people's hearts . . . the immortal Declaration with its assertion of the inalienable equality of all men."[57]

Prior to his conversion to Progressivism, Woodrow Wilson admired Burke but rarely had anything good to say about Jefferson. Completely different was the Wilson of 1912, a New Freedom candidate campaigning on the theme of renewal from the bottom and restoration of vanishing economic opportunity. Unless the government acted, ordinary Americans would suffer exclusion from the American dream. Jefferson was now Wilson's man, and the Declaration of Independence was his text, for "it is an eminently practical document, meant for the use of practical men," reformers especially. To prove his dedication to the Declaration and its notions of popular sovereignty, Wilson pointed out that the people had the right to change their government whenever they wished. "That is the foundation . . . of American institutions."[58]

William Jennings Bryan carried the Declaration of Independence into the realm of foreign policy at the time of the Spanish-American War of 1898. Inclusion, he argued, should not be forced upon the Filipinos. "If we are to govern them without their consent and give them no voice in determining the taxes which they must pay, we dare not educate them, lest they learn to read the Declaration of Independence . . . and mock us for our inconsistency."[59]

W. E. B. Du Bois, in *The Souls of Black Folk* (1903), still hoped that even though the promise of Reconstruction had been betrayed, the America of the future might yet include blacks. The "sons of the Fathers" must be reminded of what they "would fain forget": the words of the Declaration. "There are today no truer exponents of the pure human spirit of the Declaration of Independence than the American Negroes."[60]

We may conclude that over the course of American history the Declaration of Independence has consistently furnished American reform movements with their highest aspirations. It has sponsored a politics of inclusion understood as the fulfillment of the ideals of self-government, consent, and recognition of human rights. Reformers have understood that they may not rest until all have been included in the social contract signed in 1776.

Taming the Declaration

For every political action there is an equal and opposite reaction, and so it happened that the Declaration-on-the-march met with mounting resistance throughout the antebellum period. Some Southerners eventually worked up the courage to attack the Declaration root and branch; conservative Northerners, by contrast, usually preferred to attack it obliquely. The attacks came from many directions and assumed many forms. Whether by denying that the Declaration applied to everyone; or by emphasizing its original significance as an announcement of a break with England; or by pointing out its lack of constitutional authority; or, most boldly, by assaulting its Lockean preamble, its opponents had their say. Maybe the Declaration could not be destroyed, but it could at least be tamed.

Southerners learned how to cut the Declaration down to size during the Missouri crisis of 1819 to 1821, in answer to Northern efforts to play it up. Senator Nathaniel Macon of North Carolina emphasized that the Declaration was not part of the Constitution. Senator Nicholas Van Dyke, similarly, argued that the Declaration had no standing as a key to unlocking the meaning of the Constitution. Senator William Pinkney of Maryland, while willing to affirm certain forms of liberty, found that "the self-evident truths announced in the Declaration of Independence are not truths at all if taken literally." Representative John Tyler, in agreement with Pinkney, held that the Declaration's words about liberty and equality, "although lovely and beautiful," could not be taken at face value: they must never be employed to "obliterate those distinctions in society which society itself engenders and gives birth to."

For his part, Representative Louis McLane could not imagine in 1820 why anyone believed the Declaration, right or wrong, constitutional or extraconstitutional, applied to slaves: "The Revolution found them in a state of servitude, the acknowledgement of our actual independence left them so, and the Constitution of the United States perpetuated their condition." Yet another tactic for demoting the Declaration was Ben Hardin's insistence that it was about international relations: "What are the efficient parts of the Declaration of Independence? The answer is, those parts only which declare our dependence upon Great Britain to be at an end, and assume a stand and character of a sovereign people among the nations of the earth." The arsenal for the great proslavery counteroffensive of later years was stocked during the debates of 1820 over the admission of Missouri.[61]

Whether in response to Nat Turner's uprising or the growing threat from abolitionists, some Southern spokespersons turned against the Declaration in the 1830s. Thomas Roderick Dew was upset that the Virginia legislature of 1831–1832, frightened by a slave rebellion, was willing to discuss emancipation. Not ready for an all-out ideological struggle, Dew settled for showing the impracticality of freeing the slaves. Along the way, though, he could not resist taking a swipe at the Declaration's "all men are created equal." "We endeavoured to show that those maxims may be and generally are inapplicable and mischievous."[62] Five years later, in 1837, William Harper spoke with greater fervor against the Declaration in his *Memoir on Slavery:* "Is it not palpably nearer the truth to say that no man was ever born free, and that no two men were ever born equal? Man is born in a state of the most helpless dependence. . . . Then inequality is further developed, and becomes infinite in every society, and under whatever form of government." The last thing slaves need to hear is "well-sounding, but unmeaning verbiage of natural equality and inalienable rights."[63]

William Gilmore Simms's "Morals of Slavery" is another document of 1837 and is noteworthy for, among other things, its multidimensional assault on the Declaration. Southerners, he assured us, may have had their reasons to sign Jefferson's text of 1776, but belief in its preamble could not have been one of them: "It is very certain that the aristocrats of Carolina, in that day, must, if they did swallow it, have done so with monstrous wry faces." Wanting to break away from England was reason enough to sign the Declaration; quite naturally the colonists overstated their case in order to justify themselves. "We are not to subject such a performance as the declaration of independence to a too critical scrutiny, in respect to its generalizations. These are put briefly, and the circumstances of the revolutionary movement were such as required that they should be put *strongly*."[64]

No doubt, Simms surmised, the heat of the moment also accounted for the approval of Southerners in 1776 of the document they would come to regret. "They were much excited, nay, rather angry, in the days of the 'declaration,' and hence it is that what they alleged to be self-evident *then*, is, at this time, when we are comparatively cool, a source of very great doubt and disputation." And then there was the lamentable influence of the French. The only question in Simms's mind about the French connection, it seems, was whether the unfortunate wording of the preamble was the result of an effort to flatter the French for the sake of obtaining their military assistance—or was it the result of a regrettable but brief flirtation of the

Americans of that day with things French? About one matter Simms believed there was no need to speculate: The doctrine espoused in the Declaration was plainly wrong. The truth was that we alienated our rights to life, liberty, and happiness "every day," as needed to maintain a viable society.[65]

John C. Calhoun was probably the most powerful Southern political leader of the antebellum period, so his pronouncements merit attention. As abolitionist attacks upon slavery mounted, Calhoun helped move the South from the notion that slavery was a necessary evil to the view that it was a positive good. Inevitably, he eventually took to the podium to repudiate the Declaration of Independence. On June 27, 1848, Calhoun expressed his dismay that Jefferson had needlessly added the preamble, especially the line "all men are created equal," to the text of the Declaration. "It was inserted in our Declaration of Independence without any necessity. It made no necessary part of our justification in separating from the parent country, and declaring ourselves independent."[66] In the same speech, Calhoun, upping the ante, attacked the Declaration by calling the entire theory of the Lockean social contract into question—the state of nature, natural freedom and equality, the derivative status of government. Many of the same arguments, earmarked for posterity, may be found in his posthumous works, *A Disquisition on Government* and *A Disquisition on the Constitution and Government of the United States.*[67]

We move from Calhoun to the redoubtable George Fitzhugh anticipating an extreme repudiation of the Declaration of Independence, and Fitzhugh does not defeat our expectations. Both in *Sociology for the South* (1854) and in *Cannibals All!* (1857), Fitzhugh challenged the Declaration's "abstract principles" because they "are wholly at war with slavery."[68] Before the abolitionist agitation, he explained, there had been no need for the South to correct the fallacies contained in the preamble. Now, the bad philosophy and false generalizations of the Declaration could no longer be ignored. Nothing less than a systematic assault would do, which meant that Fitzhugh had to reject not only Jefferson's words of 1776 but also "Locke's theory of the Social Contract, on which Free Society rests for support."[69]

Fitzhugh sometimes brilliantly stated and at other times overstated the Southern case against the Declaration. Upbraiding the Declaration on the grounds that it was excessively abstract was the ordinary stuff of Southern thought; so were his claims that social arrangements are complex and cannot be remade overnight. Beyond the pale, however, was the statement that "constitutions should not be written till several centuries after governments have been instituted."[70] Even Calhoun, despite his hostility to the Lockean social contract, always maintained that "the people are the source of all power; that the governments of the several states and of the United States were created by them, and for them; that the powers conferred on them are not surrendered, but delegated."[71]

Fitzhugh hit his stride as a respectable spokesperson for the South when he charged that the Northern reformers who looked to the Declaration for inspiration were paving the way toward anarchy. He condemned not just abolitionists but land reformers and, in common with other Southern writers, treated feminists as destroyers of authority, hierarchy, and the very institutions of marriage and family. "The generous sentiments of slaveholders are sufficient guarantee of the rights of woman, all the world over. But there is something wrong in her condition in free society, and that condition is daily becoming worse."[72]

Frequently Fitzhugh's writings showed hostility to all versions of the theory of the social contract, not just Locke's but those of Grotius and Pufendorf, too; not so, however, in the chapter of *Sociology for the South* that he specifically devoted to a discussion of the Declaration. On this occasion he did allow that there were such things as natural rights and then adopted the standard Southern strategy of understanding those rights in the manner of Grotius rather than that of Locke. "Liberty is alien[able]; there is a natural right to alien[ate] it"; "the laws and institutions of all countries have recognized and regulated its alienation."[73] Usually eager to shock, Fitzhugh eventually realized that the Declaration's memorable "inalienable rights" were perhaps more effectively denied by claims of alienability than by abandonment of talk about natural rights.

Southerners were not isolated in their efforts to cut the Declaration down to size. If John Randolph of Virginia in 1826 dismissed the Declaration as "a fanfaronade of metaphysical abstractions," Senator Rufus Choate of Massachusetts three decades later cast aspersions upon "the glittering and sounding generalities of natural right which make up the Declaration of Independence."[74] As a loyal Whig, Choate put the Union first and therefore reacted with anger at the sight of many of his fellow Whigs joining the newly created "geographical," that is, sectional, Republican Party. When the Republicans enshrined the Declaration in their party platform of 1856, Choate supported the Democratic candidate, James Buchanan, and took out his frustration on the Declaration.

Choate's position on the Declaration was unusual but not unprecedented in the Whig Party. Calvin Colton, a leading Whig journalist, had dared to question the Declaration as early as 1839—surprisingly, because he usually took pride in bending the conservative outlook of his party in the direction of reform and progress. Against the Jacksonians, he had written that the Whigs were the true democrats, whereas the so-called Democrats were sycophantic admirers of King Andrew I.[75] When the issue was the Whig tariff, Colton cleverly voiced his support in a pamphlet titled *The Rights of Labor.* Stealing the rhetoric of the workers' movement, he wrote that "the great object of the American revolution *was to vindicate the rights of labor.*"[76] The protection afforded by the tariff, he argued, was a continuation of the Revolution because it would shield the workers no less than the capitalists. So for Colton to take on the Declaration was unexpected and striking.

Fear of the abolitionist movement was what drove Colton to search for a way to tame the Declaration. One chapter of his *Abolition a Sedition: By a Northern Man* was devoted to a discussion of liberty and equality. "Our object at this time is to correct the vague, poetic, and romantic notions which are commonly attached to these terms," he alerted the reader. "In this country, their origin may fairly be ascribed to a notable declaration, . . . 'that all men are created equal.'" Unfortunately, the abolitionists were constantly citing those words to call for illegal emancipation, no matter that the rights "set forth in the Declaration of our Independence, [were] never intended for such an application." The Constitution should interpret the Declaration, not the Declaration the Constitution.[77]

Francis Bowen was a Northerner of well-established conservative credentials who did his best to tame the Declaration of Independence, briefly but decisively, in the middle of a long essay that he wrote for the Whiggish *North American Review* in 1849. The occasion was the advent of the Second Republic of France, a historical event that deeply worried Bowen because ideas about socialism were being bandied about in Paris at a time when memories of the Anti-Rent Wars of New York were still fresh in America. It is a tribute to the prestige of the Declaration of Independence that Bowen fought off the temptation to damn it by likening it to the French Declaration of 1789. He was less successful, perhaps, in resisting the temptation to tame it by likening it to the English Declaration of 1689. Although he did not explicitly compare the Declaration of Independence to the English Declaration of Rights, his argument was bound to please anyone who wished to conflate 1776 with 1689. "When the connection between England and this country was dissolved by the Declaration of Independence, the people here did not . . . fall back into a state of nature," he wrote approvingly. "The people availed themselves of their newly acquired freedom, not to pull down their old houses and build new ones, but to restore and repair the ancient household." The American Revolution aimed at nothing beyond ending all political connection with England. "It was not a Quixotic crusade in favor of human rights in general, nor a war undertaken only to show that all men are free and equal, and have a right to govern themselves as they see fit."[78]

By no means was Bowen a reactionary. He praised the French Revolution for promoting a wider distribution of landed property and blamed the English for concentrating property.[79] Nor did he reject the Declaration; he simply refused to acknowledge the historical significance of the preamble, which, as John Quincy Adams noted, had grown greater with the passing of the years.

If spokespersons South and North raised their voices to muffle the Declaration, the same was true of the West, represented by Senator Stephen A. Douglas, chair of the committee on territories. Possibly Douglas would simply have sidestepped the Declaration had he not found himself in 1858 matching wits on the campaign trail with Abraham Lincoln. Throughout their famous debates Lincoln made repeated use of the Declaration to argue that the founders had hoped for the early death of slavery. Douglas responded by reminding Lincoln that "when Thomas Jefferson wrote that document, he was the owner, and so continued until his death, of a large number of slaves. . . . When that Declaration was put forth, every one of the thirteen colonies were slaveholding." Each time that Lincoln cited the Declaration as a call for inclusion, Douglas pointed out that "the signers of the Declaration had no reference to the negro whatever, when they declared all men to be created equal. They desired to express by that phrase white men, men of European birth and European descent."[80]

Douglas refused to judge slavery morally, always insisting that it was up to the people of the territories to vote it up or down—which way he did not care. To Lincoln this was the abandonment of principle, but not to Douglas, who believed he was standing up for the "great principle of self-government," the guiding principle of his entire career. "If there is any one principle dearer and more sacred than all the others in free governments, it is that which asserts the exclusive right of a free people to form and adopt their own fundamental law."[81] Douglas did not situate his thought outside the social contract tradition, but he did confuse the popular sovereignty of Locke's social contract with the majoritarian democracy of a working government and said little one way or the other about inconvenient natural rights. His contract and his Declaration were severely emaciated.

Nevertheless, Douglas did score a palpable hit against Lincoln simply by recalling the most commonly cited reason in 1776 for breaking with England. "Did not these colonies rebel because the British parliament had no right to pass laws concerning our property and domestic and private institutions without our consent?" he asked. "Now, Mr. Lincoln proposes to govern the Territories . . . and calls upon Congress to pass laws controlling their property and domestic concerns without their consent. . . . Thus, he asserts for his party the identical principle asserted by George III and the Tories of the Revolution."[82] Douglas knew how to appropriate the Declaration when to do so was to serve his purposes.[83]

When the Southerners withdrew from the Union, their Northern sympathizers, mostly Democrats, chose to exploit rather than abandon the Declaration. Hiding in the shadows, the Copperheads of the North had potential members recite a rewritten Declaration of Independence, reading "All men are endowed by their Creator with certain rights—equal only as far as there is equality in the capacity for the apprehension, enjoyment, and exercise of these rights."[84]

At the outbreak of the Civil War Southerners were torn between condemning the preamble and reworking it to suit their needs. One Virginia newspaper editorialized against it on the fourth of July, 1861. National independence, not equality, was the point of the Declaration, Southerners read in the *Daily Richmond Examiner:* "Never was human conduct justified by worse logic. Would that their useless preamble, their absurd pretexts and transcendental theories had been as harmless as they were sonorous."[85] Jefferson Davis, president of the Confederacy, saw matters in a completely different light. For him nothing was wrong with "the sacred Declaration of Independence"; the problem was with the gratuitous Northern claim that "the great principles" of 1776 referred to slaves. The South, he held, was appealing to "the American idea that governments rest on the consent of the governed, and that it is the right of the people to alter or abolish them at will whenever they become destructive to the ends for which they are established." As he saw it, the Confederate states had "merely asserted the rights which the Declaration . . . defined as 'inalienable.'" Then, in a typical Southern twist, Davis defined inalienable rights as the rights not of humankind but of sovereign states.[86]

Jefferson Davis was, in fact, simply repeating what various Southern states said the day they exited the Union. South Carolinians, for instance, had quoted and paraphrased the Declaration in justifying their secession. Their convention of 1860 announced that "the State of South Carolina, having resumed her separate and equal place among nations, deems it due to herself, to the remaining United States of America, and to the nations of the world, that she should declare the immediate causes which have led to this act." Continuing to paraphrase the Declaration, the rebels cited "the right of a people to abolish a government when it becomes destructive of the ends for which it was instituted."[87] Similarly, members of Tennessee's convention referred to their proclamation of secession as a "Declaration of Independence" and championed "the right of a free and independent people to alter, reform, or abolish our form of Government in such a manner as we think proper."[88]

Exactly the same arguments were made by the editors of the *New Orleans Daily Crescent*, the *Daily Nashville Patriot*, and many other Southern newspapers.[89] The Southerners, who had earlier set forth biting refutations of the Declaration of Independence, turned around in 1860 and showcased their own version of the famous document, theirs being a Declaration that justified secession but had no other implications.

After the Civil War many Northerners yearned to heal the wounds resulting from the great conflict, which explains why so many centennial speeches delivered in northern cities on July 4, 1876, depicted the Declaration as a conservative document. In Boston, Robert C. Winthrop praised a Union "recognizing a large measure of State rights" and held that the actors of 1776 "desired nothing new. Their old original rights as Englishmen were all that they sought to enjoy."[90] In New York, the Reverend R. S. Storrs took much the same approach; the sponsors of the Declaration, he told his audience, "shared the boast of Englishmen that their constitution 'has no single date from which its duration may be reckoned.'"[91] In Rochester, Theodore Bacon publicly expressed his conviction that 1776 was not "what is commonly misnamed a *revolution*. It was rather a movement of conservatism—of resistance to an innovating despotism."[92] If ever there was a distinctive moment prior to the republication of Gentz in the

1950s when some Americans were willing to minimize the Declaration by demoting 1776 into 1689 revisited, that moment came in the late nineteenth century.

Considering that the New Nationalist Progressives of the late nineteenth and early twentieth centuries were reformers, we might expect them to champion the Declaration. Exactly the opposite is true, however, because the Declaration had been transformed by a conservative Supreme Court into a doctrine serving the interests of corporate capitalism. One piece of progressive social legislation after another was struck down by the Court in the name of property rights and freedom of contract. On behalf of the conservative Supreme Court, Justice Stephen J. Field in 1884 proclaimed that "certain inherent rights lie at the foundation of all action, and upon a recognition of them alone can free institutions be maintained. These inherent rights have never been more happily expressed than in the Declaration of Independence."[93] It is not surprising, then, that when arch-Progressive Herbert Croly remarked that "American intelligence has still to issue its Declaration of Independence," he was, in truth, seeking independence from the Declaration of Independence.[94]

John R. Commons, accomplished labor historian, suggested another reason why Progressives should distance themselves from the Declaration. At the turn of the twentieth century a new wave of immigrants was coming to America from southern and eastern Europe, not to mention the Chinese already present in the United States. Knowing the Declaration had historically been used to keep America open to immigrants, he felt obliged to bracket the preamble. In the course of doing so, he overshot the mark and, like many another Progressive, indulged in racist speculations. "Race differences are established in the very blood and physical condition," he wrote, and concluded that education and environment were secondary in shaping character. "It is now nearly forty years since . . . educational advantages were given to the negro, not only on equal terms, but actually on terms of preference over the whites, and the fearful collapse of the experiment is recognized even by its partisans." On the very first page of *Races and Immigrants in America* (1907), Commons warned that the Declaration's pronouncements on equality must not be taken literally.[95]

After the Progressive Age, the Declaration faded far enough into the background that conservatives fearful of its potential radicalism usually ignored it. Not always, however. In 1953, the year Daniel Boorstin published *The Genius of American Politics,* the Cold War was very warm. While other Cold War liberals were hoping for an "end of ideology," Boorstin was spreading the good news that in America it had never started. Thanks to "the amazing poverty and inarticulateness of our theorizing about politics," we need not worry that "the marvelous success and vitality of our institutions" would ever be challenged. Ideology was the "sickness" of Europe, not America.[96] As part of his project of taking the ideas out of American history, Boorstin echoed the arguments of everyone preceding him who had ever set out to tame the Declaration of Independence.

Boorstin's Declaration was "a document of imperial legal regulations," "a bill of indictment against the king, written in the language of British constitutionalism," a call for separation and nothing more. The "technical, legalistic, and conservative character [of the Declaration] will appear at once by contrast with the comparable document of the French Revolution"; "our national birth certificate is a Declaration of Independence and not a Declaration of the Rights of Man." Boorstin wanted to steal from the English their self-satisfied theme of seamless historical continuity and to attribute it to America, so the Declaration of his construction had to be one of the greatest nonevents in American history.[97]

Removing the Declaration from revolutionary politics did not satisfy Boorstin; he also deleted its uses as a beacon of reform. His abolitionists were tough-minded purveyors of "'atrocity' journalism." Apparently none of them had even heard of the Declaration, much less cited it on every possible occasion.[98]

As late as 1976, the year of its bicentennial, a conservative set out to tame the Declaration. On that occasion Martin Diamond joined with Irving Kristol and other neoconservatives in publishing a volume on the prospects of "the American commonwealth." Along with the rest of his cohort, Diamond was determined to reverse the radical student politics and counterculture of the 1960s: the New Left. The purpose of Diamond's essay was to demonstrate that "the social contract theory upon which the Declaration is based teaches not equality as such but equal political liberty." Nor did the Declaration advocate restoring the government to the direct control of the people. The Declaration "does not say that consent is the means by which government is to operate; it says that consent is necessary only to institute or establish government."[99]

The Declaration could not be ignored on its bicentennial. Better to embrace it, then, than to permit the radicals once again to appropriate it; better to tame it, as had been attempted on so many previous occasions, over the course of so many years, in so many different ways.

The Vanishing Declaration

The 1960s was a remarkable decade, not least in respect to the fate of the Declaration of Independence. Every past effort to repudiate the Declaration had met with ultimate defeat; efforts to tame it had met with only uncertain success. But in the 1960s the Declaration vanished, replaced by the so-called Second Bill of Rights, a nationalized version of the original ten amendments to the federal Constitution. Quietly, without fanfare, almost unnoticed, the Declaration disappeared from public life by the end of the 1960s; not, however, before one last glorious moment from 1962 to 1966, one last round of calls for inclusion.

The student radicals who organized the New Left in the early 1960s were determined not to repeat the sins of the Old Left. Theirs would not be another version of the Marxist radicalism of the 1930s that had had no chance of success on this side of the Atlantic; instead, their most visible leader, Tom Hayden, was determined that his fellow student activists would "speak American."[100] After meeting at Port Huron, Michigan, in 1962, Hayden and his cohort issued a pamphlet best known for its advocacy of "participatory democracy," that is, direct political involvement on the part of a reenergized, active citizenry. Although natural rights and a social contract played little if any role in the Port Huron Statement, Hayden seemingly instinctively knew that a truly American radicalism could not be silent regarding the Declaration, especially not when the discussion turned to race. In the opening pages he observed that "the Declaration 'all men are created equal . . .' rang hollow before the facts of Negro life in the South and the big cities of the North."[101]

Without question the most famous appeal to the Declaration during the 1960s was Martin Luther King's "I Have a Dream" speech of August 28, 1963. Standing in front of the Lincoln Memorial, King remarked that "fivescore years ago, a great American . . . signed the Emancipation Proclamation," that "great beacon light of hope to millions of Negro slaves." Unfortunately, the work of emancipation was still far from complete; the "unalienable rights of life, liberty, and the pursuit of happiness" were not yet recognized for blacks as well as for whites. Nevertheless, by the grace of God and the guiding light of the Declaration of Independence, the promised day might well be not too far in the offing. "I still have a dream. It is a dream deeply rooted in the American dream that one day this nation will rise up and live out the true meaning of its creed—we hold these truths to be self-evident, that all men are created equal."[102]

Race was again the reason for reviving the Declaration when in March 1965 Daniel Patrick Moynihan, then assistant secretary of labor, drafted his influential and controversial pamphlet *The Negro Family: The Case for National Action.* On June 4 of the same year President Lyndon Baines Johnson delivered a speech at Howard University titled "To Fulfill These Rights," which transformed the "Moynihan Report" into official policy. Not all African Americans agreed with the Moynihan-Johnson claim that the repetitive cycle of poverty could be explained by positing "the breakdown of the Negro family structure." They did concur, however, with Johnson's contention, cribbed from Moynihan, that poverty was the consequence of "the devastating heritage of long years of slavery, and a century of oppression, hatred, and injustice."[103]

Basic to Moynihan's report was the idea that "the Negro American Revolution" could only succeed if it was about equality as well as liberty—equality understood as something more than the old-fashioned "equality of opportunity, [which] almost insures inequality of results." "It is not enough that all individuals start out on even terms, if the members of one group almost invariably end up well to the fore, and those of another far to the rear." Whatever the strategy the government set out to pursue, it had to be premised on the realization that African Americans suffered from severe disabilities, the legacy of "three centuries of exploitation." Working together, the government and African Americans must seek not liberty alone but also equality, newly defined "in terms of group results." If Moynihan's words sounded novel, his rationale was time-tested: Only by pursuing his ambitious program could blacks "at last redeem the full promise of the Declaration of Independence."[104]

Such has been the prestige of the Declaration that sometimes appeals to its authority have been forthcoming from the most unlikely quarters. The advent of the Black Panther Party was marked by a resurgence of impassioned black nationalist rhetoric, replete with demands that the United Nations oversee elections in the black "colonies" of America. Yet, despite their apparent contempt for things American, the gun-toting Panthers, when it came to writing their platform of 1966, chose for the finale a long quotation from the Declaration of Independence.[105]

At the time no one, in all likelihood, realized that these several striking appeals of the early to mid-1960s were the Declaration's last hurrah. How could anyone anticipate that the Bill of Rights, which had been central to sustaining the politics of exclusion, could replace the Declaration of Independence? The first ten amendments had been ratified to control the federal government but permitted the states to do as they pleased in such vital matters as race relations. That was why reformers habitually rallied to the Declaration of Independence.

To what language in the Bill of Rights, moreover, could reformers of earlier ages possibly appeal? Placed beside the theory-laden Declaration of Independence, the Bill of Rights stood exposed in all its theoretical poverty. James Madison thought that if there were to be a Bill of Rights, it should be an expansive document. He proposed that "there be prefixed to the Constitution a declaration, that all power is originally vested in, and consequently derived from, the people." He also wanted the document to state explicitly that "the people have an indubitable, unalienable, and indefeasible right to reform or change their government."[106] Had he succeeded, the Bill of Rights and thus the Constitution would have incorporated much of the vocabulary of Locke and the Declaration of Independence. Alas, the final language—matter-of-fact, tacked on, devoid of theoretical or idealistic aspirations—is not Madison's. Only by reading between the lines of the first and second amendments, or possibly the ninth and the tenth, can we infer anything resembling Madison's notions of popular sovereignty and right to revolution, and even then the Declaration's language of natural rights—of a moral imperative standing above the written laws—is wanting.[107]

All this changed, at long last, in the 1960s with the incorporation and nationalization of the Bill of Rights. The historical groundwork for this transfiguration of the amendments ratified in 1791 was laid with the passage of the Civil War amendments, especially the Fourteenth Amendment with its due process clause. Fully a century passed, however, before the Supreme Court bothered to complete the process of reconfiguring due process into the defense of individual rights against the recalcitrant state governments. Rather than employ the "due process" and "equal protection" provisions to protect emancipated slaves, the Supreme Court frequently used the Fourteenth Amendment to exempt big business from governmental regulation. In a number of cases, most notably *Plessy v. Ferguson,* the Court went so far as to side with segregationist laws passed by states.

Not until 1925 did the Supreme Court begin to alter its course and take seriously the concept of rights inherent in U.S. citizenship. The culminating point in establishing a "Second Bill of Rights," national in scope, came in the 1960s in a series of decisive cases.[108] With the nationalization of the Bill of Rights, constitutional law had undergone a major transformation and would henceforth be the focus of all groups seeking inclusion.

THE PROMOTION OF THE BILL OF RIGHTS in the 1960s entailed the demotion of the Declaration of Independence. What a century and more of critics of the preamble had failed to do—silence the Declaration—was finally and inadvertently accomplished by its friends and admirers. Its services no longer needed, the Declaration took its final bow and withdrew from public life. The parades, cookouts, and fireworks of the fourth of July continued, but the Declaration was relegated to the status of a relic.

The Declaration had taught Americans to appeal beyond the laws and the Constitution to the natural rights of all persons, to the sovereignty of the people, the consent of the governed, the social contract. The new Bill of Rights made such appeals irrelevant by offering assurances that all claims of rights, all remedies for injustice, could be pursued within the constitutional structure.

One question remains: With the disappearance of the Declaration, had the theory of the social contract also vanished into the American past?

■

SIX

The End of the Social Contract?

The theory of the social contract was never the entirety of American political thought. Before the Civil War it was, however, omnipresent and inescapable; sooner or later the proponents of seemingly every possible alternative mode of discourse had to take a bow to the social contract. After the Civil War, in striking counterpoint, the social contract was on the wane. As a natural reaction against the great upheaval of 1861 to 1865, many Americans grew weary of questions concerning political obligation and wary of those troublemakers who would dare to resurrect the dangerous old way of thinking. There was no lack of postbellum lawyers and judges who deemed "freedom of contract" under the law a far safer bet than a social contract above the law.

In the politics of Henry George and the agrarians of the late nineteenth century, the social contract once again held sway—perhaps, however, for the last time. For very soon, the movers and shakers of the Progressive movement forgot how much they owed to Henry George and congratulated themselves on surpassing and supplanting agrarian reform. Thenceforth the theory of the social contract had to struggle simply to survive in the industrial world of the twentieth century.

One fragment of social contract thinking did remain alive and is still with us today: the notion of rights. And yet the more one heard and continues to hear of rights in post–Civil War America, the less one heard and hears of social contract and consent. The theory of the social contract has undergone a process of fragmentation and diminution, with rights quite possibly the only surviving element. Rights claims have, indeed, proliferated in recent times, but problematically, for they have lost the firm grounding of bygone ages in the larger theory of the social contract and the law of nature.

Europeans long ago abandoned theories of the social contract. Americans, apparently, must now do the same; they must learn to cope with a political multiverse in which there is no language of public life that can help translate all the other languages into a common tongue, a shared idiom.

Before, During, and After the Civil War

There is a story of the social contract before the Civil War, another of the social contract thereafter, and a third of the great conflict as a turning point in the career of the social contract.

Prior to the Civil War the power of the social contract was manifest in the tribute paid to it by even the thinkers most intellectually predisposed to reject it. Then, at the outbreak of great conflict, the fate of the social contract hung in the balance, especially in the North, where a deep division arose between supporters and implacable critics. In 1861 some antislavery Northerners remained so loyal to their theories of consent and social contract that they saw no basis for denying the right of the Southerners to secede; other Northerners drew the opposite conclusion, viewing the Civil War as the occasion to launch a strong and uncompromising assault on theories of the social contract.

In the end, however, the reason why the social contract faded at the close of the nineteenth and beginning of the twentieth century was probably not because of direct denunciations; rather, it was the result of purposive neglect, combined with a refocusing of political thought away from the constituent to the constituted powers, away from the Declaration of Independence to the ever more holy words of the Constitution. The familiar contention of historians, that the Civil War was a pivotal moment in American history, holds decidedly true when applied to the fate of theories of the social contract.

THE UNDENIABLE INFLUENCE OF THEORIES of the social contract in antebellum America even in places where least expected is plainly evident in the speeches and writings of George Bancroft and Edward Everett. Trained in German historicism, both Bancroft and Everett might well have challenged antebellum theories of the social contract. Bancroft attended the University of Göttingen; Everett also studied in Germany, earning a doctoral degree. Long before it became commonplace for Americans of the Progressive Age to travel to Europe, there to imbibe the German historicism that has no use for theories of a social contract, Bancroft and Everett employed their German education to discuss all things American in the idiom of historical thought. Nevertheless, both men deferred to the entrenched American commitment to the social contract, as can be seen in their refusal to contradict the theory and in their reaffirmations of the standard wisdom on critical occasions.

Speaking on the fourth of July, 1826, Bancroft celebrated the fiftieth anniversary of the Declaration of Independence in the warmest possible terms. For the social contract language of the preamble he had nothing but praise, and he universalized its message in defiance of all the lessons of German historicism. He took pride, moreover, in the recollection that the French Revolution had been based on the principles of the American and expressed satisfaction that "a permanent consequence of the French Revolution has been the establishment of representative governments in some of the states of Europe." Popular sovereignty, too, might eventually triumph in Latin America and Europe as a long-term consequence of the American Revolution. Prospects for the future were exciting because "the history of the age is showing from actual experiments which [system of government] best promotes the ends of the social compact."[1]

Nine years later, on Washington's birthday, Bancroft accused the Whigs, unfairly but cleverly, of upholding Pufendorf's notion of a contract between rulers and ruled and congratulated his fellow Democrats on their strict adherence to the Lockean version of the social contract.[2] No matter how much "history" might beckon, Bancroft conceded that "nature" could not be denied.

Perhaps Bancroft, as a Jacksonian, was under exceptional political pressure to come to terms with the social contract of Jefferson. Everett was a Whig, hence presumably more conservative, but his party also claimed the Jeffersonian heritage, which helps explain why he never permitted his German education to stand in the way of a robust endorsement of the Lockean version of the social contract. As we have seen, Everett repudiated Burke's historicized view of rights and contract in uncompromising terms, and he made a point in his speeches of restating the "true principles" of the American Revolution, namely, the right of the sovereign people, whenever they choose, to form a new government to their liking. In any conflict between German historicism and the social contract, it was historicism that yielded.

The standard pattern of the Whigs—Daniel Webster, for instance—was to speak glowingly of the continuity of the generations in contradiction of Jefferson's "the earth belongs to the living." No sooner, however, did they take their seemingly conservative stand in favor of historical continuity than they proceeded to praise, in Webster's words, "the People's Constitution, the People's Government; made for the People; made by the People; and answerable to the People." Nor did they hesitate to affirm the very right of revolution that they ardently hoped would never be invoked by Southern plantation owners or Northern Dorrites.

The writings of Justice Joseph Story provide an excellent example of the Whiggish mind at work. There was, to begin with, the conservative streak: the fear of "ultraism of all sorts," whether of Southern secessionists or Northern abolitionists; the concern for passing down the American heritage from generation to generation; the conviction that "whatever has been found to work well in experience, should be rarely hazarded upon conjectural improvements"; and the preference for addressing "forms" rather than "principles" of government.[3] Then, in sharp contrast, there was the Story who in his *Commentaries on the Constitution of the United States* (1833) recounted but dismissed the anti–social contract theorizing of Hume, Blackstone, Paley, and Burke; the Story who sided against Americans who held that government is a compact between the rulers and the people and sided with John Quincy Adams, who held that the whole people covenanted with each citizen and each citizen with the whole people.[4]

Finishing his argument with a brief foray into comparative analysis, Story noted that it was the July Monarchy of Louis Philippe, not the Constitution of the United States, that was founded on a contract between ruler and people. England, too, was fundamentally different from America, 1688 profoundly different from 1776, Pufendorf different from Locke: "There is no analogy whatsoever between [1688] and the government of the United States, or the social compact."[5]

The positions Abraham Lincoln advanced as a Whig and later as a Republican are especially noteworthy. The Whig theme that law and reason must triumph over mob rule and mindless passion was his from the beginning, nowhere better articulated than in his early speech before the

Springfield Young Men's Lyceum in 1838, which bore the significant title "The Perpetuation of Our Political Institutions." With the recent lynching of an abolition newspaper editor in mind, Lincoln denounced the "outrages committed by mobs." It was bad enough when "the pleasure hunting masters of Southern slaves" resorted to violence; it was worse when mobs arose from the ranks of the supposedly "order loving citizens of the land of steady habits." Self-government is impossible without self-control. "Let reverence for the laws be breathed by every American mother to the lisping babe that prattles on her lap. . . . Let it be written in Primmers, spelling books, and in Almanacs;—let it be preached from the pulpit, . . . let it become the *political religion* of the nation." Bad laws should be changed as soon as possible, but while still in force, "they should be religiously observed."[6]

In the best Whig fashion, Lincoln offset his repudiation of mobs with repeated affirmations of the right of revolution. Speaking in the House of Representatives on January 12, 1848, he firmly stated that "any people anywhere, being inclined and having the power, have the *right* to rise up, and shake off the existing government, and form a new one that suits them better. This is a most valuable,—a most sacred right—a right, which we hope and believe, is to liberate the world."[7] Four years later Lincoln sounded the same theme: "Whilst we meet to do honor to Kossuth and Hungary, we should not fail to pour out the tribute of our praise and approbation to the patriotic efforts of the Irish, the Germans, and the French, who have unsuccessfully fought to establish in their several governments the supremacy of the people."[8]

While campaigning for and then when serving as president, Lincoln changed the tone and modulation of his pronouncements. Countering the claims of Southerners that they were conservatives whereas the Republicans were destructive revolutionaries, Lincoln took the stance that "you [of the South] are unanimous in rejecting and denouncing the old policy of the fathers." More importantly, Lincoln renewed the old Whig ploy of arguing that the Southerners could not leave the Union constitutionally, but only as revolutionaries. "The States have their status in the Union. . . . If they break from this, they can only do so against law, and by revolution."[9] Americans weary of the established government had two choices, and only two: "They can exercise their *constitutional* right of amending it, or their *revolutionary* right to dismember, or overthrow it."[10] Lincoln was still defending the right of revolution, but now in the old Whig hope that the South would come to its senses and stop short of such a radical measure.[11]

If Lincoln spoke in the voice of a typical Whig or Republican, he frequently did so with an unmatched depth, subtlety, and suppleness. At Gettysburg he spied the perfect opportunity to suppress the radicalism of the American social contract tradition without saying so, and without joining the growing ranks of Northerners who rejected the social contract root and branch. A few years earlier, in 1859, Lincoln had claimed for Republicans the Jefferson who had put "the man *before* the dollar" and denied Jefferson to the Democrats, who "hold the *liberty* of one man to be absolutely nothing, when in conflict with another man's right of *property*."[12] Lincoln at Gettysburg was still an admirer of Jefferson—of Jefferson's Declaration and his advocacy of human rights but not of Jefferson's "the earth belongs to the living." Gettysburg, Lincoln realized, was the perfect opportunity to delete the unwanted side of Jefferson. On that blood-stained battlefield no one could utter Jefferson's words about how the living owe nothing to the dead without committing the sin of sacrilege.

When Lincoln spoke of "us the living" in his great Gettysburg Address, it was to admonish the present generation "to be dedicated here to the unfinished work which they who fought here have thus far so nobly advanced."[13] Not the rights but the duties of the living were his concern: the obligation to honor the dead, to acknowledge the sacrifice of the fallen soldiers, and to guarantee that their deaths would become part of a history of the struggle for freedom. At the same time, then, that Lincoln deradicalized the theory of the social contract, he rededicated the preamble of the Declaration of Independence to the highest moral ends. Lincoln brilliantly fulfilled the Whig understanding of the social contract while quietly dismissing the Jeffersonian.

Not a few other Northern spokespersons, less supple and more dogmatic, did exactly what Lincoln had striven to avoid: They took one extreme or the other; they either damned America's "revolution principles" in condemnation of the rebels, or they reaffirmed the principles of the social contract and wished the Southerners Godspeed. Unlike Lincoln, many Northerners were unwilling to search for and acknowledge an acceptable middle ground between following the social contract no matter where it led or suppressing it as never before.

The most obvious example of Northerners who sanctioned secession in the name of the social contract was that of the Copperheads. Numbered among the antiwar Democrats of the North was John L. O'Sullivan, originally of "manifest destiny" fame but eventually an exile in England. In

1862 he published an angry pamphlet titled *Union, Disunion, and Reunion*. Near the beginning he vindicated "the inherent right of any and every great mass of human population, large enough for independence, to choose and change at will its form of government." Toward the end he insisted that Northerners "must learn the first principles of the political science of *confederation*." For Northerners to deny Southerners their right to secede, he argued, went against the axiom that governments "derive their just powers only *from the consent of the governed*."[14] The next year O'Sullivan published another pamphlet called *Peace: The Sole Chance Now Left for Reunion*. Ratcheting up the rhetoric, he complained that for Northerners to use violence against the South was "to blaspheme our very Declaration of Independence"; it was to justify Russia's oppression "of writhing and bleeding Poland."[15]

It is not surprising, of course, to find that the Copperheads availed themselves of the social contract tradition to support the South: Supporters of states' rights, opponents of centralized government, Democrats indifferent to slavery, Copperheads had good reasons to remain faithful to old ways of thinking. Highly remarkable, however, is that some antislavery and pronationalist Northerners took the same stance.[16] George W. Bassett, an abolitionist for two decades, granted the Southerners the right to leave the Union if they so chose: "The same principle that has always made me an uncompromising abolitionist," he explained, "now makes me an uncompromising secessionist. It is the great natural and sacred right of self-government." Echoing Southern arguments regarding "the wickedness and folly of the present war," he decided that the North was unfortunately "contending for the identical object of Lord North in his war on the American colonies."[17]

The position staked out by Bassett was not unusual. James Freeman Clarke, a widely recognized antislavery minister, stepped forth in 1861 and proclaimed that "according to the fundamental principles of our government, the secessionists are right in their main principle." Withdrawal from the Union was their prerogative, their right; the departure of the Southerners accorded perfectly well with "the principles of self-government, which are asserted in the Declaration of Independence."[18] Horace Greeley, too, added his famous name to the list of the foes of slavery who nevertheless defended the South's right of revolution. A "great principle" of the Declaration of Independence was at stake, that "governments derive their *just* powers from the *consent of the governed:* and that whenever any form of government becomes destructive of these ends, it is the *right of the people to alter or abolish it.*" Americans, Greeley added, had legitimately seceded from England, and the South had the same right to secede from the federal Union.[19]

Other Northerners, horrified by secession, thought the time ripe to abandon the social contract tradition. Henry Bellows, for example, published a pamphlet in 1863 under the eye-catching title *Unconditional Loyalty*. Whereas government for Locke was merely the "trustee" of the sovereign people and ever answerable to their ultimate authority, Bellows urged Americans to "support, encourage, cheer, and trust the Government." Our great difficulty, he complained, "is the reluctance of the people to trust the Government with all the moral and political powers it requires." Governance was his theme, "the sacred cause of Government," the need to shift attention from the constituent to the constituted authorities. "The Government is the mighty pillar that fastens . . . and holds to safety the ten thousand varying interests, rights, and obligations of a nation." From then on, Bellows averred, "the country should have but one thought . . . the upholding of the constituted authorities." All might yet be well if Americans made "a religion of patriotism," if they likewise revered their president as "a sacred person," and substituted unconditional loyalty for debates about political obligation.[20]

Bold in many respects, Bellows was nevertheless careful not to push his argument to its plausible conclusion. His plea was for permitting the president to exercise vast emergency powers in time of war, not to replace constitutional with sacred government.[21] And although he assembled every thought necessary to overthrow the social contract, he refrained from explicitly designating it as his intellectual target.

The final step, the total repudiation of the social contract, supplemented by a downgrading of the Declaration of Independence, was taken during the Civil War by Horace Bushnell, on behalf of the Northern religious ministry, and Charles J. Stillé, for the bar. Both writers lamented the weak sense of obligation in America; the lack of loyalty; the failure to appreciate the proper role of strong government in securing peaceful, civilized life. Both men placed the blame directly upon the prevalence of social contract theorizing in public discussions of the greatest import. "The most striking characteristic of the American mind at this time," and its greatest defect, thought Stillé, "is its intense activity and eagerness in the discussion of elementary political principles."[22]

Absurdly but revealingly, Bushnell announced to his Hartford congregants that the theories of the state of nature and social contract were French imports, cribbed from Rousseau and the French "infidels," then shipped to America on the orders of Thomas Jefferson.[23] "The doing [of American independence] was grand, but the doctrine of the doing was . . . a kind of latent poison against all government. . . . The true merit of this document [the Declaration of Independence], . . . lies in the bill of facts and grievances stated afterwards, not in the matter of the preamble." If there was a figure in Bushnell's writings who vied with Jefferson for the title of villain, it was Calhoun, whose speeches—to Bushnell's mind—were proof of the chaos wrought by belief that government was based on a contract.[24] If there was a flawed hero, it was Hamilton, master of governance and political institutions but unfortunately too much the man of his era to disabuse himself of the idea of the social contract.[25] In general, Bushnell championed the laws and the Constitution but complained about "the philosophy that is given of their grounds and underlying principles."[26]

Bushnell conceded that "our current political philosophy [of the social contract], figuring always in the speeches and political speculations of our statesmen, [hails] from the Revolution downward."[27] Stillé's contrasting ploy was to deny the existence of America's revolutionary principles. Taking as his theme "the historical character of our civilization," he saw no reason to waste time discussing "some fancied compact of society." In his estimation, "it is remarkable how few of the great principles of our liberty can be deduced in any way from any pure and unmixed general theory of human rights." Our liberty was an offshoot of England's; our meaningful rights were those sanctioned by common, not natural, law.[28]

In every way that he could imagine, Stillé portrayed American political culture as if it were a replica of England's. Did we not encounter in America the same disdain for "speculative theorists" as in England; the same approval not of natural but of "chartered rights," of "rights and duties as a member of society" rather than as an isolated individual; the same contempt for the French Declaration of Rights—that monument to "pure reason" and futility? Far different was the Declaration of Independence: "Although general axioms are laid down, yet the complaint is that of the violation of positive laws." Consistently enough, Stillé beamed with satisfaction at the thought that "the glory of our system is that there is nothing revolutionary about it"; or if a revolution, then "a political, not a social revolution."[29]

Stillé shows us how vehement a Northern intellectual could be in his efforts to erase the social contract from the records of the American past. Inadvertently, he also tells us that efforts to remove principles of revolution from the history of America are themselves a revolutionary break with tradition. In order to read the social contract out of the past, he drew upon "the safest books we have in modern times upon the philosophy of history—the works of Guizot, Thierry, Arnold, Stephen, and Lieber"; that is, he turned to the French, English, and German liberals who had substituted history for nature, constitutional for natural rights.[30] He imposed European categories of thinking upon American history, not so much to criticize notions of natural rights, consent, and social contract as to pretend they had never existed in the United States. His study titled "The Historical Development of American Civilization" is a systematic distortion of American history.

The retreat from the social contract tradition in postbellum times would require a less confrontational approach than that of Bellows, Bushnell, and Stillé. Conservatives of the late nineteenth century hit upon a workable solution: They chose to maintain a discreet silence on the social contract while keeping intact everything the Civil War conservatives had suggested concerning the vital necessity of governance and strong political institutions. "Have you thought what a vindication this [ongoing civil] war is of Alexander Hamilton?" asked publicist George W. Curtis. The vogue of Hamilton that was an outgrowth of the Civil War continued through the rest of the century, with Henry Cabot Lodge, for instance, publishing his *Hamilton* in 1882 and editing Hamilton's writings in 1885. The reputation of Hamilton, master of institution-building and governance, was on the ascent in the late nineteenth century; the reputation of Jefferson, master of political principles, was in relative decline.[31]

The revival of Hamilton was part of a much larger reorientation of postbellum thought. Governance, political institutions, and the Constitution had always had their place in American political thought, but in the postbellum era they received a noteworthy promotion at the expense of the constituent power of the people—at the expense, that is, of political conventions, the consent of the governed, the right of revolution, and the Declaration of Independence.

One sign of the changing times was the deification of the Constitution during the final decades of the nineteenth century. Henry Estabrook, a widely respected member of the New York bar, exhausted every rhetorical flourish he could muster, every exclamation mark his typewriter could tolerate, in the cause of commanding his compatriots to adore their Constitution: "O Marvellous Constitution! Magic Parchment! Transforming word! Maker, Monitor, Guardian of Mankind!"[32] Estabrook did what many another conservative commentator did in the late nineteenth century to assure that a nation based on a renegotiable social contract would have a permanent "foundation." He asked all eyes to gaze with reverence on the document of 1787 rather than on the process of drawing up and ratifying the Constitution.

Another unmistakable sign of the dawn of a new era was the demotion during the Gilded Age of constitutional conventions. The process of rendering them insignificant had begun even before the Civil War had ended, with occasional explicit calls to shut them down. Joseph P. Thompson, a Congregational minister of New York, in the course of declaring "revolution against free government not a right but a crime," made a special point in 1864 of vilifying Jefferson's "the earth belongs to the living" and opined that the "perfect" Constitution of the framers had foreclosed any and all claims to a future convention.[33]

State constitutional conventions North and South had been prominent before the Civil War; state conventions, again, had carried the Southerners out of the Union; and state conventions permitted Southerners to reenter after the end of the fighting. The sovereign people of the entire United States might have assembled only once in American history, in 1787, but the sovereign people of the various states had met frequently. If the powers of the sovereign people were to be stymied in the postbellum age, state constitutions would have to be domesticated or eliminated, and that was exactly what happened.

Once Southern racists had resumed power, they had little interest in calling for additional conventions; in the North, reformers such as Horace Greeley and E. L. Godkin opposed significant state constitutional change because they feared the new wave of immigrants, who were being courted by the political machines. Carefully screened and specific constitutional amendments rather than thoroughgoing constitutional revision would henceforth be a favorite means of preventing "the people" from wreaking havoc at constitutional conventions.[34] Availing themselves of the process of amendment, the gathering forces of late-nineteenth-century conservatism had found a quietly effective way of paying lip service to popular sovereignty while denying it in practice.

The theory of the social contract took a direct hit at the time of the Spanish-American War of 1898. Democratic Senator George Vest objected that the United States should not "govern millions without their consent," in defiance of the Declaration of Independence.[35] The Republican Party, however, and especially Theodore Roosevelt, accepted imperialism despite its reversal of the doctrine that just governments derive their authority from the consent of the governed. Roosevelt derided those "who cant about 'liberty' and the 'consent of the governed.' . . . Their doctrines, if carried out, would make it incumbent upon us to leave the Apaches of Arizona to work out their own salvation, and to decline to interfere in a single Indian reservation." The American West had been gloriously won by blood and force, remarked Roosevelt, and now the time had come for America to apply the same methods across the globe.[36] The sons of the men who had worn blue and gray fought side by side against Spain and were prepared to join hands in spreading American grandeur far and wide, said a triumphal Roosevelt. Suspending the quest for consent when dealing with foreigners or Indians was, in Roosevelt's view, a small price to pay for the emergence of America as a world power.

Teddy Roosevelt hailed the reunion of Northern and Southern men, even though their rediscovered "brotherhood" came at the expense of the social contract tradition.[37] In a parallel development, the Northern women's suffrage movement of the late nineteenth century successfully incorporated Southern women, but not without sacrificing the same intellectual heritage. As late as 1894 Elizabeth Cady Stanton published *Suffrage a Natural Right,* in which she clung to the words of the Declaration of Independence as tenaciously as had the women at Seneca Falls in 1848.[38] Overall, however, the 1890s was the moment when the earlier abolitionist-inspired members yielded leadership of the National American Women Suffrage Movement to a younger and more conservative generation. To placate the racist Southern women, the movement dropped talk of natural rights, consent, and equality, or relabeled such notions under the heading "for whites only."[39]

At least one additional end-of-the-century strategy for jettisoning the social contract merits consideration: the practice of speaking of society as a series of contractual, but not social contractual, relations. Lawyers, judges, and businessmen built their vision of postbellum times on the idea that contract had replaced bondage for emancipated blacks and that "free labor" was contractual labor.[40] The newly professionalized bar association

held sway and placed "freedom of contract," as defined by it, where the social contract had previously held the high ground.

Writers such as E. L. Godkin, William Graham Sumner, and Woodrow
Wilson stated the same theme more theoretically by Americanizing Sir
Henry Maine's contention that the course of history was an evolution
"from status to contract." The Mugwump Godkin in 1867 explicitly endorsed Maine's view, supplementing it with the suggestion that the time
had come to apply the Englishman's insight to the working class.[41] Social
Darwinist Sumner, who despised notions of social contract and natural
rights, held in 1883 that "in the United States more than anywhere else, the
social structure is based on contract, and status is of the least importance."[42] Woodrow Wilson exploited Maine's theme in his early writings
and almost simultaneously wrote that Jefferson's "French" predilection for
theories of the social contract proved he was "not a great American."[43]

There were occasions in antebellum times when abuse was poured on
the theory of the social contract.[44] Nothing, however, in that earlier age
prepares us for the damage it suffered in the decades following the Civil
War—the retreat, one by one, from notions of popular sovereignty, consent, natural rights, and, more generally, from the idea of the social contract as founding and refounding moment.

From Agrarianism to Progressivism

The upsurge of Henry George's agrarianism in the late nineteenth century
came at a critical moment in the history of the social contract. Even as
many efforts were afoot to ignore the social contract or to dismantle it one
piece at a time, the land reformers stepped forth and reasserted the old notions in fully developed and uncompromising language. If, in the end, these
agrarians lost out, it was not so much to the conservatives as to the Progressives, the very group that was indebted to Henry George for many of
its most important concepts. The Progressive intellectuals eventually
turned against their agrarian mentors, penning perhaps the most systematic critiques of agrarianism and social contract theory ever written on
American soil.

On many of the most vital points, the Progressives had much in common with the latest generation of land reformers. Herbert Croly, one of the
most ardent Progressives and a direct influence on Bull Moose candidate
Teddy Roosevelt, was in perfect if unacknowledged agreement with the

likes of Henry George when he wrote that "the American problem is the social problem."[45] Three decades earlier, Henry George had already recognized that the question of the day was the future of labor, and he had freely admitted that the old political debate about republics versus monarchies could not successfully address the problems of an industrial society. "Political liberty," observed George, was hollow when it amounted to little more than "the liberty to compete for employment at starvation wages."[46]

Progressives and agrarians agreed, once again, that the frontier had been but could no longer be the American answer to class conflict. Well in advance of Progressive historian Frederick Jackson Turner's famous essay on the closing of the frontier, Henry George had warned that "our advance has reached the Pacific"; "the public domain is almost gone."[47] Progressives and agrarians also agreed that the Republican Party's postbellum formulas, "from bondage to contract" and "freedom of contract," were for the workers little more than rationalizations of what labor groups since antebellum times had been calling "wage slavery."[48] Convinced that fundamental reforms were essential, both Progressives and agrarians were willing to risk offering selective praise of socialists. "The principles or methods which the Socialists advocate and which I believe to be in the interest of the people I support," said New Nationalist Teddy Roosevelt.[49] Henry George, likewise, wanted "to realize the dream of socialism," if by other means.[50]

Agrarians could also argue that they and their social contract theory had always been "progressive," long before there were any Progressives. A primitive evolutionary anthropology, a sketch of stages of social development, may be found in Pufendorf, in Locke, in Paine; and no one believed more in progress than the agrarian Thomas Jefferson. John Randolph might mock Jefferson's plow, with its "moldboard of least resistance," but to the rest of the world it was an advance in scientific agriculture.[51] Henry George sounded exactly like Jefferson when he asserted that "human progress goes on as the advances made by one generation are . . . secured as the common property of the next, and made the starting point for new advances."[52]

Finally, agrarians and Progressives were as one in rejecting the pervasive Constitution-worship of their age. "At the present time," wrote Croly, "there is a strong, almost a dominant, tendency to regard the existing Constitution with religious awe," to elevate it into "a monarchy of the Word," and to stifle creative political intelligence.[53] Croly included the Democrats when he drew up his list of persons unduly under the influence of the Constitution because the Jeffersonian and Jacksonian heroes of the party, wanting the federal government to do little or nothing, had resorted to a strict reading of the Constitution that had the effect of turning it into holy writ. Had Croly examined the Jeffersonian tradition more thoroughly, he would have encountered another strain of Jeffersonian thought, the stress on the constituent rather than the constituted power. He might also have learned that Henry George identified with this latter Jeffersonian tradition that was hostile to Constitution-worship.

The second generation of Progressives sometimes forgot how many of the arguments of their movement were derived from the formulations of the land reformers. Croly, for instance, was typical of the Progressives in his insistence that wealth is "created by social rather than individual activity."[54] To all appearances he did not know that Tom Paine in *Agrarian Justice* had written that "it is as impossible for an individual to acquire personal property without the aid of Society, as it is for him to make land originally."[55] The Progressive case for a "social debt" that the wealthy should repay to society was originally argued by the land reformers.

Whereas a first-generation Progressive might appreciate the theoretical accomplishments and cosmopolitanism of the land reformers and concede that an intellectual debt was owed to them, Croly saw only provincialism and foolishness in the thought of his predecessors. The novelty he claimed for himself was that "of applying ideas, long familiar to foreign political thinkers, to the subject-matter of American life." His admiration was for Progressives who went to Continental Europe for insights because at home intellectual life had been about as vigorous "as that of the domestic animals."[56] He failed to appreciate that the land reformers had earlier gone to Europe—not to Continental Europe but to England and Ireland, and not simply to learn but to teach. American agrarianism held its own in conversations with the likes of English progressives T. H. Green and L. T. Hobhouse, and spoke effectively both to the Irish workers and to their Irish American brethren.

T. H. Green might as well have been quoting a great many antebellum American land reformers when he remarked that land was similar to air, light, and water in being given to all in common but different in that it had been problematically appropriated for private use. He did not doubt that "the landless countrymen . . . are the parents of the proletariat of great towns" and thought it appropriate to regulate distribution in the public interest.[57] Although L. T. Hobhouse thought Green's social understanding of human beings a vast improvement over what he took to be the narrow individualism of the social contract tradition, he spoke approvingly of Henry George. The American land reformer had correctly condemned the institution of private property in land. All a good Progressive had to do, thought Hobhouse, was to expand George's findings to other parts of the modern economy that cried out for collective ownership in a just industrial order.[58]

Many figures both in America and England took the claim that land should not be held as private property as the point from which they commenced the intellectual odysseys that frequently ended in progressivism and/or socialism.[59] Labor, the fate of the working classes, and the transformation of the workplace were the overriding concerns. In America the working-class movement was largely Irish, which made Henry George's thought and his trips to Ireland especially pertinent. Terence Powderly of the Knights of Labor sounded exactly like Henry George when he announced in 1882 that "the soil is the heritage of all men and can neither be bought or sold." At the same time Robert Blissert, speaking on behalf of New York's Central Labor Union, proclaimed that "labor today declared its right to the soil—to the land—which should belong to everyone in general and no one in particular."[60]

No matter how much the Progressives and socialists owed to Henry George, be it ever so great, eventually they had little choice but to abandon him. Always the Jeffersonian, George believed his land reform was a cure-all that would accomplish a social revolution while minimizing the role of government. Quite consistently and yet to the surprise of many agrarians, he sided against the Populists because their platform of 1892 stated that "the powers of government—in other words, of the people—should be expanded."[61] Henry George sharply disagreed with them; their call for a graduated income tax, in his opinion, would empower "a large number of officials clothed with inquisitorial powers."[62] He disappointed labor as well with his denial of the legitimacy of strikes because, in his view, they necessitated "tyrannical" organization within labor unions.[63]

Two events in particular forced the Progressives to turn their backs on Henry George. In 1888, fearful of socialists, George wrote a free trade tract for Grover Cleveland. In 1890, when the American Social Science Association held its annual meeting, the breach between Georgists and the younger generation of reformers was palpable. The aging followers of

George spoke of natural rights, justice, and the social contract; the contrasting words from the mouths of the youthful professionals were value, price, market, and state.[64]

For Progressives, the problem was not only that the agrarians opposed the political measures necessary for reform; it was also that the conservatives of the Gilded Age and thereafter had captured the doctrines of natural rights and a social contract. Standard fare in the works of Progressives was the unmasking of natural rights as the doctrine behind which the fat and exploitative business classes hid their vested interests.[65] When anti-Progressive William Howard Taft complained in 1912 that the Declaration of Independence had been "erroneously interpreted" to mean that "each child as it came into the world was entitled to as much of this world's goods as any other," Progressive jurist Learned Hand predictably answered not by returning to Henry George but by asserting that "certainly we do not want to get mixed up with any inalienable rights of man arising from the social compact."[66]

Progressive intellectuals, convinced that the social contract was reactionary, availed themselves of the resources of European historicism in an effort to drive the old doctrine out of public life. Of the many possible Progressive spokespersons, two will suffice: Herbert Croly, editor of the *New Republic*, author of *The Promise of American Life* (1909) and *Progressive Democracy* (1914), and John Dewey, philosopher and educator, whose many publications include *Individualism Old and New* (1929–1930).

For both Croly and Dewey, as for Progressives in general, the first mistake of the old theorizing came in the form of its misunderstanding of the individual human being. Society, argued the Progressives, makes individuals; individuals do not make society. If Americans thought otherwise, that was due to the narrowly individualistic political culture that had shaped and molded them—their inheritance from Locke and Adam Smith, reinforced by a crassly commercial culture, a gospel of acquisitiveness and accumulation that glorified the economic winners and stigmatized the losers.[67]

We are all the products of collective social and cultural forces, all socially constituted, argued Croly and Dewey. The great misfortune of the Americans was that their culture had habituated them to take "the individual" as a given, even though true individuality was an achievement that could be attained only through constructing a new culture of mutuality and cooperation in an ever more collective economic order. American individualism must be surpassed because it was the foremost obstacle to the emergence of genuine individuality.

Croly ended his first book with a section called "Constructive Individualism," itself part of a chapter titled "The Individual and National Purpose." His second book closed with a discussion of the "Social Education" that would train managers and unionized workers to find the fulfillment of their higher selves in the company of others, working together for their mutual benefit. Dewey, pursuing the same theme, addressed "The Crisis in Culture," the need to redefine individualism and to foster "the creation of a type of individual whose pattern of thought and desire is enduringly marked by consensus with others."[68] The old individualism was social conformity and injustice; the new would be social justice and the full development of selfhood and personality.

To Croly and Dewey the American fascination with theories of the social contract was a major part of what was wrong with the culture of the United States. So unsympathetic were they to the social contract, so eager to dismiss it as a relic from a bygone era, that much of the damage they did to the old ideas was based upon a highly biased and misleading portrayal of the views they rejected. It was not true, as they implied, that social contract theory hinged on the notion of an abstract, disembodied individual. Far from it; Grotius had postulated sociability as naturally given; Pufendorf had refuted the individualism of Hobbes; and Locke's natural man was engaged in myriad social relationships, making him seem like an English gentleman taking a Sunday walk in the woods. Nor was it obviously true that the emphasis on natural rights was at the expense of duties. Pufendorf had written a treatise on the topic of duties, and, in general, the stress on sociability in social contract theory led quite naturally to an affirmation of our duties. If Croly and Dewey had bothered to reread the Declaration of Independence, they would have encountered the claim that, in the case of an oppressed people, "it is their right, it is their *duty* to throw off such government."

Less than entirely fair in their treatment of social contract theory, Croly and Dewey, rather predictably, rejected agrarianism out of hand. Neither man, apparently, remembered its uses as a reform doctrine; neither realized it had ever been a training school for Progressives. Their only concern was to label agrarianism passé in an industrial age. "We may say that the United States has steadily moved from an earlier pioneer individualism to a condition of dominant corporateness," wrote Dewey, who shed no tears at the interment of an outmoded ideology.[69] Croly at an earlier date had noted with satisfaction the demise of "pioneer democracy."[70]

There was one difference, perhaps, between Croly and Dewey on the topic of agrarianism. Dewey was willing to concede that there had been a moment in history, long ago, when the doctrine had worked on behalf of freeing Europeans from feudal oppressions and liberating Americans from Europe.[71] Croly, by contrast, could not hide his contempt for a doctrine he thought ignoble yet pervasive in American history. Herbert Croly despised the Jeffersonians, advocates of natural rights and a social contract; it was they who "began that career of intellectual lethargy, superficiality, and insincerity which ever since has been characteristic of official American thought."[72] Even Woodrow Wilson's "New Freedom" version of Progressivism, thought Croly, was compromised insofar as it was "a revival of the old Jeffersonian individualism." Happily, "in practice the 'New Freedom' has approximated in certain respects to the 'New Nationalism.'"[73]

The social contract was nevertheless so embedded in the American psyche that it had a way of coming back from the grave. Despite their efforts to purge agrarianism, natural rights, and the social contract from the new culture, the Progressives sometimes found it necessary to restate the old beliefs in an updated form. Croly's *Progressive Democracy* contains a chapter titled "Popular Sovereignty" that features words previously spoken by many a devotee of the social contract: "Constitutionalism necessarily remains; but the constitutions are intrusted frankly to the people instead of the people to the constitutions." The ongoing consent of the governed, rebaptized as public opinion, also reemerges in his pages: "The really sovereign power is to be found in public opinion, and public opinion is always in the making."[74]

The reappearance of the language of the social contract in the utterances of the New Nationalists was not simply the unconscious resurgence of an unsuccessfully repressed cultural residue—they had good reasons to revert to the old vocabulary. Judges were voiding social legislation, so Teddy Roosevelt felt compelled to revisit the familiar language of popular sovereignty. In one of his most daring proposals, Roosevelt demanded that laws struck down by state judges be taken directly to the people for a popular vote. "The people shall themselves have the right to declare whether or not the proposed law is to be treated as constitutional," he told his audience. Lincoln was the historical figure in whom Roosevelt took explicit refuge, but he could just as readily have cited Jefferson.[75]

At the Progressive Party convention in 1912 Roosevelt and the delegates endorsed measures such as direct primaries, popular election of senators, the initiative and referendum, and an expedited process of constitutional amendment—all in the name of returning government to the sovereign people. "Public opinion," the public voice of the people, particularly if educated by Progressive leaders, was infinitely superior to the whispers emanating from political machines and corrupt political parties. The platform issued by the Bull Moose Progressives was named a "Covenant with the People."

At least one more example may be cited of the implicit return of the Progressives to the themes of social contract traditions. The notion of natural rights, thrown out the front door by the New Nationalists, had a way of reentering through the back door. Croly's message on this topic was the perfectly unambiguous statement of a man not running for office and hence free to speak his mind: "Of all the perverted conceptions of democracy, one of the most perverted and dangerous is that which identifies it exclusively with a system of natural rights."[76] Roosevelt followed Croly in many matters, but not where rights were concerned. As Bull Moose candidate, Roosevelt spoke frequently of rights, and although he preferred to call them "human rights," the difference between "human" and "natural" rights was impossible to discern. The courts and the unenlightened heads of corporations were "upholders of property rights against human rights"; the Progressives and trade unionists were the guardians of the "fundamental human rights," "the rights of life, liberty, and the pursuit of happiness."[77]

Teddy Roosevelt understood that Progressivism could not forgo the notion of inalienable rights if it were to meet the challenge of the working class. He apparently did not understand that the Progressives also needed the old faith to combat their substantial racism. Several lines after Croly denounced natural rights, he voiced his conviction that "the Southern slave owners . . . were right in believing that the negroes were a race possessed of moral and intellectual qualities inferior to those of the white men." Disappointingly but perhaps not surprisingly, the Bull Moose convention lacked the courage to pass a proposed civil rights plank.

Other Progressives, faced in Northern cities with blacks who had relocated from the South and a new wave of immigrants from southern and eastern Europe, indulged their prejudices by applying theories of eugenics and scientific racism in local courts.[78] Progressive intellectuals even carried their bias into the new field of Soviet studies, where, under cover of study-ing "national character," they all too often permitted their racial bias to dictate their findings.[79] Only in response to the Nazi experience did the Progressives finally cleanse themselves of the last taint of racism.

Inadvertently more than intentionally, the Progressive movement gives us reasons to appreciate why it is so difficult to relinquish the idea of natu-ral, inalienable, "human" rights.

Fragmentation and Dilution

The Progressives forgot their debt to Henry George, dismissed all agrarians as reactionaries, and subjected social contract theories to the kinds of criti-cism that in Europe spelled the doom of the social contract as early as the writings of Hegel. And yet, as we have just seen, they sometimes slipped back into the old way of thinking. Perhaps there is a lesson for us to learn from their experience: If the social contract came to an end, it probably met its demise not at once but in phases and piecemeal. The theory broke into fragments, some of which could not survive on their own, while others refused to die but suffered dilution.

The "state of nature" was probably the first concept to disappear from social contract theory in America, and the least mourned. "We were re-duced to the state of nature," lamented Patrick Henry.[80] Colonial Ameri-cans feared the final break with England because they did not look forward to being thrown into a possibly turbulent state of nature. Slowly pushed to the point of no return, they reluctantly admitted that the state of nature was their lot, but always they insisted that the state of society in America remained intact, no matter that internationally their fate was to sail in un-charted waters. One might say, then, that at the outbreak of the Revolu-tion, the international predicament of the Americans was such that, even if they had wanted to, they could not avoid thinking in terms of the concept of a state of nature.

Enthusiasm for the state of nature was not entirely absent from the American tradition, frequently assuming the form of sympathy for the In-dians. Thomas Jefferson spoke of them in his second inaugural address as "breathing an ardent love of liberty and independence." In his earlier *Notes on Virginia* he similarly praised them on the grounds that they had "never submitted themselves to any laws, any coercive power, any shadow of government. Their only controls are their manners, and that moral sense of right and wrong, which, like the sense of tasting and feeling, in every man makes a part of his nature." Such compliments alternated in his thought, however, as circumstances dictated, with condemnations. The Declaration of Independence accused King George of "endeavor[ing] to bring on the inhabitants of our frontiers the merciless Indian savages."[81]

Perhaps the most typical use Jefferson and some of his followers made of the Indians was to suggest, contra Locke, that the plight of the workers was worse than that of the Indians. Locke had remarked that the Indians of America "are rich in land, and poor in all the comforts of life." In his view "a king of a large and fruitful territory there feeds, lodges, and is clad worse than a day laborer in England."[82] Jefferson, writing from Paris, witness to the poverty of the lower classes, saw things differently: "I am convinced that those societies (as the Indians) which live without government enjoy in their general mass an infinitely greater degree of happiness than those who live under the European governments."[83] Tom Paine in *Agrarian Justice* made the same point, but much more forcefully, and so did later Jeffersonians and land reformers, all afraid that the misery of European workers was about to descend upon America.

During the second-party system, Americans split on the state of nature, with Jacksonians embracing it and Whigs looking to jettison the concept. It was a commonplace of Jacksonian sentiments, borrowed from the likes of Jefferson and Paine, that human woes were the result of external coercions, the removal of which would restore social harmony. Just underneath the artificial political surface of banking monopolies and undemocratic governments lay original, natural, pristine human nature, awaiting its retrieval by the Jeffersonians and Jacksonians. Remove the banks, remove the tariff, allow free trade full play, and nature would have its way, to the benefit of everyone. Paine had said it all in *Common Sense:* America was a country still in the state of nature, unspoiled, needing little government, which was good because "society in every state is a blessing, but government even in its best state is but a necessary evil. . . . Government, like dress, is the badge of lost innocence."[84]

Disagreeing with their Jacksonian opponents, the Whigs expressed fear of the state of nature on those occasions when they conceded its reality. Although Democrats admired the frontier, where settlers were mixing their labor with the land, transforming the state of nature into the state of civil society, the Whigs feared the lawlessness of the wild West, its invitation to humans to lose self-control. John Quincy Adams gave voice to the anxiety of many another Whig when he fretted that the pioneers, left to their own devices, might degenerate into beasts.[85]

Some Whigs fought against the state of nature as part of their larger fight against the abolitionists, who posed a greater threat to stability than the unregulated frontier. "We do not undertake to *disprove* that man has 'natural rights,'" remarked Whig journalist Calvin Colton in a polemic written against the abolitionists; he did insist, however, that the state of nature was one of despotism and wretchedness. "The best authority, therefore, is not to go back to a state of nature . . . but it is to consult that system of jurisprudence, which the wisdom and justice of many ages, and the most civilized and Christian nations, have established." Colton's disdain for the state of nature was intimately tied to his larger insistence that the law of nature and natural rights "are for extremities, as a necessity, not for common use."[86] Efforts of abolitionists to introduce the paraphernalia of social contract theory into everyday politics must be repudiated.

Probably the favorite Whig treatment of the state of nature was to ignore it and address other topics. Self-improvement was the Whig theme, with variations encompassing self-regulation rather than laissez-faire, self-overcoming rather than self-indulgence, evangelical striving rather than the easy and "natural" religion of Tom Paine. Institutions, traditions, cultural practices, and socially constructed identities were to Whigs what made humans truly human.[87] It would seem, then, that the Whigs had the intellectual wherewithal to toss out the state of nature on historicist grounds if they wished, but since they had no intention of abandoning the theory of the social contract in toto, the path of least resistance was quietly to drop talk of the state of nature while holding on to the rest of the theory—the notions of natural rights, the higher law, and the social contract. Slowly but surely the concept of the state of nature receded from American political discourse.

More vital in American thought than the state of nature was the related idea of a social contract. Even the Whigs, as previously noted (chapters 2 and 4), took pride that in America, David Hume notwithstanding, there actually had been a constitutional convention; a social contract had in fact been signed. Some antebellum Southerners such as George Fitzhugh eventually tried their hand at living without a social contract, but the more popular intellectual move in the South was to retain the contract and restate it in the terms of Grotius and Pufendorf, which permitted slaveholders to make the argument that blacks had signed away their rights.

Northerners prior to the Civil War sometimes sounded as if they were ready to refute the idea of a social contract, but typically they pulled up short. Theodore Parker, for instance, told his audience that "society, government, politics come not from a social compact which men made and may unmake." The rest of his paragraph made it clear, however, that his intent was not to reject the theory of the social contract but only those versions, the ones cited by slave owners, that allow us to bargain away our inherent rights.[88]

Both antebellum Northerners and Southerners reaffirmed the social contract, moreover, when they offered disputing claims as to the identity of the sovereign people who had ratified the Constitution, whether it was the people of the nation, as the Northerners held, or of the states, the position of the Southerners. Who are the people? Those of John Taylor and John C. Calhoun or those of Daniel Webster and Abraham Lincoln? Either way, the discussion was undeniably about the actual signing of a social contract.

All the more, then, does the significance come to light of the Civil War as the turning point in the career of social contract theory. "The state of nature" could be downplayed or dropped by the Whigs, and yet the theory of the social contract could survive in American life. The same was not true of the idea of signing a social contract. Once the Civil War had made it difficult ever to raise again the question of political obligation—Have I consented? Am I obliged?—the entire theory of the social contract was in deep trouble. With both the state of nature and the contractual transition to civil society in abeyance, was the social contract still alive?

The outlook for the theory of the social contract would be even bleaker, of course, if it lost another of its critical components: the concept of a "higher law." Theories of natural rights quite typically included provisions for appeals, when necessary, to a moral law of nature. Subjects or citizens could not be unconditionally bound; an agreement that breached the rights of a minority, for instance, could be rejected on the grounds that it conflicted with the law of nature. "There is a higher law than the Constitution," proclaimed Senator William H. Seward in response to the proposed Compromise of 1850, opening the lands taken from Mexico to slavery.[89] Seward's willingness as a Conscience Whig to defy the Cotton Whigs was an American high point in the history of the law of nature—the higher law, the escape clause that the theory of the social contract had provided against consensual, politically expedient, but morally unconscionable compromises.

By the turn of the twentieth century the higher law, formerly the trump card of the reformers, had become the tool of the conservatives on the Supreme Court. In the celebrated case of *Lochner v. New York*, 1905, Justice Peckham and the majority struck down a law limiting the hours of bakers to ten per day or sixty per week. The official judicial rationale was that the regulation interfered with the due process clause of the Fourteenth Amendment, which the conservatives believed gave legal sanction to the morally transcendent "right of free contract." Voting in dissent was Oliver Wendell Holmes Jr., who famously objected that "the Fourteenth Amendment does not enact Mr. Herbert Spencer's *Social Statics*." The idea of so-called freedom of contract had no sanction in a higher, transcendental law of nature.

Holmes was not himself a Progressive, but he taught the Progressives how to destroy the very notion of a law of nature. "The jurists who believe in natural law seem to me to be in that naïve state of mind that accepts what has been familiar and accepted by them and their neighbors as something that must be accepted by all men everywhere," he wrote in a brief but pungent essay titled "Natural Law." Behind "the philosopher's effort to prove that truth is absolute and . . . the jurist's search for criteria of universal validity" lay a refusal to face up to the need to make moral decisions in a world bereft of moral certainty. There was, in fact, no principle on which we could all agree, applicable at all times and places, not even the sanctity of life. "The most fundamental of the supposed preexisting rights—the right to life—is sacrificed without a scruple not only in time of war, but whenever the interest of society . . . is thought to demand it."[90]

Holmes was a genial skeptic, not a nihilist, whose denial of dogmatic absolutes opened the door to respect for differing political points of view and invited the social experimentation of the Progressives. Although the Social Gospel type of Progressives might have felt slightly ill at ease in his irreverent company, the smiling skeptics of the movement—figures such as Thurman Arnold and Walter Lippmann—could admire Holmes as their muse.[91] As Progressives, they had every reason to applaud his demolition of the "higher law" that had evolved into the tool of the plutocrats.

Lippmann is worth special notice because his career as a Progressive led him, eventually, to an attempted revival of the "higher law" that accomplished little more than to show how lifeless the idea had become after being severed from the rest of social contract theory. His earliest writings, such as *A Preface to Politics* (1913) and *Drift and Mastery* (1914), are those of a New Nationalist, scornful of the conservatism of the lawyers and the common law, convinced that Americans needed to leave their pioneer past behind them, annoyed that Woodrow Wilson's New Freedom might amount to a failure to face up to a modern world composed of large-scale economic units. Trained in Pragmatism at Harvard University, Lippmann believed political philosophy should be regarded as "an instrument to fit a need," not a revelation of ultimate truths. Policies should answer to the only possible standard, "the pragmatic test by results." The purpose of politics was to solve specific problems; "politics is not concerned with prescribing the ultimate qualities of life."[92]

The pivotal moment for Lippmann, it seems clear in retrospect, came with his book *Public Opinion*, published in 1922. Progressives, as we have seen, had placed their bets on public opinion, sometimes advancing the notion that it was the modern version of popular sovereignty and the consent of the governed. But to Lippmann's mind the events of World War I proved how unenlightened public opinion actually was, how readily political leaders lowered themselves to the level of the audience—issuing unfortunate calls for a war to end wars, demanding impolitic unconditional surrender, resorting to empty phrases about the "Rights of Humanity" that everyone interpreted according to his or her predilection. Progressives had appealed over the heads of the parties to the people, but the persons they actually trusted were the "experts," and so it was that Lippmann ended his book with the proposal that experts, trained by a new generation of political scientists, should shape and mold the information submitted to the press.[93]

In 1955 Walter Lippmann issued a book titled *The Public Philosophy* that was based on the premise that public opinion continued to be uninformed and irrational. By this time the former Progressive had refashioned himself into a Cold War liberal afraid of the "totalitarian democracy" of the Soviet Union, afraid also of McCarthyism at home, afraid that "the people" could not be counted on to uphold the fundamentals of constitutional government. If he had his way, Lippmann would strengthen the executive to limit the power of the all-too-popular legislature. If possible, he would also infuse the educational system and public life with adulation of the higher moral law, which teaches that reason must triumph over passion, civility over impulse. Lippmann had little use for the dangerous modern philosophy of natural rights and only metaphorical use for a social contract. His emphasis was on the old-fashioned natural law philosophy of Greece, Rome, and the Middle Ages—an odd selection for an intellectual who had never abjured his Pragmatic past, but a choice that reflected his desperation over the absence of a trustworthy public.

Lippmann was part of a larger intellectual movement of the 1950s, a return to the "great books," to the classic texts of Plato, Aristotle, Cicero, the Stoics, and Aquinas, especially to their teaching of a "law of nature." In his earlier incarnation as a Progressive, Lippmann had remarked approvingly on the diversity of modern culture: "the fact that this culture is multiform and often contradictory is a sign that more and more of the interests of life are finding expression," he wrote in 1914.[94] Political leaders, he then believed, should serve these interests, each on its own terms, rather than striving to impose an impossible unity. Later, as a Cold Warrior, he joined in the pretence of the day that the Western tradition was one-dimensional, spoke with one voice only, and was unproblematically universal in applicability.

The only missing element in Lippmann's performance was conviction. On the final page of *The Public Philosophy* the former Pragmatist reappeared in all but name: "What is necessary to continuous action," concluded Lippmann, "is that [the public philosophy] shall be *believed* to be right."[95] The italics are in the original, and the similarity to William James's "The Will to Believe" is far more than an analogy. Lippmann had begun *Public Opinion* with an explicit quotation from Plato's "allegory of the cave"; one wonders whether he ended *The Public Philosophy* with an implicit nod to Plato's "noble lie."

The revived natural law philosophy of the 1950s was cut off from the rest of the social contract tradition—the state of nature, the contract, natural rights. Or, rather, it hearkened back to premodern, pre–social contract versions of natural law. It could not last. Soon its ethnocentrism would be exposed, and the multiplicity of conflicting voices in Western thought would be restored to the account of intellectual history. The repeated claim of its devotees that failure to accept its comforting moral absolutes led to nihilism suffered from two fatal defects: the first that no proof was forthcoming, the second that the argument was about consequences instead of truth.[96] Before long the fragmented but bloated "higher law" of the 1950s faded from public discourse.

The theory of the social contract had shattered at great cost to each of the resulting fragments; the state of nature, the contract forming civil society, the higher law were for all practical purposes lost and gone. Only one element still remained in apparent vigor, and that was the notion of natural rights. Whether for better or for worse, to the present day one of the most inescapable languages of American politics has been and still is that of rights. It is worth remembering how frequently Americans over the course of the last century, when the rest of the theory of the social contract was falling by the wayside, continued to stake their claims in the language of rights.

The Populist movement of the late nineteenth century, for example, seldom renewed the full-blown theory of the social contract. It did, however, foster a reassertion of the notion of natural rights, so vigorous as to remind one of antebellum times. Standard conduct for the Populists was the portrayal of their revolt as a return to 1776, and they frequently reissued the old Jacksonian slogan "Equal rights to all; special privileges to none." Texas Populist James H. Davis, having immersed himself in the collected works of Jefferson, repeated his hero's words about generational autonomy; he proclaimed, moreover, that "all men's rights to the earth (the unborn as well as the present) should be protected and secured in every way consistent with the common rights of all."[97] James B. Weaver, Populist presidential candidate in 1892, expressed similar sentiments: "The child . . . comes into this world clothed with all the natural rights which Adam possessed. . . . Liberty to occupy the soil in his own right, . . . and to live upon the fruits of his toil . . . are among the most sacred and essential of these rights."[98]

At the same time that Populists were reviving the language of natural rights, Eugene V. Debs was Americanizing socialism by peppering his speeches with references to the philosophy of Jefferson. Time and again Debs asserted that life, liberty, and pursuit of happiness were meaningless without recognition of the right to the fruits of one's labors. "Equal rights" was also one of his themes, but whereas Jacksonians had applied that slogan to white men only, Debs invoked it on behalf of all men and women. One of the many rights he demanded was "the inalienable right of all to work," which had previously played almost no role in America except for a few antebellum spokespersons of labor who had quickly moved on to land reform.[99]

Perhaps most tellingly, Debs—knowingly or unknowingly?—reiterated the metaphor of a banquet that had been employed with considerable rhetorical success by labor and land reformers Thomas Skidmore, Frederick Robinson, and Henry George: "Nature has spread a great table bounteously for all the children of men," announced Debs. "There is room for all and there is a plate and a place and food for all, and any system of society that denied a single one the right . . . to freely help himself to nature's bounties is an unjust and iniquitous system."[100] Echoes, at least, of the great rhetoric of antebellum times can still be heard in the speeches of Debs and the Populists.

The Progressives, too, made considerable use of the language of rights. When he became a New Freedom Progressive, Woodrow Wilson, in an about-face, insisted that he was more interested in human than in property rights.[101] As a New Nationalist Progressive, Theodore Roosevelt preferred to continue speaking, as he had before his conversion to Progressivism, of civic duties; he never stopped warning citizens against permitting claims of rights to undermine their sense of duty.[102] Nevertheless, as we know, he found it essential, as a Progressive, to speak in favor of human rights over property rights.

Herbert Hoover was a Bull Mooser in 1912, a member of Wilson's war cabinet, and then an "independent Progressive" in 1920. His was the Progressivism of Associational Activities, which stressed a partnership between business and government, with the leadership coming mainly from enlightened managers. During this early phase of his career, Hoover insisted that "private property is not a fetish in America," and he did not hesitate to place human above property rights.[103] The presidency of Franklin Delano Roosevelt led Hoover to reverse field, but even as he seemingly abandoned his Progressive past, he did so in the name of human and natural rights. FDR's "collectivist" program, Hoover explained, was really a perversion of human rights and had to be answered by an uncompromising reassertion of "the great individual rights," which had always been about limitations on, not enhancement of, the powers of government.[104]

Franklin Roosevelt understood from the beginning that he had to disabuse the public of the charge that his proposals were in any way collectivist, anti-individualist, or of foreign origin. On the campaign trail in 1932 he wanted to make certain his proposals sounded perfectly American; to that end, in his Commonwealth Club address of September 23, he framed his proposals in terms that seemed like a revival of the social contract tradition. "I want to speak not of parties, but of universal principles," he began. The Declaration of Independence "discusses the problem of government in terms of a contract," of consent accorded on the condition that rights are respected. "The task of statesmanship has always been the re-definition of these rights in terms of a changing and growing social order."[105]

Roosevelt in 1932 readily agreed that, under pioneer conditions, "individualism was made the great watchword of American life." He did not, however, follow the likes of Croly and Dewey in socializing the individual; he retained the old individualism, asking only that Americans admit that new measures were required to permit them to retain their time-honored ideals. "There is no safety valve in the form of a Western prairie." Under the conditions of the Industrial Age, the rights of the individual could only be guaranteed by "an economic declaration of rights, an economic constitutional order." Just before assuming office, FDR was binding together rights and social contract into a package that, on the surface at least, looked a great deal like the fully realized social contract theory of yesteryear.[106]

Alas, the gap between what Franklin Roosevelt said before his election and the deals he had to make in office was enormous. Welfare measures of the New Deal distinguished between deserving and undeserving poor, which was a far cry from welfare as a natural right guaranteed by a social contract. To pass Social Security, New Dealers had to sell it as something "earned," an insurance program, in contrast to color-coded welfare. The vision articulated in the fall of 1932 fell by the wayside, and nothing like it reappeared in Roosevelt's speeches until 1944, when he attempted to reclaim the domestic ideals he feared might be lost in the preoccupation with the war. "We are not going to turn the clock back!" he announced in that year. On January 11, 1944, and again on October 28 he promised "a second Bill of Rights," an "economic bill of rights."[107]

There was a major difference between these speeches of 1944 and his speech of 1932: No longer was Roosevelt trying to integrate his rights talk into a broader speech of social contract. This theoretical downgrading had practical consequences. The unacknowledged result was that his welfare program appeared to be exactly what he had originally wished to avoid, less a statement of "universal principles" than the position of a political party. He and some of his fellow Democrats would fight to sustain and enhance the welfare state and would embellish their efforts with talk of rights. But the social contract had disappeared from their speech, even as metaphor.

Franklin Roosevelt should not be blamed for this outcome. A brief exercise in comparative analysis suffices to show that the problem was a matter of historical timing over which he had no control. In France the idea that our natural rights include social rights had been floated as early as 1789, had become a specific plank of the never-enacted Constitution of 1793, and had come again to the fore in 1848. Thus, in France there was an actual historical basis for the claim that the social contract had recognized social rights. In America, by contrast, where open land had always been the answer to the social problem, social rights were a late development, clearly a legislative add-on, not part of the contract signed at the start of the republic. Try as he might to confer constitutional invulnerability on social rights, Roosevelt could not elevate them above the unstable realm of party politics.[108] Economic rights, despite his best efforts, remained far removed from the saving larger context of the social contract to which FDR had originally aspired.

In the 1970s something new happened: a "rights revolution" sponsored by the Democratic Party that arguably diluted rights in the process of expanding them exponentially. Rights of women, gays and lesbians, the handicapped, and consumers; rights to drink clean water and breathe clean air were among the many policies that Democratic politicians in Congress phrased in the language of rights. Reform policies were passed off as legally enacted because they were rights rather than as rights because legally enacted.

There was no mistaking the motivation of the Democrats. The presidency, which had been theirs to lose since the days of Franklin Roosevelt, was passing over to the Republicans. Conservative presidents would undo reform, so a Democratic Congress forged an alliance with the courts. The heirs of the New Deal welcomed judicial activism on behalf of their programs as much as FDR had condemned the courts for blocking his measures. Through statutory interpretation, the judges of the 1970s, and beyond, protected and enhanced the new rights, frequently using the open-ended language of rights to overlook the question of costs.[109]

Thanks in large part to the "rights revolution" of the 1970s, the rhetoric of rights continues to figure to the present day as the default language of the American polity in a way that distinguishes the United States from the democracies of Europe. Only in America, it has been remarked, do environmentalists champion their cause by endowing trees with rights rather than speaking the language of moral stewardship.[110] Where everything is a right, the concept is empty, diluted beyond recognition. It may be more accurate to view the "rights revolution" as the final demise of the social contract tradition than as its contemporary manifestation.

Afterword

Dissolution, decomposition, fragmentation, and dilution would seem to be the ultimate fate of the once proud and highly influential tradition of the social contract in America. Only within the academy, thanks to the debate over John Rawls's *A Theory of Justice* (1971), has there been serious talk in recent decades about anything resembling social contract theory. Rawls's neo-Kantian book succeeded in restoring political philosophy to life after it had been pronounced dead by analytical philosophers; Hegel once again confronted Kant, this time on American soil, when the communitarians attacked Rawls. One may question, however, whether Rawls is a theorist of the social contract, considering he held that "the content of the relevant agreement is not to enter a given society or to adopt a given form of government"; considering, furthermore, his Kantian denial that obligation arises from consent or his insistence that rights do not inhere in individuals but are "legitimate expectations" arising from principles of justice.[111] For our purposes, possibly the most decisive missing dimension is that the "Rawls and his critics" debate is confined to the academy, unlike the historical American debate over the social contract, which filled the pages of newspapers, pamphlets, campaign speeches, and the like.

The consequence of the presence or absence of the social contract for public speech in America is worth comment. Obviously its presence did not guarantee harmony when we remember that the North and South, availing themselves of theories of the social contract, talked themselves into a bloody civil war. It is nonetheless true that in antebellum times the many different voices of the day—evangelical, common-law, and constitutional, among others—sometimes met on the common ground of the vocabulary of social contract and thus were able to carry on a genuine dialogue.

Less harm would presumably follow from the decline of the social contract if its heir apparent had succeeded historically. Progressivism claimed to take over where the social contract had left off and did have its moment in the sun. After World War II, in particular, Progressive theories of modernization, purged of the racism of the past, emerged victorious in American social, economic, and political thought. Whether the topic was the advanced industrial states or the many new decolonized nations, the method of inquiry began with a discussion of the transition from traditional to modern society. The unstoppable progressive unfolding of history, onward and upward, appeared to be the undeniable reality. Theories of modernization dominated the curriculum and reached well beyond the academy into public life.

With the incorporation of the trade unions into the structure of government and the establishment of a kind of welfare state, the working class had been absorbed into industrial citizenship, argued the Progressives of the 1950s. Another of their contentions was that religious fanaticism would increasingly be a thing of the past because modernization entailed secularization. Admittedly there would be bumps in the road, cultural lags, temporary reversals. John Dewey said of "our older creeds" that "the more we depart from them in fact, the more loudly we proclaim them."[112] About the ultimate outcome, the final victory of the Progressives, he had, however, no doubt.

Today we have doubts aplenty. Labor is in disarray; the welfare state is imperiled; and the most shrill forms of religion threaten to intrude into all matters of public life, both domestically and internationally. History has abandoned the Progressive philosophy that always counted history as its best friend. To all appearances the vocabulary of Progressivism is as imperfect a fit with the times as that of the social contract, which it replaced. Fragments from all the political languages of the past—evangelical, original intent, Progressive, and others—speak past one another, and public life suffers accordingly.

Echoes of the popular social contract of times past are sometimes still heard, as when public figures ask that the contract be restored, renewed, or updated, usually without further elaboration. Certainly the concept of human rights, whatever its rationale, cannot be permitted to die in a world where genocide is common and some cultural practices, such as genital mutilation, are so abhorrent that they cry out for condemnation. It does appear, however, that there is no privileged road map available for negotiating our way through the political and moral quandaries of our age, no language that can serve to translate all the other languages. We must do our best with what we have, however piecemeal and uncertain it may be, in an age that is intolerant of uncertainty.

■
Notes

Prologue

1. Bill Clinton, "The New Covenant: Responsibility and Rebuilding the American Community," speech delivered October 23, 1991, at Georgetown University.

2. Samuel Pufendorf, *Of the Law of Nature and Nations* (Clark, NJ: Lawbook Exchange, 2005), and *On the Duty of Man and Citizen According to Natural Law* (Cambridge: Cambridge University Press, 1991). On the disappearing act of natural rights in Pufendorf's thought, see Richard Tuck, *Natural Rights Theories: Their Origin and Development* (Cambridge: Cambridge University Press, 1979), p. 1. See also Knud Haakonssen, *Natural Law and Moral Philosophy: From Grotius to the Scottish Enlightenment* (New York: Cambridge University Press, 1996).

3. R. Shep Melnick, *Between the Lines: Interpreting Welfare Rights* (Washington, DC: Brookings Institution, 1994); Mary Ann Glendon, *Rights Talk: The Impoverishment of Political Discourse* (New York: Free Press, 1991).

4. "Great men, in teaching the feeble to think, have put them on the route to error." Michael Oakeshott, *Rationalism in Politics and Other Essays* (London: Methuen, 1962).

5. J. G. A. Pocock, *The Ancient Constitution and the Feudal Law: A Study of English Historical Thought in the Seventeenth Century* (Cambridge: Cambridge University Press, 1957); J. G. A. Pocock, "Burke and the Ancient Constitution," in *Politics, Language and Time* (New York: Atheneum, 1971), ch. 6.

6. Quoted in Eric Foner, *Tom Paine and Revolutionary America* (New York: Oxford University Press, 1976), p. 114.

7. *U.S. Term Limits, Inc. v. Thornton*, 514 U.S. 846 (1995).

8. James Madison, *Notes on the Debates in the Federal Constitution* (New York: W. W. Norton, 1987), pp. 88–89, 92, 304–305, 518.

9. *Federalist*, no. 39.

10. Newt Gingrich, *Contract with America* (New York: Random House, 1994), p. 5; Newt Gingrich, *To Renew America* (New York: HarperCollins, 1996), pp. 9, 168, 223.

11. Gingrich, *Contract with America*, p. 192; Gingrich, *To Renew America*, pp. 34–35.

12. Hans Reiss, ed., *Kant's Political Writings* (Cambridge: Cambridge University Press, 1970), pp. 57, 59, 79, 81–83, 144–145.

13. Thomas Babington Macaulay, *The History of England from the Accession of James the Second,* vol. 2 (London: Longman, Roberts, and Green, 1863), pp. 662–671.

14. Daniel Rodgers, *Atlantic Crossings: Social Politics in a Progressive Age* (Cambridge, MA: Harvard University Press, 1998).

15. Friedrich Gentz, *The French and American Revolutions Compared* (New York: Gateway, 1955); Bernard Bailyn, *The Ideological Origins of the American Revolution* (Cambridge, MA: Harvard University Press, 1967); Louis Hartz, *The Liberal Tradition in America* (New York: Harcourt, Brace and World, 1955); R. R. Palmer, *The Age of the Democratic Revolution* (Princeton, NJ: Princeton University Press, 1959).

16. See, for example, Ronald J. Pestritto and Thomas G. West, eds., *The American Founding and the Social Compact* (Lexington, MA: Lexington Books, 2003); Michael P. Zuckert, *The Natural Rights Republic: Studies in the Foundation of the American Political Tradition* (Notre Dame, IN: University of Notre Dame Press, 1996).

Chapter 1. Principles, Forms, Foundations

1. Edmund S. Morgan, ed., *Prologue to Revolution: Sources and Documents on the Stamp Act Crisis, 1764–1766* (Chapel Hill: University of North Carolina Press, 1959), p. 114.

2. Pauline Maier, *From Resistance to Revolution: Colonial Radicals and the Development of American Opposition to Britain, 1765–1776* (New York: Vintage, 1974).

3. Robert Filmer, *Observations upon Aristotles Politiques, Touching Forms of Government, Together with Directions for Obedience to Governours,* in Johann P. Sommerville, ed., *Filmer: Patriarcha and Other Writings* (Cambridge: Cambridge University Press, 2000), p. 252; Robert Filmer, *Observations Concerning the Original of Government,* in ibid., pp. 184–185.

4. In common with other Loyalists, Jonathan Boucher admired the English constitution and thought that what the Patriots called its corruption was, instead, exactly the kind of influence necessary to keep its complex mechanism from grinding to a halt. See Jonathan Boucher, *A View of the Causes and Consequences of the American Revolution* (1797) (New York: Russell and Russell, 1967), dedication of 1797 to George Washington and pp. 208, 217.

5. L. T. Hobhouse observed that in England "the Liberal movement has often sought to dispense with general principles." The "Whig tradition," he further explicated, is "the Conservative element in Liberalism." L. T. Hobhouse, *Liberalism* (1911),

6th ed. (London: Thornton Butterworth, 1934), p. 51. The American situation, we shall see, has been quite the opposite.

6. Stephen Hopkins, *The Rights of Colonies Examined,* in Merrill Jensen, ed., *Tracts of the American Revolution* (Indianapolis, IN: Hackett, 2003), p. 43.

7. John Adams, *Novanglus,* in C. Bradley Thompson, ed., *The Revolutionary Writings of John Adams* (Indianapolis, IN: Liberty Fund, 2000), p. 234.

8. David Hume, "Of the Independency of Parliament" and "Of the First Principles of Government," in *Essays, Moral, Political, and Literary* (Indianapolis, IN: Liberty Fund, 1984), pp. 36, 45.

9. Janice Potter, *The Liberty We Seek: Loyalist Ideology in Colonial New York and Massachusetts* (Cambridge, MA: Harvard University Press, 1983).

10. Candidus [James Chalmers], *Plain Truth,* in Jensen, ed., *Tracts of the American Revolution,* pp. 451, 453, 461; Hume, "Of the Original Contract," in *Essays,* pp. 465–487.

11. William Blackstone, *Commentaries on the Laws of England* (Chicago: University of Chicago Press, 1979), Bk. 2, ch. 1, p. 2.

12. Adam Ferguson, *Remarks on Dr. Price's Observations on the Nature of Civil Liberty* (London: Printed for G. Kearsley, 1776), pp. 36–37.

13. Edmund Burke, "Speech on a Bill for Shortening the Duration of Parliaments," in *The Works of the Right Honorable Edmund Burke,* vol. 7 (Boston: Little, Brown, 1866), p. 71.

14. Samuel Seabury, *Letters of a Westchester Farmer* (White Plains, NY: Westchester County Historical Society, 1930), p. 110.

15. Ibid., pp. 79, 83.

16. See Thomas Hutchinson's *A Dialogue Between an American and a European Englishman,* with an introduction by Bernard Bailyn, *Perspectives in American History* 9 (1975): 343–410.

17. On the continuing importance of the will in social contract theory, see Patrick Riley, *Will and Political Legitimacy* (Cambridge, MA: Harvard University Press, 1982).

18. Hugo Grotius, *The Law of War and Peace* (Indianapolis, IN: Bobbs-Merrill, 1925), Bk. 1, ch. 3, no. 8, pp. 103, 109; Bk. 2, ch. 5, no. 27, p. 255; Bk. 7, ch. 7, no. 1, p. 690; Samuel Pufendorf, *Of the Law of Nature and Nations* (Clark, NJ: Lawbook Exchange, 2005), Bk. 6, ch. 3, nos. 4 and 5, pp. 615, 616; Bk. 7, ch. 3, no. 1, p. 654; Bk. 7, ch. 8, no. 6, pp. 720–722.

19. Grotius, *Law of War and Peace,* Bk. 1, ch. 4, no. 2, p. 139.

20. Ibid., Bk. 1, ch. 3, no. 8, p. 110.

21. Pufendorf, *Law of Nature and Nations,* Bk. 7, ch. 8, no. 6, p. 720.

22. Grotius, *Law of War and Peace,* Bk. 1, ch. 3, no. 8, p. 109; Pufendorf, *Law of Nature and Nations,* Bk. 7, ch. 2, no. 12, p. 645.

23. Michael Zuckert, *Natural Rights and the New Republicanism* (Princeton, NJ: Princeton University Press, 1994), chs. 4 and 5.

24. Jean-Jacques Rousseau, *On the Social Contract,* Bk. 1, ch.2.

25. Ferguson, *Remarks on Dr. Price's Observations,* p. 49. William Warburton drew upon both Grotius and Pufendorf and criticized Rousseau in *The Alliance Between*

Church and State, in *Collected Works,* vol. 7 (Bristol, England: Thoemmes Continuum, 2005). For a cogent overview, see H. T. Dickinson, "Whiggism in the Eighteenth Century," in John Cannon, ed., *The Whig Ascendancy: Colloquies on Hanoverian England* (New York: St. Martin's Press, 1981), ch. 2.

26. Seabury, *Letters of a Westchester Farmer,* pp. 91, 93, 111.

27. Ibid., pp. 107, 109–110; Hutchinson, *A Dialogue,* pp. 373, 390–392.

28. Hutchinson, *A Dialogue,* pp. 370, 398, 400.

29. Seabury, *Letters of a Westchester Farmer,* p. 130.

30. Pufendorf, *Law of Nature and Nations,* Bk. 7, ch. 2, nos. 7–8, pp. 639–641.

31. Hutchinson, *A Dialogue,* pp. 391–392.

32. Joseph Galloway, *A Candid Examination of the Mutual Claims of Great Britain and the Colonies,* in Jensen, ed., *Tracts of the American Revolution,* pp. 352, 364, 367, 377.

33. See, for example, ibid., pp. 354, 356, 362, 364, 368; Hutchinson, *A Dialogue,* p. 394.

34. John Locke, *Second Treatise of Government,* nos. 149–150.

35. Blackstone, *Commentaries,* Bk. 1, ch. 1, p. 122; intro., p. 53, intro., p. 43, on the state of nature; Bk. 2 on property; Bk. 1, ch. 2, p. 157.

36. Seabury, *Letters of a Westchester Farmer,* p. 133.

37. Pufendorf, *Law of Nature and Nations,* Bk. 7, ch. 1, no. 11, p. 633; Bk. 7, ch. 8, no. 6, pp. 720–721.

38. Ibid., Bk. 7, ch. 2, no. 5, p. 638, nos. 9, 11, pp. 642, 644.

39. On the Whigs of the Glorious Revolution and their notions of a double contract, see Lois G. Schwoerer, *The Declaration of Rights, 1689* (Baltimore, MD: Johns Hopkins University Press, 1981).

40. John Wise, *A Vindication of the Government of New England Churches,* in Edmund S. Morgan, ed., *Puritan Political Ideas, 1558–1794* (Indianapolis, IN: Bobbs-Merrill, 1965), pp. 252–253.

41. Pufendorf, *Law of Nature and Nations,* Bk. 2, ch. 2, nos. 5–8, pp. 109–113; Bk. 7, ch. 1, nos. 3–4, pp. 625–627.

42. Wise, *A Vindication,* pp. 251–267.

43. Henry St. John Viscount Bolingbroke, *The Idea of a Patriot King* (Indianapolis, IN: Bobbs-Merrill, 1965), pp. 24, 58. This pamphlet was penned sometime around 1738 and published in 1749.

44. Morgan, ed., *Prologue to Revolution,* p. 114 (emphasis added).

45. Maier, *From Resistance to Revolution,* p. 13.

46. Francis Hutcheson, *A Short Introduction to Moral Philosophy,* in *Collected Works,* vol. 4 (Hildesheim, Germany: G. Olms, 1969), Bk. 3, chs. 5 and 7, pp. 286, 287, 304.

47. Samuel Adams (?), *A State of the Rights of the Colonists,* in Jensen, ed., *Tracts of the American Revolution,* pp. 237–238; Locke, *Second Treatise,* no. 23.

48. Benjamin Franklin, *Rules by Which a Great Empire May Be Reduced to a Small One,* in Ralph L. Ketcham, ed., *The Political Thought of Benjamin Franklin* (Indianapolis, IN: Bobbs-Merrill, 1965), p. 256.

49. Ferguson, *Remarks on Dr. Price's Observations,* pp. 34, 36.

50. Ibid., p. 25.

51. Ibid., pp. 23, 30, 45, 64, 56.

52. Ibid., pp. 41, 42, 47.

53. Ibid., pp. 64–65; D. O. Thomas, ed., *Richard Price: Political Writings* (Cambridge: Cambridge University Press, 1991), pp. 56, 144–145.

54. Jean-Jacques Rousseau, *Discourse on Inequality,* in *Oeuvres complètes,* vol. 3, Pléiade edition (Paris: Gallimard, 1969), p. 211; Adam Ferguson, *An Essay on the History of Civil Society* (Cambridge: Cambridge University Press, 1995), p. 8.

55. Rousseau, *Discourse on Inequality,* p. 182.

56. See James T. Boulton, *The Language of Politics in the Age of Wilkes and Burke* (London: Routledge, 1963), p. 94, on Arthur Young's *Travels in France* (1792–1794). As Boulton noted, Young later adopted the anti-French position in *The Example of France, a Warning to Britain* (1793).

57. Burke admitted to the émigré Calonne, "In reality my object was not France, in the first instance, but this country," October 25, 1790. Alfred Cobban and Robert A. Smith, eds., *The Correspondence of Edmund Burke,* vol. 6 (Cambridge: Cambridge University Press, 1967), p. 141.

58. Gary B. Nash, "The American Clergy and the French Revolution," *William and Mary Quarterly* 22, no. 3 (July 1965): 392–412.

59. Colin Bonwick, *English Radicals and the American Revolution* (Chapel Hill: University of North Carolina Press, 1977); H. T. Dickinson, *British Radicalism and the French Revolution, 1789–1815* (Oxford: Basil Blackwell, 1985); Isaac Kramnick, *Republicanism and Bourgeois Radicalism: Political Ideology in Late Eighteenth-Century England and America* (Ithaca, NY: Cornell University Press, 1990).

60. Benjamin Rush, *Observations on the Government of Pennsylvania,* in Dagobert D. Runes, ed., *The Selected Writings of Benjamin Rush* (New York: Philosophical Library), p. 78.

61. James Axtell, ed., *Educational Writings of John Locke* (London: Cambridge University Press, 1968), p. 400.

62. James Otis, *The Rights of the British Colonies Asserted and Proved,* in Bernard Bailyn, ed., *Pamphlets of the American Revolution* (Cambridge, MA: Harvard University Press, 1965), pp. 423, 436, 424, 426.

63. Blackstone, *Commentaries,* Bk. 1, ch. 2, p. 157.

64. Adams, "Novanglus," p. 152.

65. Thomas Jefferson to Thomas Mann Randolph, May 30, 1790, in Paul Leicester Ford, ed., *The Writings of Thomas Jefferson,* vol. 5 (New York: G. P. Putnam's, 1895), p. 173.

66. Richard Henry Lee, *Letters from a Federal Farmer,* in Forrest McDonald, ed., *Empire and Nation* (Indianapolis, IN: Liberty Fund, 1999), pp. 90, 92. It should be noted that Lee's identity as "Federal Farmer" is a matter of continuing scholarly dispute.

67. John Taylor, *Construction Construed and Constitutions Vindicated* (1820) (New York: Da Capo Press, 1970), p. 13.

68. Grotius, *Law of War and Peace,* Bk. 1, ch. 3, no. 8, p. 104.

69. Otis, *Rights of the British Colonies*, p. 426.

70. Thomas, ed., *Richard Price*, p. 79.

71. Peter N. Miller, ed., *Joseph Priestley: Political Writings* (Cambridge: Cambridge University Press, 1993), pp. 28, 62; Thomas, ed., *Richard Price*, pp. 79, 95–96, 164–165. Paine sometimes sounded indifferent to forms of government; see *Rights of Man* (New York: Penguin, 1984), p. 42.

72. John Adams to Mercy Warren, January 8, 1776, in Adrienne Koch and William Peden, eds., *The Selected Writings of John and John Quincy Adams* (Westport, CT: Greenwood Press, 1981), p. 49.

73. Thomas Paine, *Common Sense* (New York: Penguin, 1986), p. 68.

74. John Adams, *Thoughts on Government*, in Thompson, ed., *Revolutionary Writings*, pp. 287–293.

75. Jack N. Rakove, *Original Meanings: Politics and Ideas in the Making of the Constitution* (New York: Vintage, 1997), esp. ch. 4.

76. Herbert J. Storing, ed., *The Complete Antifederalist* (Chicago: University of Chicago Press, 1981), 3.3.43.

77. See Rakove's account, *Original Meanings*, pp. 102–105, for the difficulties of the delegates in dealing with the legality of their proceedings.

78. Robert Green McCloskey, ed., *The Works of James Wilson* (Cambridge, MA: Harvard University Press, 1967), pp. 759–772.

79. James Madison, *Federalist*, no. 46.

80. Alexander Hamilton, *Federalist*, no. 22.

81. Morton J. Frisch, ed., *Selected Writings and Speeches of Alexander Hamilton* (Washington, DC: AEI, 1985), p. 21.

82. *Federalist*, nos. 15, 16, 20.

83. Frisch, ed., *Selected Writings*, pp. 19–22.

84. Storing, ed., *Complete Antifederalist*, 2.9.196; 2.8.50–51.

85. Gordon Wood, *The Creation of the American Republic, 1776–1787* (New York: W. W. Norton, 1972), pp. 268–273.

86. Storing, ed., *Complete Antifederalist*, 5.1.22; 5.6.11.

87. Merrill Jensen, John P. Kaminski, and Gaspare J. Saladino, *The Documentary History of the Ratification of the Constitution*, vol. 2 (Madison: State Historical Society of Wisconsin, 1976), pp. 421, 434; *Federalist*, no. 84. I am indebted to Edmund S. Morgan's account, *Inventing the People: The Rise of Popular Sovereignty in England and America* (New York: W. W. Norton, 1989), pp. 282–284, although I find his phraseology about popular sovereignty in England misleading.

88. Niccolò Machiavelli, *Discourses on Livy*, Bk. 3, ch. 1; John Dickinson, *Letters from a Farmer in Pennsylvania*, in McDonald, ed., *Empire and Nation*, p. 69.

89. James Wilson, *Considerations on the Nature and Extent of the Legislative Authority of the British Parliament*, in McCloskey, ed., *The Works of James Wilson*, pp. 723, 727.

90. "Virginia Bill of Rights" (June 12, 1776), in Samuel Eliot Morison, ed., *Sources and Documents Illustrating the American Revolution, 1764–1788* (Oxford: Oxford University Press, 1965), pp. 149–151.

91. Machiavelli, *Discourses on Livy,* Bk. 1, ch. 9.

92. Carl J. Richard, *The Founders and the Classics: Greece, Rome, and the American Enlightenment* (Cambridge, MA: Harvard University Press, 1994).

93. Adams, *Thoughts on Government,* p. 293.

94. *Federalist,* no. 14.

95. Ibid., no. 38.

96. James Wilson, "Speech of 26 November [1787], Convention of Pennsylvania," in McCloskey, ed., *The Works of James Wilson,* p. 762.

97. Machiavelli, *Discourses on Livy,* Bk. 1, chs. 11, 13.

98. John Locke, *A Letter Concerning Toleration* (Indianapolis, IN: Hackett, 1983).

99. Patrick Henry, "In Defense of Religious Liberty," in William Addison Blakely, ed., *American State Papers and Related Documents on Freedom in Religion* (Washington, DC: Review and Herald, 1949), pp. 178–181.

100. Note the analogy of the sculptor shaping a block of marble in Machiavelli, *Discourses on Livy,* Bk. 1, ch. 11.

101. I have presented my interpretation of the remarkable Florentine in *Citizen Machiavelli* (Princeton, NJ: Princeton University Press, 1983).

102. John Adams, *A Dissertation on the Canon and Feudal Law,* in Thompson, ed., *Revolutionary Writings,* p. 31.

103. Paine, *Common Sense,* pp. 94, 98.

104. Montesquieu, *The Spirit of the Laws,* Bk. 3, ch. 1.

105. Adams, *Thoughts on Government,* p. 288.

106. John Adams to Hezekiah Niles, February 13, 1818, in Charles Francis Adams, ed., *The Works of John Adams,* vol. 10 (Boston: Little, Brown, 1850–1856), p. 282.

107. Benjamin Rush to Richard Price, May 25, 1786, in Lyman Butterfield, ed., *Letters of Benjamin Rush,* vol. 1 (Princeton, NJ: Princeton University Press, 1951), p. 388.

108. Montesquieu, *The Spirit of the Laws,* Bk. 4, ch. 1; Benjamin Rush, *A Plan for the Establishment of Public Schools and the Diffusion of Knowledge in Pennsylvania,* in Frederick Rudolph, ed., *Essays on Education in the Early Republic* (Cambridge, MA: Harvard University Press, 1965), ch. 1.

109. Merrill Peterson, ed., *Thomas Jefferson: Writings* (New York: Library of America, 1984), pp. 944, 1425.

110. Hannah Arendt, *Between Past and Future* (New York: Meridian Books, 1963), p. 120.

111. Runes, ed., *Selected Writings of Benjamin Rush,* p. 62.

112. Peterson, ed., *Thomas Jefferson,* p. 1176; *Federalist,* no. 5.

113. *Federalist,* no. 56.

114. Paine, *Common Sense,* p. 120.

115. Peterson, ed., *Thomas Jefferson,* p. 1086.

116. *Federalist,* no. 14. See also James Madison's preface to his *Notes of Debates in the Federal Convention of 1787* (New York: W. W. Norton, 1987), p. 3, in which he again observed with pride that America had shown the world "a system without a[n] example ancient or modern." Madison wrote the preface to his notes late in life, sometime between 1830 and 1836.

117. Boucher, *View of the Causes and Consequences of the American Revolution*, p. 313.

118. Peterson, ed., *Thomas Jefferson*, pp. 959–964, 1395–1403, 1490–1496.

119. Ibid., pp. 1401, 1428.

120. *Federalist*, no. 49.

121. James Madison to Thomas Jefferson, February 4, 1790, in Jack N. Rakove, ed., *James Madison: Writings* (New York: Library of America, 1999), pp. 473–477.

122. Peterson, ed., *Thomas Jefferson*, p. 911.

123. *Federalist*, no. 28.

124. Pufendorf, *Law of Nature and Nations*, Bk. 7, ch. 8, nos. 1–5, pp. 716–719.

125. Locke, *Second Treatise*, nos. 73, 118.

126. Ibid., no. 121; Gordon J. Schochet, *Patriarchalism in Political Thought* (New York: Basic Books, 1975), p. 253.

127. Otis, *Rights of the British Colonies*, p. 425.

128. Richard Bland, *An Inquiry into the Rights of the British Colonies*, in Jensen, ed., *Tracts of the American Revolution*, pp. 112–113.

129. Thomas Jefferson, *A Summary View of the Rights of British America*, in Peterson, ed., *Thomas Jefferson*, p. 105; Thomas Jefferson to Albert Gallatin, June 26, 1806, in Ford, ed., *Writings of Thomas Jefferson*, vol. 8, p. 458.

130. *The Constitution of Pennsylvania, 1776*, in Samuel Eliot Morison, ed., *Sources and Documents Illustrating the American Revolution, 1764–1788*, p. 164.

131. McCloskey, ed., *The Works of James Wilson*, pp. 244–245.

132. St. George Tucker, *View of the Constitution of the United States* (Indianapolis, IN: Liberty Fund, 1999), p. 358.

133. Edward J. Erler, "From Subjects to Citizens: The Social Compact Origins of American Citizenship," in Ronald J. Pestritto and Thomas G. West, eds., *The American Founding and the Social Compact* (Lexington, MA: Lexington Books, 2003), ch. 6.

134. Joel Barlow, *Advice to the Privileged Orders in the Several States of Europe, Resulting from the Necessity and Propriety of a General Revolution in the Principle of Government* (Ithaca, NY: Great Seal Books, 1956), pp. 7–8, 46.

Chapter 2. Social Contracts in Antebellum America

1. My disagreement is with Louis Hartz, *The Liberal Tradition in America* (New York: Harcourt, Brace, & World, 1955).

2. Quoted in Hezekiah Niles, ed., *Principles and Acts of the Revolution in America* (Baltimore, MD, 1822), p. 77; see also Thad W. Tate, "The Social Contract in America, 1774–1787: Revolutionary Theory as a Conservative Instrument," *William and Mary Quarterly* 22, no. 3 (July 1965): 375–391.

3. Forrest McDonald, *Novus Ordo Seclorum: The Intellectual Origins of the Constitution* (Lawrence: University Press of Kansas, 1985), pp. 60, 66.

4. Between 1776 and 1784 eleven of the thirteen states adopted the common law.

5. William Blackstone, *Commentaries on the Laws of England* (Chicago: University of Chicago Press, 1979), Bk. 1, pp. 148, 204, 206, 238, 204–206.

6. Ibid., Bk. 1, p. 234; intro., p. 9.

7. Robert McCloskey, ed., *The Works of James Wilson* (Cambridge, MA: Harvard University Press, 1967), pp. 70, 71, 77, 80, 82.

8. Blackstone, *Commentaries*, Bk. 1, pp. 53, 121, 134.

9. McCloskey, ed., *The Works of James Wilson*, pp. 587–588.

10. Blackstone, *Commentaries*, Bk. 1, p. 77.

11. McCloskey, ed., *The Works of James Wilson*, pp. 102, 122, 180, 183, 184.

12. Blackstone, *Commentaries*, Bk. 1, p. 39.

13. McCloskey, ed., *The Works of James Wilson*, p. 121.

14. Blackstone, *Commentaries*, Bk. 1, p. 157; McCloskey, ed., *The Works of James Wilson*, p. 185.

15. McCloskey, ed., *The Works of James Wilson*, pp. 186, 110, 169.

16. St. George Tucker, *View of the Constitution of the United States*, ed. Clyde Wilson (Indianapolis, IN: Liberty Fund, 1999), pp. 3, 5, 89n.

17. Ibid., pp. 6, 339, 19.

18. Daniel T. Rodgers, *Contested Truths: Keywords in American Politics Since Independence* (New York: Basic Books, 1987), pp. 93–94. See also Morton Keller, "The Politics of State Constitutional Revision, 1820–1930," in Kermit Hall, Harold Hyman, and Leon Sigal, eds., *The Constitutional Convention as an Amending Device* (Washington, DC: American Historical Association and American Political Science Association, 1981), ch. 2.

19. C. Bradley Thompson, ed., *The Revolutionary Writings of John Adams* (Indianapolis, IN: Liberty Fund, 2000), p. 297.

20. *Journal of Debates and Proceedings in the Convention of Delegates Chosen to Revise the Constitution of Massachusetts* (Boston: Office of the Daily Advertiser, 1821), pp. 84–86 (hereafter cited as *MA Convention, 1821*).

21. Ibid., p. 176.

22. Thompson, ed., *Revolutionary Writings*, p. 297.

23. *MA Convention, 1821*, p. 121.

24. Ibid., p. 134.

25. Thompson, ed., *Revolutionary Writings*, pp. 297, 300.

26. See, for example, *MA Convention, 1821*, p. 136b, for Joseph Story's use of "life, liberty, and property" to defend the conservative cause.

27. "The Virginia Convention of 1829–30 was the last of the great constituent assemblies in American history. As an arena of ideological encounter it was unexcelled." Merrill Peterson, ed., *Democracy, Liberty, and Property: The State Constitutional Conventions of the 1820s* (Indianapolis, IN: Bobbs-Merrill, 1966), p. 271. See also Dickson D. Bruce Jr., *The Rhetoric of Conservatism: The Virginia Convention of 1829–30 and the Conservative Tradition in the South* (San Marino, CA: The Huntington Library, 1982).

28. *Proceedings and Debates of the Virginia State Convention of 1829–30* (Richmond, VA: S. Shepherd, 1830), pp. 54–55, 57, 120, 130, 193. Hereafter cited as *VA Convention, 1829–1830*.

29. Ibid., pp. 158, 161.

30. Ibid., pp. 69–70, 193, 70.

31. Montesquieu, *The Spirit of the Laws*, Bk. 5, ch. 19; Mark Hulliung, *Montesquieu and the Old Regime* (Berkeley: University of California Press, 1976). See Frances Acomb, *Anglophobia in France, 1763–1789* (Durham, NC: Duke University Press, 1950), for evidence that Montesquieu's view of England as a republic won out in eighteenth-century France.

32. *Federalist*, no. 2.

33. Herbert J. Storing, ed., *The Complete Antifederalist* (Chicago: University of Chicago Press, 1981), 2.9.16.

34. Ibid., 4.6.16.

35. Ibid., 5.17.1.

36. *Writings and Speeches of Daniel Webster*, vol. 16 (Boston: Little, Brown, 1903), p. 423.

37. Peter S. Onuf, "Liberty, Development, and Union: Visions of the West in the 1780s," *William and Mary Quarterly* 43, no. 2 (April 1986): 179–213; Gilbert Chinard, "Looking Westward," in *Meet Mr. Franklin* (Philadelphia: Franklin Institute, 1943), pp. 135–150.

38. Frederick Merk, *Manifest Destiny and Mission* (New York: Random House, 1963), pp. 33, 46.

39. Ibid., pp. 17–18. See also Charles F. Adams, ed., *Memoirs of John Quincy Adams*, vol. 4 (New York: AMS Press, 1970), pp. 438–439.

40. Vattel's chapter was something of a favorite in antebellum America. Andrew Johnson, for instance, cited it when arguing for a homestead bill (*The Papers of Andrew Johnson*, vol. 1 [Knoxville: University of Tennessee Press, 1967], pp. 558, 564). Emmerich de Vattel, *The Law of Nations: or, Principles of the Law of Nature, Applied to the Conduct and Affairs of Nations and Sovereigns* (Philadelphia: T. & J. W. Johnson, Law Booksellers, 1854), Bk. 1, ch. 7, pp. 35–36. Anders Stephanson briefly noted the importance of Vattel to Americans seeking a justification for "Indian removal" in *Manifest Destiny: American Expansion and the Empire of Right* (New York: Hill and Wang, 1998), p. 25.

41. "Nothing testifies so effectively to the strength of Jacksonian ideals as their power to inspire their victims as well as their beneficiaries," wrote Harry L. Watson in *Liberty and Power: The Politics of Jacksonian America* (New York: Hill and Wang, 1990), p. 14.

42. Richard Walsh, ed., *The Writings of Christopher Gadsden, 1746–1805* (Columbia: University of South Carolina Press, 1966), pp. 66–67.

43. Tucker, *View of the Constitution*, pp. 7, 91–92, 95–96, 101–103, 106, 120–121, 252, 315, 356, 364.

44. Thomas Jefferson to Archibald Thweat, January 19, 1821, in Paul Leicester Ford, ed., *The Writings of Thomas Jefferson*, vol. 10 (New York: G. P. Putnam's, 1899), p. 184. On Taylor and his background, see Robert E. Shalhope, *John Taylor of Caroline, Pastoral Republican* (Columbia: University of South Carolina Press, 1980). See also Loren Baritz, *City on a Hill: A History of Ideas and Myths in America* (New York: John Wiley & Sons, 1964), ch. 4; and Norman K. Risjord, *The Old Republicans: Southern Conservatism in the Age of Jefferson* (New York: Columbia University Press, 1965).

45. John Taylor, *Construction Construed and Constitutions Vindicated* (New York: Da Capo Press, 1970), pp. 13, 17, 22, 37, 52, 67.

46. Ibid., pp. 234, 171.

47. Ibid., p. 26.

48. On the confusions of the old Federalist vocabulary, see Patrick Riley, *Historical Development of the Theory of Federalism, 16th–19th Centuries* (unpublished Ph.D. dissertation, Harvard University, 1968).

49. Taylor, *Construction Construed*, p. 47.

50. John Taylor, *An Inquiry into the Principles and Policy of the Government of the United States* (Indianapolis, IN: Bobbs-Merrill, 1969), p. 79 (emphasis added).

51. Taylor, *Construction Construed*, pp. 43, 172 (emphasis added).

52. Ibid., p. 43; Articles of Confederation, article 3, in Henry Steele Commager, ed., *Documents of American History*, 9th ed. (Englewood Cliffs, NJ: Prentice-Hall, 1973), pp. 376–384.

53. John C. Calhoun, "Speech on the Force Bill, 15–16 February 1833," in Ross M. Lence, ed., *Union and Liberty: The Political Philosophy of John C. Calhoun* (Indianapolis, IN: Liberty Fund, 1992), pp. 437–438.

54. *State Papers on Nullification: Including the Public Acts of the Convention of the People of South Carolina, November 19, 1832 and March 11, 1833* (Boston: Dutton and Wentworth, 1834), pp. 23–25, 47. I have profited from reading Pauline Maier's insightful article "The Road Not Taken: Nullification, John C. Calhoun, and the Revolutionary Tradition in South Carolina," *South Carolina Historical Magazine* 82 (1981): 1–19. For a general study, see William W. Freehling, *Prelude to Civil War: The Nullification Controversy in South Carolina, 1816–1836* (New York: Harper & Row, 1966).

55. For an example of the radical rhetoric, read the selection from Robert J. Turnbull's *The Crisis* (1827) in William J. Freehling, ed., *The Nullification Era: A Documentary Record* (New York: Harper TorchBooks, 1967), pp. 26–47.

56. Clyde N. Wilson, ed., *The Papers of John C. Calhoun*, vol. 12 (Columbia: University of South Carolina Press, 1979), pp. 110–111, 118.

57. Ibid., vol. 10, p. 545; vol. 11, pp. 421, 489; Maier, "The Road Not Taken."

58. Hugo Grotius, *The Law of War and Peace* (Indianapolis, IN: Bobbs-Merrill, 1925), Bk. 3, ch. 7, nos. 1–2, pp. 690–691.

59. Samuel Pufendorf, *Of the Law of Nature and Nations* (Clark, NJ: Lawbook Exchange, 2005), Bk. 6, ch. 3, nos. 3–5; Bk. 7, ch. 3, no. 1, ch. 8, no. 6, pp. 615, 616, 654, 722.

60. Thomas R. Dew, "Review of the Debate in the Virginia Legislature, 1831–32," in *The Proslavery Argument as Maintained by the Most Distinguished Writers of the Southern States* (1852) (New York: Negro Universities Press, 1968), pp. 308–310.

61. Quoted in William Sumner Jenkins, *Pro-Slavery Thought in the Old South* (Chapel Hill: University of North Carolina Press, 1935), p. 112.

62. Albert Taylor Bledsoe, *An Essay on Liberty and Slavery* (Philadelphia: J. B. Lippincott, 1856), pp. 91, 94; Kenneth S. Greenberg, "Revolutionary Ideology and the Proslavery Argument: The Abolition of Slavery in Antebellum South Carolina," *Journal*

of *Southern History* 42, no. 3 (August 1976): 377; Jenkins, *Pro-Slavery Thought*, p. 108.

63. See Drew Gilpin Faust, ed., *The Ideology of Slavery: Proslavery Thought in the Antebellum South, 1830–1860* (Baton Rouge: Louisiana State University Press, 1981), p. 238, for Josiah C. Nott's explicit use of the phrase as a conclusion to his thoughts on ethnology and phrenology. Southern natural rights thought was less outspoken but delivered the same message.

64. John Locke, *Second Treatise of Government*, no. 103.

65. Thomas Paine, *Rights of Man* (New York: Penguin, 1984), p. 66.

66. Grotius, *Law of War and Peace*, prolegomena, no. 46, p. 26.

67. James Henry Hammond, *Letters on Slavery*, in *Proslavery Argument*, p. 154.

68. William Harper, *Memoir on Slavery*, in Faust, ed., *Ideology of Slavery*, pp. 79–80, 89. Compare James Shannon, *The Philosophy of Slavery as Identified with the Philosophy of Human Happiness* (Frankfort, KY: A. G. Hodges, 1849), p. 8: "We have the universal consent of mankind . . . that some are incapable of making a proper use of freedom."

69. Drew Gilpin Faust, *A Sacred Circle: The Dilemma of the Intellectual in the Old South, 1840–1860* (Baltimore, MD: Johns Hopkins University Press, 1977), pp. 83–84.

70. Harper, *Memoir on Slavery*, p. 83; William Harper, *Anniversary Oration: The South Carolina Society for the Advancement of Learning, 9 December 1835* (Columbia, SC: Telescope Office, 1836), p. 18.

71. Grotius, *Law of War and Peace*, Bk. 2, ch. 5, no. 27, p. 255; Jenkins, *Pro-Slavery Thought*, p. 108.

72. Harper, *Memoir on Slavery*, p. 98.

73. William Gilmore Simms, "The Morals of Slavery" (1837), in *Proslavery Argument*, p. 267n; compare Henry Pinckney, *The Spirit of the Age* (Raleigh, NC: J. Gales, 1836), p. 9.

74. Samuel Pufendorf, *On the Duty of Man and Citizen* (Cambridge: Cambridge University Press, 1991); Richard Tuck, *Natural Rights Theories: Their Origin and Development* (Cambridge: Cambridge University Press, 1979), p. 1.

75. Simms, "Morals of Slavery," p. 259.

76. Harper, *Memoir on Slavery*, p. 84.

77. Pufendorf, *Law of Nature and Nations*, Bk. 7, ch. 8, no. 6, p. 721.

78. On Simms, see William R. Taylor, *Cavalier and Yankee: The Old South and American National Character* (New York: George Braziller, 1961), ch. 8; and Faust, *A Sacred Circle*.

79. Simms, "Morals of Slavery," pp. 251, 266–267.

80. Ibid., pp. 233, 264, 274.

81. Ibid., pp. 251, 258.

82. Lence, ed., *Union and Liberty*, pp. 44, 565, 569, 67, 75–78.

83. George Fitzhugh, "Southern Thought" (1857), in Faust, ed., *Ideology of Slavery*, pp. 277, 285.

84. George Fitzhugh, *Cannibals All! or Slaves Without Masters* (Cambridge, MA: Harvard University Press, 1960), p. 8. See also p. 134.

85. Ibid., pp. 13, 71; George Fitzhugh, *Sociology for the South: Or the Failure of Free Society* (1854) (New York: Burt Franklin, 1965), pp. 175, 187; Fitzhugh, "Southern Thought," p. 294.

86. John Taylor, *Arator* (Indianapolis, IN: Liberty Classics, 1992), pp. 52, 94, 96; Fitzhugh, *Sociology for the South*, p. 156.

87. Fitzhugh, *Sociology for the South*, pp. 189–193, 94, 139, 142, 145, 157–158; Fitzhugh, *Cannibals All!* p. 59.

88. Fitzhugh, *Cannibals All!* ch. 7; Fitzhugh, "Southern Thought," p. 292.

89. Fitzhugh, *Sociology for the South*, p. 33.

90. Fitzhugh, "Southern Thought," p. 282; Fitzhugh, *Cannibals All!* pp. 40, 255.

91. Fitzhugh, *Sociology for the South*, pp. 45, 94–95.

92. Ibid., p. 26; Fitzhugh, *Cannibals All!* p. 190.

93. Fitzhugh, *Sociology for the South*, pp. 27, 185.

94. Fitzhugh, *Cannibals All!* p. 130.

95. Ibid., pp. 8, 133.

96. Fitzhugh, *Sociology for the South*, pp. 209, 176–177.

97. Taylor, *Inquiry*, pp. 346, 405–406.

98. Fitzhugh, *Cannibals All!* pp. 53, 135.

99. Fitzhugh, *Sociology for the South*, p. 170.

100. Dwight Lowell Dumond, ed., *Southern Editorials on Secession* (Gloucester, MA: Peter Smith, 1964), p. 402.

101. William W. Freehling and Craig M. Simpson, eds., *Secession Debated: Georgia's Showdown in 1860* (New York: Oxford University Press, 1992), p. 58; Dumond, ed., *Southern Editorials*, p. 8.

102. Dumond, ed., *Southern Editorials*, pp. 7, 35, 37, 57, 76, 87, 101, 102, 151, 195, 223, 227, 229, 241, 242, 245–247, 256, 259, 260, 272, 274, 288, 296, 324, 333, 424, 435; Freehling and Simpson, eds., *Secession Debated*, pp. 43, 45, 58; John Amasa May and Joan Reynolds, eds., *South Carolina Secedes* (Columbia: University of South Carolina Press, 1960), p. 87.

103. May and Reynolds, eds., *South Carolina Secedes*, p. 82.

104. Dumond, ed., *Southern Editorials*, pp. 435, 515.

105. May and Reynolds, eds., *South Carolina Secedes*, p. 7.

106. Ibid., pp. 44, 76–77, 91.

107. David Brion Davis, ed., *Antebellum American Culture: An Interpretive Anthology* (University Park: Pennsylvania State University Press, 1997), p. 171.

108. Joseph L. Blau, ed., *Social Theories of Jacksonian Democracy* (Indianapolis, IN: Hackett, 2003), pp. 164, 168, 169.

109. An indispensable source for any comments on the Loco-Focos is Fitzwilliam Byrdsall's book *The History of the Loco-Foco or Equal Rights Party: Its Movements, Conventions and Proceedings* (1842) (New York: Burt Franklin, 1967). Also quite pertinent is William Leggett, *Democratick Editorials* (Indianapolis, IN: Liberty Classics, 1984). Secondary studies include Arthur M. Schlesinger Jr., *The Age of Jackson* (Boston: Little, Brown, 1945), ch. 15; and Brad Clarke, *"The True Prosperity of Our Past"* (unpublished Ph.D. dissertation, Brandeis University, 1997), ch. 7.

110. Quoted in Philip S. Foner, ed., *History of the Labor Movement in the United States* (New York: International Publishers, 1998), p. 158.

111. Byrdsall, *History of the Loco-Foco . . . Party*, p. 151.

112. Ibid., p. 53.

113. Ibid., pp. 39, 68, 72, 126, 168.

114. Ibid., p. 165, for evidence that the Loco-Focos, too, sometimes vigorously attacked the common-law courts. On the workers' movement, see Edward Pessen, *Most Uncommon Jacksonians: The Radical Leaders of the Early Labor Movement* (Albany: State University of New York Press, 1967).

115. Christopher L. Tomlins, *Law, Labor, and Ideology in the Early American Republic* (New York: Cambridge University Press, 1993); Karen Orren, *Belated Feudalism: Labor, the Law, and Liberal Development in the United States* (New York: Cambridge University Press, 1991).

116. Theophilus Fisk, *An Oration upon the Freedom of the Press,* in Fisk, *Orations on Freedom of the Press* (New York: Arno, 1970), p. 35. See also Theophilus Fisk, *Labor, the Only Source of Wealth,* in Leon Stein and Philip Taft, eds., *Labor Politics: Collected Pamphlets,* vol. 1 (New York: Arno, 1971), p. 16.

117. Seth Luther, *An Address Delivered Before the Mechanics and Workingmen of the City of Brooklyn* (Brooklyn, NY: Alden Spooner, 1836), pp. 6, 7, 8, 10.

118. Frederick Robinson, *An Oration Delivered Before the Trades Union of Boston* (Boston: Charles Douglas, 1834), pp. 12–13, 15, 16.

119. Ely Moore, *Address Delivered Before the General Trades' Union of the City of New York* (New York: James Ormond, 1833), p. 13.

120. Byrdsall, *History of the Loco-Foco . . . Party,* p. 165.

121. Locke, *Second Treatise,* no. 16; Ely Moore, *Speech of the Honorable Ely Moore in Reply to the Honorable Waddy Thompson and Others, in the House of Representatives, May 5, 1836* (Washington, DC: Blair & Rives, 1836), p. 11.

122. Locke, *Second Treatise,* no. 12.

123. Matthew Tindal, *Christianity as Old as the Creation* (Stuttgart, Germany: Friedrich Frommann Verlag, 1967), p. 134.

124. Robert E. Collins, ed., *Theodore Parker: American Transcendentalist* (Metuchen, NJ: Scarecrow Press, 1973), pp. 143, 146, 167.

125. Nathaniel Hawthorne, *The House of the Seven Gables* (New York: Buccaneer Books, 1987), p. 163. The character in question alters his view in the closing pages, deciding in favor of a permanent stone house, the interior of which will be redesigned by each generation as it wishes.

126. Collins, ed., *Theodore Parker,* pp. 55, 57, 58, 66.

127. Ibid., pp. 66–67.

128. William Ellery Channing, *Slavery* (Boston: James Munroe & Co., 1835), pp. 30, 35–37. Daniel Walker Howe offered a brief overview of Channing's thought in *Making the American Self: Jonathan Edwards to Abraham Lincoln* (Cambridge, MA: Harvard University Press, 1997), pp. 131–135.

129. Channing, *Slavery,* pp. 1, 35.

130. *Selections from the Writings and Speeches of William Lloyd Garrison* (1852) (New York: Negro Universities Press, 1968), pp. 68–69, 238, 295.

131. Nathaniel Chipman, *Principles of Government: A Treatise on Free Institutions, Including the Constitution of the United States* (1833) (New York: Da Capo, 1970), pp. 64, 186.

132. James Kirke Paulding, *Slavery in the United States* (New York: Harper & Brothers, 1836), pp. 37, 44.

133. Locke, *Second Treatise*, no. 85; Dew, "Review of the Debate," pp. 309–310. On the willingness of many Northern intellectuals to accommodate the South, see Larry E. Tise, *Proslavery: A History of the Defense of Slavery in America, 1701–1840* (Athens: University of Georgia Press, 1987).

134. Calvin Colton, *The Junius Tracts* (New York: Greeley & McElrath, 1844), p. 66.

135. Calvin Colton, *Abolition a Sedition: By a Northern Man* (Philadelphia: Geo. W. Donohue, 1839), pp. 121–123.

136. Ibid., p. 73.

137. Rufus Choate, *The Importance of Illustrating New England History*, in Daniel Walker Howe, ed., *The American Whigs: An Anthology* (New York: John Wiley, 1973), pp. 159–171. Surely the most famous repudiation of the Puritans by a Jacksonian was also a work of fiction: Hawthorne's *The Scarlet Letter* (1850).

138. G. E. Baker, ed., *The Works of William H. Seward*, vol. 4 (Boston: Houghton, Mifflin, 1889), p. 190; Daniel Webster, *First Settlement of New England*, in *Writings and Speeches of Daniel Webster*, vol. 1, p. 198.

139. John Quincy Adams, *An Oration Delivered at Plymouth, December 22, 1802, at the Anniversary Commemoration of the First Landing of Our Ancestors at That Place* (Plymouth: Joseph Avery, 1820), pp. 7, 13. The date of this speech suggests that Adams was a Whig long before the formation of the Whig Party. For an effective repudiation of the claim that the ideology of the American Revolution was foreshadowed by Puritan America, see Michael Zuckert, *The Natural Rights Republic* (Notre Dame, IN: University of Notre Dame Press, 1996), ch. 5.

140. Other examples include Joseph Story, *History and Influence of the Puritans*, in *Miscellaneous Writings* (New York: Da Capo Press, 1972), pp. 408–474; Edward Everett, "First Settlement of New England," in *Orations and Speeches on Various Occasions*, vol. 1 (Boston: Little, Brown, 1878), pp. 45–72; Edward Everett, "The Pilgrim Fathers," in ibid., vol. 2, pp. 232–243; Edward Everett, "The Departure of the Pilgrims," in ibid., vol. 2, pp. 639–645.

141. On the manner in which American judges used the common law to foster economic development, see Morton J. Horwitz, *The Transformation of American Law, 1780–1860* (Cambridge, MA: Harvard University Press, 1977).

142. Story, *Miscellaneous Writings*, p. 236.

143. For Story's position on the English Whigs and on the inapplicability of 1688 to America, see his *Commentaries on the Constitution of the United States: With a Preliminary Review of the Constitutional History of the Colonies and States, Before the Adop-*

tion of the Constitution (Boston: Charles C. Little & James Brown, 1851), pp. 216–217, 233. Story identifies with Marshall in the Preface, pp. vii–viii.

144. *The Writings of John Marshall* (Boston: James Munroe & Co., 1839), p. 163; Herman Belz, ed., *The Webster/Hayne Debate on the Nature of the Union* (Indianapolis, IN: Liberty Classics, 2000), p. 126; Webster, *The Constitution Not a Compact Between Sovereign States,* in *Writings and Speeches of Daniel Webster,* vol. 6, p. 205.

145. Belz, ed., *Webster/Hayne Debate,* pp. 124–125; Webster, *Constitution Not a Compact,* p. 211.

146. See, for example, Francis Bowen, "The Recent Contest in Rhode Island," *North American Review* 58 (April 1844): esp. 421–426. For background, see Daniel Walker Howe, *The Unitarian Conscience: Harvard Moral Philosophy* (Cambridge, MA: Harvard University Press, 1970).

147. Daniel Webster, *The Rhode Island Question* (Washington: J. & G. S. Gideon, 1848), pp. 4, 5, 16, 20.

148. Jackson's "proclamation" of December 10, 1832, was similar in argument to the position staked out by Webster and other Whigs. James D. Richardson, ed., *Messages and Papers of the Presidents,* vol. 3 (New York: Bureau of National Literature, 1897), pp. 1203–1219.

149. An excellent history of the continuing viability of doctrines of states' rights is Forrest McDonald, *States' Rights and the Union: Imperium in Imperio, 1776–1876* (Lawrence: University Press of Kansas, 2000).

150. J. Q. Adams, *Oration Delivered at Plymouth, 1802,* p. 5; Everett, *Orations and Speeches,* vol. 1, p. 172; William Seward, *The Destiny of America* (Albany, NY: Weed, Parsons, 1853).

151. Richard Hildreth, *Despotism in America: An Inquiry into the Nature, Results, and Legal Basis of the Slave-Holding System in the United States* (Boston: John P. Jewett & Co., 1854), pp. 9–10.

Chapter 3. The Right to Land in the Land of Rights

1. John Locke, *Second Treatise of Government,* no. 49.

2. Merrill Peterson, ed., *Thomas Jefferson: Writings* (New York: Library of America, 1984), pp. 290–291.

3. Jack N. Rakove, ed., *James Madison: Writings* (New York: Library of America, 1999), p. 132.

4. Marvin Meyers, ed., *The Mind of the Founder: Sources of the Political Thought of James Madison* (Hanover, NH: University Press of New England, 1981), p. 415.

5. Thomas Paine, *Rights of Man* (New York: Penguin, 1984), pp. 211, 218.

6. Ibid., pp. 212, 242, 243, 248, 251.

7. Ibid., pp. 217–218.

8. Ibid., p. 41.

9. Thomas Paine, *Agrarian Justice,* in Eric Foner, ed., *Thomas Paine: Collected Writings* (New York: Library of America, 1995), pp. 405, 407, 411.

10. Paine, *Agrarian Justice,* pp. 397, 399; Thomas Jefferson to Edward Carrington, January 16, 1787, in Peterson, ed., *Thomas Jefferson,* p. 880.

11. Paine, *Rights of Man*, p. 211; Paine, *Agrarian Justice*, p. 397.

12. Paine, *Agrarian Justice*, pp. 398, 399, 400.

13. Ibid., pp. 399, 400, 401, 405.

14. Ibid., p. 399.

15. Ibid., p. 408.

16. See, for instance, the writings of the French Solidarists at the end of the nineteenth century and the beginning of the twentieth.

17. Thomas Paine, *The Age of Reason*, in Foner, ed., *Collected Writings*, p. 677.

18. Eric Foner, *Tom Paine and Revolutionary America* (New York: Oxford University Press, 1976), ch. 7.

19. Thomas Skidmore, *The Rights of Man to Property!* (New York: Burt Franklin, 1964), pp. 174, 72, 71, 57, 126, 358, 67.

20. Ibid., pp. 22, 125.

21. Paine, *Rights of Man*, p. 42.

22. Skidmore, *The Rights of Man to Property!* pp. 60, 91, 101, 112, 221; on the generations, see pp. 86, 89, 111–112, 115, 117–118, 226–227, 266, 284, 372.

23. Edward Pessen, *Most Uncommon Jacksonians: The Radical Leaders of the Early Labor Movement* (Albany: State University of New York Press, 1967), p. 146.

24. *Working Man's Advocate*, October 31, November 7, November 14, 1829.

25. Helene Zahler, *Eastern Workingmen and National Land Policy, 1829–1862* (New York: Greenwood Press, 1969), p. 52n.

26. George Henry Evans, "History of the Origin and Progress of the Working Men's Party in New York," *The Radical in Continuation of the Working Man's Advocate* 2 (January 1842): 9.

27. *The Radical* 1 (January 1841); *Working Man's Advocate*, October 5, 1844.

28. I have found especially helpful Thomas A. Horne's important book, *Property Rights and Poverty: Political Argument in Britain, 1605–1834* (Chapel Hill: University of North Carolina Press, 1990).

29. Hugo Grotius, *The Free Sea* (Indianapolis, IN: Liberty Fund, 2005); Hugo Grotius, *The Law of War and Peace* (Indianapolis, IN: Bobbs-Merrill, 1925), Bk. 2, ch. 2, nos. 2 and 3, pp. 186, 187, 190.

30. Grotius, *Law of War and Peace*, Bk. 2, ch. 2, no. 2, pp. 189–190.

31. Ibid., Bk. 2, ch. 2, no. 6, p. 193.

32. Samuel Pufendorf, "On the Origin of Dominion or Property," *Of the Law of Nature and Nations* (Clark, NJ: Lawbook Exchange, 2005), Bk. 4, ch. 4, pp. 361–378.

33. "Of the Right and Privilege of Necessity," ibid., Bk. 2, ch. 6, pp. 202–212.

34. Horne, *Property Rights and Poverty*, pp. 34–40.

35. Paine, *Common Sense* (New York: Penguin, 1976), p. 65.

36. Skidmore, *The Rights of Man to Property!* p. 80.

37. Henry George, *Progress and Poverty* (New York: Robert Schalkenbach Foundation, 1942), pp. 320, 454–456.

38. Locke, *Second Treatise*, nos. 12, 103.

39. Ibid., nos. 40, 42.

40. Ibid., nos. 6, 23; *Working Man's Advocate* (October 5, 1844).

41. Robert Filmer, *Observations Concerning the Originall of Government,* in Johann P. Sommerville, ed., *Filmer: Patriarcha and Other Writings* (Cambridge: Cambridge University Press, 2000), p. 234.

42. Locke, *Second Treatise,* no. 25 (emphasis added).

43. Ibid., no. 27.

44. Skidmore, *The Rights of Man to Property!* p. 7: "I am undertaking a work, which, as Rousseau said of his *Confessions,* has no example, and whose execution, perhaps, will find no approval"; Rousseau, *Discourse on Inequality,* in Roger Masters, ed., *The First and Second Discourses* (New York: St. Martin's, 1964), p. 158.

45. Skidmore, *The Rights of Man to Property!* p. 117; see also pp. 8, 33, 34, 37, 42, 376.

46. Thomas Spence, *The Real Rights of Man,* in M. Beer, ed., *The Pioneers of Land Reform* (New York: Alfred A. Knopf, 1920), pp. 7–11. The *Working Man's Advocate* sometimes directly quoted Spence, e.g., the issue of March 30, 1844.

47. See, for example, Arthur M. Schlesinger Jr., *The Age of Jackson* (Boston: Little, Brown, 1945), p. 184, for a dismissal of Skidmore.

48. From the beginnings in the 1780s, Americans were remarkably unsentimental in their enthusiasm for land. See Peter S. Onuf, "Liberty, Development, and Union: Visions of the West in the 1780s," *William and Mary Quarterly* 43, no. 2 (April 1986): 179–213; Leo Marx, *The Machine in the Garden: Technology and the Pastoral Ideal in America* (New York: Oxford University Press, 1964).

49. Thomas Jefferson to John Adams, August 1, 1816, in Lester J. Cappon, ed., *The Adams-Jefferson Letters* (Chapel Hill: University of North Carolina Press, 1959), p. 485.

50. Skidmore, *The Rights of Man to Property!* pp. 355–356.

51. Frederick Robinson, *An Oration Delivered Before the Trades Union of Boston* (Boston: Charles Douglas, 1834), p. 10.

52. George, *Progress and Poverty,* p. 390.

53. Leviticus 25: 23.

54. John Pickering, *The Working Man's Political Economy, Founded upon the Principle of Immutable Justice, and the Inalienable Rights of Man; Designed for the Promotion of National Reform* (1847) (New York: Arno Press, 1971), pp. 3, 77.

55. William Paley, *The Principles of Moral and Political Philosophy* (Indianapolis, IN: Liberty Fund, 2002), p. xxxv.

56. Anna Haddow, *Political Science in American Colleges and Universities, 1636–1900* (New York: Appleton-Century, 1939), p. 67.

57. Pickering, *Working Man's Political Economy,* p. 11.

58. Paley, *Principles,* pp. 70, 63–64, 66.

59. Pickering, *Working Man's Political Economy,* p. 25.

60. Ibid., p. 27; Paley, *Principles,* pp. 141, 68.

61. Pickering, *Working Man's Political Economy,* pp. 105, 179.

62. William Blackstone, *Commentaries on the Laws of England* (Chicago: University of Chicago Press, 1979), Bk. 1, p. 120.

63. Pickering, *Working Man's Political Economy,* p. 104.

64. Blackstone, *Commentaries,* Bk. 2, p. 2.

65. Paley, *Principles*, p. 64.

66. Blackstone, *Commentaries*, Bk. 1, pp. 53, 121, 134.

67. Pickering, *Working Man's Political Economy*, pp. 108, 17, 23–24.

68. Ibid., pp. 6, 7, 154.

69. On political parties and their relationship to the National Reform movement, see Zahler, *Eastern Workingmen;* Roy M. Robbins, *Our Landed Heritage: The Public Domain, 1776–1936* (New York: Peter Smith, 1950); and Brad Clarke, *"The True Prosperity of Our Past"* (unpublished Ph.D. dissertation, Brandeis University, 1997), ch. 9.

70. *Speeches of Gerrit Smith in Congress* (New York: Mason Brothers, 1855), pp. 10, 41, 296–297.

71. Ibid., pp. 78–79, 49–50, 75.

72. Ibid., pp. 101–102, 79–80.

73. The Equal Rights or Loco-Foco Party, a short-lived offshoot of the Democratic Party, to the limited extent that it took up the question of land reform, was highly supportive. See F. Byrdsall, *The History of the Loco-Foco or Equal Rights Party* (New York: Burt Franklin, 1967), pp. 149–150; and William Leggett, *Democratick Editorials* (Indianapolis, IN: Liberty Fund, 1984), p. 391.

74. LeRoy P. Graf and Ralph W. Haskins, eds., *The Papers of Andrew Johnson*, vol. 1 (Knoxville: University of Tennessee Press, 1967), pp. 563–564.

75. James D. Richardson, ed., *Messages and Papers of the Presidents*, vol. 3 (New York: Bureau of National Literature, 1897), pp. 1163–1164, 1169.

76. *Papers of Andrew Johnson*, pp. 565, 570–571.

77. The party platforms of 1848 and 1852 are reprinted as appendix A and appendix B in Frederick J. Blue, *The Free Soilers: Third Party Politics, 1848–54* (Urbana: University of Illinois Press, 1973), pp. 295, 299.

78. George W. Julian, *Speeches on Political Questions, 1850–1868* (Westport, CT: Negro Universities Press, 1970), pp. 50–66.

79. Charles F. Adams, ed., *Memoirs of John Quincy Adams*, vol. 10 (New York: AMS Press, 1970), p. 19.

80. Horace Greeley, *Hints Toward Reforms* (New York: Harper & Brothers, 1850), pp. 8, 140, 325, 311.

81. Ibid., pp. 20, 24, 27, 28, 184, 317, 133, 172–173, 311, 316, 321.

82. Edward Everett explicitly spoke of a "holy alliance" between labor and capital. Daniel Walker Howe, ed., *The American Whigs: An Anthology* (New York: John Wiley, 1973), pp. 30–31. Alonzo Potter warned that calls for class struggle were an unwanted import from Europe; see Potter's essay "Trades' Unions," *New York Review* (January 1838): 5–48.

83. George Henry Evans's "Vote Yourself a Farm" is reprinted in Zahler, *Eastern Workingmen,* appendix 2, pp. 207–208. It originally appeared in the *Working Man's Advocate,* March 15, 1845.

84. Calvin Colton, *The Rights of Labor* (New York: A. S. Barnes, 1846), p. 7.

85. Henry Nash Smith, *Virgin Land: The American West as Symbol and Myth* (Cambridge, MA: Harvard University Press, 1950), ch. 15.

86. Galusha Grow delivered his speech in Congress on March 30, 1852.

87. Eric Foner, *Politics and Ideology in the Age of the Civil War* (New York: Oxford University Press, 1980), ch. 7.

88. William Ogilvie, *The Right of Property in Land* (1781), reprinted in M. Beer, ed., *The Pioneers of Land Reform* (New York: Alfred A. Knopf, 1920).

89. George, *Progress and Poverty,* pp. 390, 391, 10.

90. David Hume, "Of the Original Contract," in *Essays Moral, Political, and Literary* (Indianapolis, IN: Liberty Fund, 1984), p. 471.

91. George, *Progress and Poverty,* p. 370.

92. Ibid., p. 340.

93. Henry George, *Our Land and Land Policy* (1871) (New York: Doubleday & McClure, 1901), p. 86.

94. Evans had turned to education during the early period, when he was trying to distance himself from Skidmore. Eventually he moved to the position that educational reform, though desirable, was a far from adequate response to the situation of the workers. See George, *Progress and Poverty,* p. 394.

95. Ibid., pp. 285–286, 390, 227, 287, 295, 468.

96. Ibid., p. 387.

97. Ibid., pp. 326, 384 (compare 336, 389), 328, 399.

98. Ibid., pp. 403, 405.

99. Ibid., pp. 365–366, 421.

100. Eric Goldman, *Rendezvous with Destiny: A History of Modern American Reform* (New York: Vintage, 1952), p. 28.

101. See, for example, *Papers of Andrew Johnson,* vol. 1, p. 559; Greeley, *Hints Toward Reforms,* p. 24; Julian, *Speeches on Political Questions,* p. 60; *Speeches of Gerrit Smith in Congress,* pp. 76, 103.

102. Henry George, *The Land Question: What It Involves and How Alone It Can Be Settled* (New York: Robert Schalkenbach Foundation, 1941), p. 8 (originally published under the title *The Irish Land Question*).

103. George, *Progress and Poverty,* pp. 360–365.

104. John Stuart Mill, *England and Ireland* (1868), in *John Stuart Mill on Ireland* (Philadelphia: Institute for the Study of Human Issues, 1979), pp. 11, 18.

105. Herbert Spencer, *Social Statics* (New York: Robert Schalkenbach Foundation, 1970), p. 113.

106. Malcolm Chase, *"The People's Farm": English Radical Agrarianism, 1775–1840* (Oxford: Clarendon Press, 1988). See also Richard Ashcraft, "Liberal Political Theory and Working-Class Radicalism in Nineteenth-Century England," *Political Theory* 21, no. 2 (May 1993): 249–272.

107. Robert Kelley, *The Transatlantic Persuasion: The Liberal-Democratic Mind in the Age of Gladstone* (New York: Alfred A. Knopf, 1969), chs. 5 and 6.

108. John Stuart Mill, *Considerations on Representative Government* (Indianapolis, IN: Bobbs-Merrill, 1958), p. 2.

109. E. D. Steele, "J. S. Mill and the Irish Question: Reform and the Integrity of the Empire, 1865–1870," *Historical Journal* 13, no. 3 (September 1970): 419–450.

110. Remarkably, in his "Speech on Mr. Fox's East India Bill," Burke briefly went so

far as to speak the language of Locke, government as a trust, and natural rights. *The Works of the Right Honorable Edmund Burke* (Boston: Little, Brown, 1866), vol. 2, pp. 437–441.

111. Debate on the Quebec Government Bill, May 6, 9, and 11, 1791, *Parliamentary History of England from the Earliest Period to the Year 1803*, vol. 29, pp. 364–374, 380–388, 395–426.

112. Mill, *England and Ireland*, pp. 14, 23.

113. Quoted in Daniel T. Rodgers, *Contested Truths: Keywords in American Politics Since Independence* (New York: Basic Books, 1987), p. 37.

114. Jeremy Bentham, "A Critical Examination of the Declaration of Rights," in John Bowring, ed., *Works of Bentham*, vol. 2 (London: Simpkin, Marshall, 1843), pp. 496–503; John Offer, ed., *Herbert Spencer: Political Writings* (Cambridge: Cambridge University Press, 1994), pp. 150–166.

115. Herbert Spencer, *The Man Versus the State*, in Offer, ed., *Spencer: Political Writings*, pp. 94, 136.

116. Henry George, *A Perplexed Philosopher: Being an Examination of Mr. Herbert Spencer's Various Utterances on the Land Question* (1892) (New York: Robert Schalkenbach Foundation, 1965), pp. 272, 275.

117. William L. Miller, "Herbert Spencer's Drift to Conservatism," *History of Political Thought* 3, no. 3 (November 1982): 483–497.

118. Richard Hofstadter, *Social Darwinism in American Thought* (Boston: Beacon Press, 1955), ch. 2.

Chapter 4. Burke in America?

1. Perhaps the best example is Daniel Walker Howe, *The Political Culture of the American Whigs* (Chicago: University of Chicago Press, 1979).

2. See R. Kent Newmyer, *Supreme Court Justice Joseph Story: Statesman of the Old Republic* (Chapel Hill: University of North Carolina Press, 1985), p. 169, for an example of a strong claim of Burkean influence backed by no actual evidence.

3. Jonathan Boucher, *A View of the Cause and Consequences of the American Revolution* (1797) (New York: Russell & Russell, 1967), pp. v, xv–xvii, lxii–lxiii, 233, 368–369, 416, 499.

4. Benjamin Franklin to William Franklin, April 16, 1768, in John Bigelow, ed., *Complete Works of Benjamin Franklin*, vol. 4 (New York: G. P. Putnam, 1887), p. 149; Sons of Liberty to John Wilkes, June 6, 1768, in Worthington C. Ford, ed., "John Wilkes and Boston," Massachusetts State Historical Society *Proceedings* 48 (1914): 191. See Pauline Maier's illuminating article "John Wilkes and American Disillusionment with Britain," *William and Mary Quarterly* 20, no. 3 (1963): 373–395.

5. Edmund Burke, *Thoughts on the Cause of the Present Discontents*, in *The Works of the Right Honorable Edmund Burke*, vol. 1 (Boston: Little, Brown, 1866), pp. 497, 499, 500. A year later, in 1771, Burke again rose to demand that Wilkes be seated: "Speech Relative to the Middlesex Election," in ibid., vol. 7, pp. 59–67.

6. Edmund Burke, "A Letter to the Sheriffs of the City of Bristol on the Affairs of America," in ibid., vol. 2, p. 209.

7. Edmund Burke, "Speech on Conciliation with the Colonies," in ibid., vol. 2, pp. 120, 125, 118, 120–121.

8. Ibid., pp. 124–125, 122–123.

9. Ibid. pp. 153, 136; Edmund Burke, "Speech on American Taxation," in ibid., vol. 2, p. 74.

10. Burke, "Speech on American Taxation," pp. 72–73.

11. Burke's *Thoughts on the Cause of the Present Discontents* is a vigorous Whig attack upon the governing clique.

12. Quoted in C. R. Ritcheson, *British Politics and the American Revolution* (Norman: University of Oklahoma Press, 1954), p. 41.

13. Burke, "Speech on American Taxation," p. 79.

14. Burke's 1777 "Address to the British Colonists in North America," in *Works,* vol. 6, pp. 183–196, although meant to be sympathetic to the Americans, actually demonstrated his failure to comprehend the ideological terms in which they had declared independence the year before.

15. Edmund Burke, "Speech to the Electors of Bristol," in *Works,* vol. 2, p. 96.

16. Alexander Hamilton, "Speech in the Constitutional Convention on a Plan of Government, June 18, 1787," in Joanne B. Freeman, ed., *Alexander Hamilton: Writings* (New York: Library of America, 2001), pp. 153, 156.

17. See, for example, "Brutus of New York": "Representatives . . . are supposed to know the minds of their constituents, and to be possessed of integrity to declare this mind." Herbert J. Storing, ed., *The Complete Antifederalist* (Chicago: University of Chicago Press, 1981), 2.9.14.

18. James Madison, *Federalist,* no. 10.

19. Burke, "Speech to the Electors of Bristol," pp. 89–98.

20. Burke's opposition to triennial elections was temperate in his *Thoughts on the Cause of the Present Discontents* (1770) but quite shrill in his "Speech on a Committee to Inquire into the State of the Representation of the Commons in Parliament" (1782). See also his "Speech on a Bill for Shortening the Duration of Parliaments" (1780). The two speeches appear in *Works,* vol. 7, pp. 69–104.

21. Robert McCloskey, ed., *The Works of James Wilson* (Cambridge, MA: Harvard University Press, 1967), pp. 574, 586–592.

22. Philip S. Foner, ed., *The Democratic-Republican Societies, 1790–1800: A Documentary Sourcebook of Constitutions, Declarations, Addresses, and Toasts* (Westport, CT: Greenwood Press, 1976), pp. 55–56, 64, 83, 85, 95, 97, 104, 168–170, 174–175, 185, 201, 203, 217–218, 222, 229, 231–232, 235, 237, 245, 266–268, 352, 363, 380, 383, 393.

23. W. B. Allen, ed., *Works of Fisher Ames* (Indianapolis, IN: Liberty Fund, 1983), p. 303. One important Federalist countersociety was the Constitutional Association of the Borough of Elizabeth, New Jersey.

24. *Columbian Centinel* (Boston), July 23, 1814, cited by James M. Banner, *To the Hartford Convention: The Federalists and the Origins of Party Politics in Massachusetts* (New York: Alfred A. Knopf, 1970), p. 6.

25. Fisher Ames to Oliver Wolcott, March 9, 1803, cited by Linda K. Kerber, *Feder-*

alists in Dissent: Imagery and Ideology in Jeffersonian America (Ithaca, NY: Cornell University Press, 1970), p. 162.

26. Allen, ed., *Works of Fisher Ames,* pp. 201, 1473–1474. See David Hackett Fischer, *The Revolution of American Conservatism: The Federalist Party in the Era of Jeffersonian Democracy* (New York: Harper, 1965), and Banner, *To the Hartford Convention,* for accounts of the process by which the Federalists learned to compete with the Jeffersonians in electoral politics.

27. Burke, *Thoughts on the Cause of the Present Discontents,* p. 530: "Party is a body of men united for promoting by their joint endeavors the national interest upon some particular principle in which they are all agreed."

28. Edmund Burke, *Reflections on the Revolution in France* (Indianapolis, IN: Hackett, 1987), p. 69; Lewis M. Ogden to William Meredith, February 26, 1801, cited by Fischer, *The Revolution of American Conservatism,* p. 97.

29. Foner, *Democratic-Republican Societies,* pp. 212, 215; Philip H. Marsh, ed., *The Prose Works of Philip Freneau* (New Brunswick, NJ: Scarecrow Press, 1955), pp. 300, 395.

30. Kerber, *Federalists in Dissent,* pp. 97–100. For an examination of the relationship between Noah Webster and other Federalists, see chapter 4 of Kerber's book.

31. John Adams to Thomas Jefferson, June 22, 1819, in *The Works of John Adams,* vol. 10 (Boston: Little, Brown, 1856), p. 380; L. H. Butterfield, Leonard C. Faber, and Wendell D. Garnett, eds., *Diary and Autobiography of John Adams,* vol. 3 (Cambridge, MA: Harvard University Press, 1961), pp. 330–333; David Freeman Hawke, *Paine* (New York: Harper & Row), p. 7.

32. John Adams to Benjamin Rush, September 27, 1809, in John A. Schutz and Douglass Adair, eds., *The Spur of Fame* (Indianapolis, IN: Liberty Fund, 1966), p. 169. Adams also repudiated Charles James Fox in this letter—the same Fox who had once described the new French constitution as "the most stupendous and glorious edifice of liberty which had been erected on the foundation of human integrity in any time or country."

33. George W. Carey, ed., *The Political Writings of John Adams* (Washington, DC: Regnery, 2000), p. 418.

34. Zoltán Haraszti, *John Adams and the Prophets of Progress* (New York: Grosset & Dunlap, 1952), pp. 213, 339.

35. Mary Wollstonecraft attacked Burke's rhetoric in *A Vindication of the Rights of Woman* (New York: Cambridge University Press, 1995); Tom Paine in *Rights of Man* (New York: Penguin, 1984).

36. Edward Handler, *America and Europe in the Political Thought of John Adams* (Cambridge, MA: Harvard University Press, 1964), pp. 157–158.

37. Michael Foot and Isaac Kramnick, eds., *The Thomas Paine Reader* (New York: Penguin, 1987), p. 506.

38. Jefferson's comment was printed without his permission when a new edition of *Rights of Man* was published. He admitted that he had been thinking of Adams.

39. John Stevens, *Observations on Government* (New York: W. Ross, 1787); John Taylor, *An Inquiry into the Principles and Policy of the Government of the United States* (Indianapolis, IN: Bobbs-Merrill, 1969).

40. John Adams, *Defence of the Constitutions of the United States,* vol. 1 (New York: Da Capo, 1971), pp. xvii–xviii.

41. Ibid., p. 121.

42. John Quincy Adams's "Publicola" papers were published anonymously—and wrongly attributed to his father—in the *Columbian Centinel,* beginning June 8, 1791. I am quoting from *An Answer to Pain's Rights of Man* (Dublin: printed for P. Byrne, J. Moore, & W. Jones, 1793), pp. 6, 10, 11.

43. Ibid., pp. 24, 28, 31.

44. Ibid., pp. 17, 24, 44.

45. Ibid., pp. 28, 30–31.

46. John Quincy Adams, *American Principles: A Review of the Works of Fisher Ames* (Boston: Everett and Munroe, 1809), pp. 32–33, 35, 47. Later he made much the same argument in *Parties in the United States* (New York: Greenberg, 1941), pp. 9, 54–56, 96–98.

47. Quoted in Shaw Livermore Jr., *The Twilight of Federalism: The Disintegration of the Federalist Party, 1815–1830* (Princeton, NJ: Princeton University Press, 1962), p. 220.

48. Edmund Burke, *An Appeal from the New to the Old Whigs,* in *Works,* vol. 4, pp. 121–125, 133, 141, 161–162, 169–170; Burke, *Reflections on the Revolution in France,* p. 24.

49. John Quincy Adams, *The Jubilee of the Constitution* (1839) (New York: Bedford and Co., 1848), pp. 40–41; John Quincy Adams, *The Social Compact Exemplified in the Constitution of the Commonwealth of Massachusetts* (Providence, RI: Knowles and Vose, 1842), p. 29.

50. Adams, *Social Compact Exemplified,* p. 25.

51. John Quincy Adams, *An Oration Addressed to the Citizens of the Town of Quincy on the Fourth of July, 1831* (Boston: Richardson, Lord & Holbrook, 1831), p. 18; see also Paine, *Rights of Man,* p. 159.

52. Adams, *Jubilee of the Constitution,* pp. 12, 16, 40.

53. Adams, *Social Compact Exemplified,* pp. 21, 23, 24, 29.

54. John Quincy Adams, "An Oration Delivered Before the Cincinnati Astronomical Society, November 10, 1843," in Adrienne Koch and William Peden, eds., *The Selected Writings of John and John Quincy Adams* (Westport, CT: Greenwood, 1981), pp. 398–399.

55. Charles F. Adams, ed., *Memoirs of John Quincy Adams,* vol. 8 (New York: AMS Press, 1970), p. 433.

56. Nathaniel Hawthorne, *The Scarlet Letter* (New York: Bantam, 2003), pp. 122, 178, 180.

57. "Veneration for our forefathers and love for our posterity . . . form links between the selfish and the social passions." John Quincy Adams, *An Oration Delivered at Plymouth, December 22, 1802, at the Anniversary Commemoration of the First Landing of our Ancestors at That Place* (Plymouth: Joseph Avery, 1820), p. 5.

58. Burke, *Reflections on the Revolution in France,* p. 85.

59. Adams, *Oration to the Citizens of Quincy,* p. 38.

60. Linda Kerber and Walter John Morris, "Politics and Literature: The Adams Family and the *Port Folio*," *William and Mary Quarterly* 23, no. 3 (July 1966): 450–476.

61. Adams, "Oration Before the Cincinnati Astronomical Society," p. 405.

62. Daniel Webster, "Appeal to the Old Whigs of New Hampshire," in *The Writings of Daniel Webster*, vol. 15 (Boston: Little, Brown, 1903), pp. 522–531.

63. Edward Everett, "Principle of the American Constitutions" (1826), in *Orations and Speeches on Various Occasions*, vol. 1 (Boston: Little, Brown, 1878), p. 120.

64. Edward Everett, "First Settlement of New England," in *Orations*, vol. 1, p. 64.

65. Burke, *Appeal from the New to the Old Whigs*, pp. 99–101.

66. Everett, "Principle of the American Constitutions," pp. 107, 117.

67. Everett, "First Settlement of New England," p. 54.

68. Ibid., p. 65.

69. Everett, "Principle of the American Constitutions," p. 111.

70. Edward Everett, "The History of Liberty," in *Orations*, vol. 1, pp. 160, 171–172; Edward Everett, "The Departure of the Pilgrims," in *Orations*, vol. 2, p. 645.

71. Everett, "First Settlement of New England," p. 59; Everett, "Principle of the American Constitutions," pp. 120–122, 112–113.

72. Hubbard Winslow, *The Means of the Perpetuity and Prosperity of Our Republic* (Boston: John H. Eastburn, 1838), p. 9.

73. Gary B. Nash, "The American Clergy and the French Revolution," *William and Mary Quarterly* 22, no. 3 (July 1965): 392–412.

74. Winslow, *Means,* pp. 41n, 20, 17n, 17.

75. Edmund Burke, "First Letter on a Regicide Peace," in *Works*, vol. 5, pp. 312, 313; Joseph Tracy, *A Sermon Before the Vermont Colonization Society* (Windsor, VT: Chronicle Press, 1833), pp. 7–8.

76. Winslow, *Means,* pp. 22–24.

77. Howe, *Political Culture of the American Whigs,* p. 227.

78. Thomas E. Woods Jr., ed., *The Political Writings of Rufus Choate* (Washington, DC: Regnery, 2001), pp. 193, 202, 349.

79. Ibid., p. 202.

80. Ibid., pp. 204–205, 197, 203–204 (emphasis added), 195.

81. William Sumner Jenkins, *Pro-Slavery Thought in the Old South* (Chapel Hill: University of North Carolina Press, 1935), p. 290.

82. Burke, "Speech on Conciliation," pp. 123–124.

83. Herman Belz, ed., *The Webster-Hayne Debate* (Indianapolis, IN: Liberty Fund, 2000), pp. 50, 80.

84. Thomas Roderick Dew, "Abolition of Negro Slavery," in Drew Gilpin Faust, ed., *The Ideology of Slavery: Proslavery Thought in the Antebellum South, 1830–1860* (Baton Rouge: Louisiana State University Press, 1981), p. 66; Thomas Roderick Dew, "Review of the Debate in the Virginia Legislature, 1831–32," in *The Proslavery Argument as Maintained by the Most Distinguished Writers of the Southern States* (1852) (New York: Negro Universities Press, 1968), p. 461.

85. William Harper, *Anniversary Oration: The South Carolina Society for the Advancement of Learning, 9 December 1835* (Columbia, SC: Telescope Office, 1836), p. 20.

86. George Fitzhugh, "Southern Thought" (1857), in Faust, ed., *Ideology of Slavery*, p. 287.

87. George Fitzhugh, *Sociology for the South: Or the Failure of Free Society* (1854) (New York: Burt Franklin, 1965), p. 93.

88. Harper, *Anniversary Oration*, p. 13.

89. Winslow, *Means*, p. 22.

90. I am not taking up in this section the question of John Randolph's Burkean credentials, mainly because I find them highly exaggerated. In this matter I find that my judgment coincides with Robert Dawidoff's in his *The Education of John Randolph* (New York: W. W. Norton, 1979), pp. 217–229.

91. Woodrow Wilson, *Division and Reunion, 1829–1889* (1893) (New York: Longmans, Green & Co., 1902), pp. 105, 107.

92. Ibid., pp. 125–126, 181; Woodrow Wilson, *A History of the American People*, vol. 4 (New York: Harper, 1902), pp. 160, 196–197.

93. Woodrow Wilson, *Mere Literature and Other Essays* (Port Washington, NY: Kennikat Press, 1965), p. 105.

94. Ibid., pp. 142, 128, 156.

95. Edmund Burke, *A Vindication of Natural Society*, in *Works*, vol. 1, pp. 4–5.

96. Wilson, *Mere Literature*, pp. 118–119.

97. Ibid., pp. 109, 114–115, 159.

98. Ibid., p. 131.

99. Woodrow Wilson, *The State, Elements of Historical and Practical Politics: A Sketch of Institutional History and Administration* (Boston: D. C. Heath, 1889), p. 575.

100. J. W. Burrow, *Whigs and Liberals: Continuity and Change in English Political Thought* (Oxford: Clarendon Press, 1988), p. 46.

101. Henry Maine, *Ancient Law* (New York: Dutton, 1954), pp. 67–68, 100.

102. Wilson, *The State*, pp. 9–10, 13.

103. Wilson, *Mere Literature*, pp. 155–156.

104. Wilson, *A History of the American People*, vol. 3, p. 130.

105. Wilson, *Division and Reunion*, p. 15; Wilson, *Mere Literature*, pp. 196–197.

106. Wilson, *Division and Reunion*, p. 111; Wilson, *The State*, p. 643; Wilson, *A History of the American People*, vol. 5, p. 6; Woodrow Wilson, *Constitutional Government in the United States* (New York: Columbia University Press, 1908), p. 16.

107. Wilson set the stage for *Congressional Government* with his earlier (August 1879) essay "Cabinet Government in the United States," in Arthur S. Link, ed., *The Papers of Woodrow Wilson*, vol. 1 (Princeton, NJ: Princeton University Press, 1966), pp. 493–510.

108. Woodrow Wilson, *Congressional Government* (New Brunswick, NJ: Transaction, 2002), p. 5.

109. William Gladstone, "Kin Beyond Sea," *North American Review* 127 (September 1878): 185. On the influence of Gladstone's remark in America, see Michael Kammen, *A Machine That Would Go of Itself: The Constitution in American Culture* (New York: Random House, 1986), p. 162.

110. Walter Bagehot, *The English Constitution* (Ithaca, NY: Cornell University Press, 1966), pp. 277, 281.

111. Henry Maine, *Popular Government* (Indianapolis, IN: Liberty Classics, 1976), ch. 4.

112. Wilson, *Mere Literature,* pp. 99–100.

113. Woodrow Wilson, *Leaders of Men* (Princeton, NJ: Princeton University Press, 1952), p. 20.

114. Wilson, *A History of the American People,* vol. 3, p. 117.

115. Woodrow Wilson, *The New Freedom* (Englewood Cliffs, NJ: Prentice-Hall, 1961), p. 35.

116. Wilson, *The State,* p. 668.

117. Wilson, *New Freedom,* p. 40.

118. See the preface to the 1900 edition of *Congressional Government* and Wilson's work of 1908, *Constitutional Government in the United States.*

119. Wilson, *New Freedom,* pp. 50, 57, 59, 114.

120. Ibid., p. 164, and Woodrow Wilson, "What Would Jefferson Do?" April 14, 1912, in Link, ed., *Papers of Woodrow Wilson,* vol. 24, pp. 331–332. Wilson revised his view of Jefferson in the years leading up to his run for the presidency; see, for instance, "An Address on Thomas Jefferson," April 16, 1906, in Link, ed., *Papers of Woodrow Wilson,* vol. 16 (1973), pp. 362–369.

121. Wilson, *New Freedom,* p. 159.

122. Woodrow Wilson, "A Memorial Day Address," May 30, 1916, in Link, ed., *Papers of Woodrow Wilson,* vol. 37 (1981), p. 125.

123. Woodrow Wilson, "An Appeal to the American People," April 15, 1917, in Link, ed., *Papers of Woodrow Wilson,* vol. 42 (1983), p. 72.

124. Burke, "Address to the British Colonists," pp. 188, 191–192, 194.

125. Burke, "A Letter to the Sheriffs of the City of Bristol," p. 211.

126. Burke, *An Appeal from the New to the Old Whigs,* pp. 100–101.

127. Friedrich Gentz, *The French and American Revolutions Compared* (New York: Gateway, 1955), pp. 84, 62, 69, 77, 47.

128. Nash, "The American Clergy and the French Revolution."

129. Gentz, *French and American Revolutions Compared,* pp. 63, 66.

130. For an example of a denial of America's "revolution principles," see the very conservative Francis Bowen's essay written in response to the Revolution of 1848, "French Ideas of Democracy and a Community of Goods," *North American Review* 69 (1849): 277–325.

Chapter 5. Declarations of Independence

1. John Adams to Abigail Adams, July 3, 1776, in Charles Francis Adams, ed., *The Works of John Adams,* vol. 9 (Boston: Little, Brown, 1850–1856), p. 420. See also Charles Warren, "Fourth of July Myths," *William and Mary Quarterly* 2, no. 3 (July 1945): 237: "The fact is that Independence Day was properly the day on which Congress passed the resolution which actually established our independence; and that day was July 2 and not July 4, 1776."

2. On the theme of inclusion, see John P. Roche, *The Quest for the Dream: The Development of Civil Rights and Human Relations in Modern America* (New York:

Macmillan, 1963); Judith N. Shklar, *American Citizenship: The Quest for Inclusion* (Cambridge, MA: Harvard University Press, 1991); and Cal Jillson, *Pursuing the American Dream: Opportunity and Exclusion over Four Centuries* (Lawrence: University Press of Kansas, 2004).

3. David Armitage, "The Declaration of Independence and International Law," *William and Mary Quarterly* 59, no. 1 (2002): 1–32. Armitage, I believe, did not dismiss the preamble; it simply was not his focus.

4. John Phillip Reid, "The Irrelevance of the Declaration," in Hendrik Hartog, ed., *Law in the American Revolution and the Revolution in the Law* (New York: New York University Press, 1981), pp. 46–89. Reid takes seriously Daniel Boorstin's claims about Jefferson in *The Lost World of Thomas Jefferson* (New York: Henry Holt, 1948). As we shall see, Boorstin is a dubious source because his work was so much a product of the ideological excesses of the Cold War.

5. Reid's essay "The Irrelevance" contains many relevant citations. Also helpful is Pauline Maier, *American Scripture: Making the Declaration of Independence* (New York: Vintage Books, 1998), pp. 50–59. Edmund S. Morgan's *Inventing the People: The Rise of Popular Sovereignty in England and America* (New York: W. W. Norton, 1988) seems to me to reverse Reid's error. To speak of England in terms of popular sovereignty is highly problematical.

6. Lois G. Schwoerer, *The Declaration of Rights, 1689* (Baltimore, MD: Johns Hopkins University Press, 1981).

7. "The Petition of Right" [1628], in David Wooton, ed., *Divine Right and Democracy: An Anthology of Political Writing in Stuart England* (New York: Penguin, 1986), p. 168.

8. For an excellent comparison of the Declaration of Independence with the English Declaration of Rights, see Michael Zuckert, *Natural Rights and the New Republicanism* (Princeton, NJ: Princeton University Press, 1994), pp. 4–14.

9. Edmund Burke, *An Appeal from the New to the Old Whigs*, in *The Works of the Right Honorable Edmund Burke*, vol. 4 (Boston: Little, Brown, 1866), p. 121; Edmund Burke, *Reflections on the Revolution in France* (Indianapolis, IN: Hackett, 1987), p. 24.

10. Isaac Kramnick, *Republicanism and Bourgeois Radicalism: Political Ideology in Late Eighteenth-Century England and America* (Ithaca, NY: Cornell University Press, 1990).

11. John Locke, *Second Treatise of Government*, no. 225.

12. Eugene N. Curtis, "American Opinion of the French Nineteenth-Century Revolutions," *American Historical Review* 29, no. 2 (January 1924): 249–270.

13. For a brief overview of the Southern response to the French Revolution, see Elizabeth Fox-Genovese and Eugene D. Genovese, "Political Virtue and the Lessons of the French Revolution: The View from the Slaveholding South," in Richard K. Matthews, ed., *Virtue, Corruption, and Self-Interest: Political Values in the Eighteenth Century* (Bethlehem, PA: Lehigh University Press, 1994).

14. David Brion Davis, ed., *Antebellum American Culture: An Interpretive Anthology* (University Park, PA: Pennsylvania State University Press, 1997), pp. 185–187;

Richard Hofstadter, *The Paranoid Style in American Politics* (Cambridge, MA: Harvard University Press, 1996), ch. 1.

15. Thoughtful overviews of the role of the Declaration in American history include Philip F. Detweiler, "The Changing Reputation of the Declaration of Independence," *William and Mary Quarterly* 19, no. 4 (October 1962): 557–574; and Maier, *American Scripture*.

16. Constitution of the United States of America, Article IV, section 4.

17. I am making use of Philip F. Detweiler's excellent article "Congressional Debate on Slavery and the Declaration of Independence, 1819–1821," *American Historical Review* 63, no. 3 (April 1958): 598–616.

18. John Quincy Adams, *Address Delivered at the Request of a Committee of the Citizens of Washington, on the Occasion of Reading the Declaration on the Fourth of July, 1821* (Washington, DC: Davis and Force, 1821), pp. 5, 8–9, 26.

19. Ibid., pp. 12, 21.

20. John Quincy Adams, *The Jubilee of the Constitution* (1839) (New York: Bedford and Co., 1848), pp. 45, 46.

21. Ibid., pp. 15, 19, 68, 40, 41.

22. Wendell Phillips, *Speeches, Lectures, and Letters* (Boston: Walker, Wise & Co., 1864), p. 414.

23. Richard Hildreth, *Despotism in America: An Inquiry into the Nature, Results, and Legal Basis of the Slave-Holding System in the United States* (Boston: John P. Jewett & Co., 1854), pp. 249–251.

24. *Speeches of Gerrit Smith in Congress* (New York: Mason Brothers, 1855), pp. 130, 135.

25. George W. Julian, *Speeches on Political Questions, 1850–1868* (1872) (Westport, CT: Negro Universities Press, 1970), pp. 4, 5, 72, 152, 166, 12–15.

26. Robert E. Collins, ed., *Theodore Parker: American Transcendentalist* (Metuchen, NJ: Scarecrow Press, 1973), pp. 155, 66, 143, 151–152.

27. Garry Wills, *Lincoln at Gettysburg: The Words That Remade America* (New York: Simon & Schuster, 1992), p. 108; Julian, *Speeches on Political Questions*, p. 139.

28. *Selections from the Writings and Speeches of William Lloyd Garrison* (New York: Negro Universities Press, 1968), pp. 35, 70, 53, 62–63.

29. Thomas Jefferson, *Notes on Virginia*, in Merrill Peterson, ed., *Thomas Jefferson: Writings* (New York: Library of America, 1984), p. 270.

30. David Walker, "Appeal in Four Articles to the Coloured Citizens of the World, But in Particular to Those of the United States of America," in Sterling Stuckey, ed., *The Ideological Origins of Black Nationalism* (Boston: Beacon Press, 1972), pp. 56, 113.

31. Davis, ed., *Antebellum American Culture*, pp. 293–295.

32. Frederick Douglass, "What to the Slave Is the Fourth of July?" in William L. Andrews, *The Oxford Frederick Douglass Reader* (New York: Oxford University Press, 1996), pp. 109–130.

33. Philip S. Foner, ed., *We, the Other People: Alternative Declarations of Independence by Labor Groups, Farmers, Woman's Rights Advocates, Socialists, and Blacks,*

1829–1975 (Urbana: University of Illinois Press, 1976), pp. 78–83; Eleanor Flexnor, *Century of Struggle: The Women's Rights Movement in the United States* (Cambridge, MA: Harvard University Press, 1959), p. 74.

34. Lawrence Frederick Kohl, *The Politics of Individualism: Parties and the American Character in the Jacksonian Era* (New York: Oxford University Press, 1989), p. 34.

35. Donald Bruce Johnson, ed., *National Party Platforms* (Urbana: University of Illinois Press, 1978), pp. 1–2, 4, 11, 17, 24.

36. Sean Wilentz, *Chants Democratic: New York City and the Rise of the American Working Class, 1788–1850* (New York: Oxford University Press, 1984), pp. 88–91, 246.

37. Joseph Blau, ed., *Social Theories of Jacksonian Democracy* (Indianapolis, IN: Hackett, 2003), p. 137.

38. Frederick Robinson, *An Oration Delivered Before the Trades Union of Boston* (Boston: Charles Douglas, 1834), p. 3.

39. Ely Moore, *Oration Delivered Before the Mechanics and Workingmen of the City of New York* (New York: John Windt, 1843), pp. 14–15.

40. Seth Luther, *An Address to the Working Men of New England on the State of Education and on the Condition of the Producing Classes in Europe and America* (Boston: published by the author, 1832); Seth Luther, *An Address on the Origin and Progress of Avarice and Its Deleterious Effects on Human Happiness* (Boston: published by the author, 1834), pp. 6–7.

41. Luther, *Address on Education*, p. 5. Luther, *An Address Delivered Before the Mechanics and Workingmen of the City of Brooklyn, on the Celebration of the Sixtieth Anniversary of American Independence* (New York: Alden Spooner & Sons, 1836), p. 3.

42. Ely Moore, *Address on Civil Government Delivered Before the New York Typographical Society* (New York: B. R. Barlow, 1847).

43. "The Working Men's Declaration of Independence, December, 1829," in Foner, ed., *We, the Other People*, pp. 48–50.

44. George Henry Evans, *The Radical*, no. 1, vol. 2 (1842), p. 1.

45. See, for example, *Working Man's Advocate*, May 25, 1844, July 6, 1844, October 5, 1844.

46. Ibid., March 16, 1844.

47. Charles Sumner, *The Promises of the Declaration of Independence: Eulogy of Abraham Lincoln* (Boston: Ticknor & Fields, 1865), pp. 7, 10, 17.

48. Quoted in Richard N. Current, ed., *The Political Thought of Abraham Lincoln* (New York: Macmillan, 1967), pp. 73, 83.

49. Ibid., pp. 89, 90.

50. Frederick Saunders, ed., *Our National Centennial Jubilee* (New York: E. B. Treat, 1877), pp. 129, 263.

51. Charles Francis Adams, "The Progress of Liberty," in Saunders, ed., *Our National Centennial Jubilee*, pp. 200, 209.

52. William L. Riordon, *Plunkitt of Tammany Hall* (Boston: Bedford and St. Martin's, 1994), p. 86.

53. Henry George, *Progress and Poverty* (New York: Robert Schalkenbach Foundation, 1942), p. 545.

54. Norman Pollack, ed., *The Populist Mind* (Indianapolis, IN: Bobbs-Merrill, 1967), pp. 21, 53, 60, 204–205, 216.

55. Arthur M. Schlesinger Jr., ed., *Writings and Speeches of Eugene V. Debs* (New York: Hermitage Press, 1948), pp. 6, 9.

56. Foner, ed., *We, the Other People,* pp. 47–55, 64–76, 84–104, 115–162.

57. Edward Bellamy, *Equality* (New York: AMS Press, 1970), p. 332.

58. Woodrow Wilson, *The New Freedom* (Englewood Cliffs, NJ: Prentice-Hall, 1961), pp. 43, 143.

59. *Speeches of William Jennings Bryan,* vol. 2 (New York: Funk & Wagnalls, 1909), p. 39; compare pp. 24, 26, 48.

60. W. E. B. Du Bois, *The Souls of Black Folk* (1903) (New York: Bantam, 1989), pp. 8, 42.

61. I am indebted, again, to Detweiler, "Congressional Debate on Slavery and the Declaration of Independence."

62. Thomas Roderick Dew, "Abolition of Negro Slavery," in Drew Gilpin Faust, ed., *The Ideology of Slavery: Proslavery Thought in the Antebellum South, 1830–1860* (Baton Rouge: Louisiana State University Press, 1981), p. 28.

63. William Harper, *Memoir on Slavery,* in Faust, ed., *Ideology of Slavery,* pp. 83, 87.

64. William Gilmore Simms, "The Morals of Slavery," in *The Proslavery Argument as Maintained by the Most Distinguished Writers of the Southern States* (1852) (New York: Negro Universities Press, 1968), p. 253.

65. Simms, "Morals of Slavery," pp. 251, 253, 259.

66. Ross M. Lence, ed., *Union and Liberty: The Political Philosophy of John C. Calhoun* (Indianapolis, IN: Liberty Fund, 1992), p. 566.

67. Ibid., pp. 44, 45, 84, 90.

68. George Fitzhugh, *Sociology for the South: Or the Failure of Free Society* (1854) (New York: Burt Franklin, 1965), p. 175.

69. George Fitzhugh, *Cannibals All! or Slaves without Masters* (Cambridge, MA: Harvard University Press, 1960), pp. 12–13.

70. Fitzhugh, *Sociology for the South,* p. 187.

71. Lence, ed., *Union and Liberty,* p. 82.

72. Fitzhugh, *Sociology for the South,* pp. 189, 216–217. Chapter 23 of the book is on "woman's rights"; chapter 20, which follows the chapter on the Declaration, is on "the marriage relation."

73. Ibid., pp. 181, 179.

74. *The Works of Rufus Choate,* vol. 1 (Boston: Little, Brown, 1862), p. 215.

75. Calvin Colton, "Democracy," in *The Junius Tracts* (New York: Greeley & McElrath, 1844), ch. 6.

76. Calvin Colton, *The Rights of Labor* (New York: A. S. Barnes, 1846), p. 9.

77. Calvin Colton, *Abolition a Sedition: By a Northern Man* (Philadelphia: Geo. W. Donohue, 1839), pp. 120–121, 127.

78. Francis Bowen, "French Ideas of Democracy and a Community of Goods," *North American Review* 69 (1849): 325, 308–309.

79. Ibid., pp. 312–313.

80. Robert W. Johannsen, ed., *The Lincoln-Douglas Debates* (New York: Oxford University Press, 1965), pp. 215, 127–128, 299.

81. Ibid., p. 22.

82. Ibid., p. 328.

83. In *Harper's Magazine* (September 1859), Douglas wrote that the inalienable right of each colony to self-government was the meaning of the Declaration. Merrill Peterson, *The Jefferson Image in the American Mind* (New York: Oxford University Press, 1960), p. 195.

84. Quoted in Morton Keller, *Affairs of State: Public Life in Late Nineteenth Century America* (Cambridge, MA: Harvard University Press, 1977), p. 27.

85. Robert Pettus Hay, *Freedom's Jubilee: One Hundred Years of the Fourth of July, 1776–1876* (unpublished Ph.D. dissertation, University of Kentucky, 1967), p. 255.

86. William J. Cooper Jr., ed., *Jefferson Davis: The Essential Writings* (New York: Modern Library, 2003), pp. 193, 199.

87. John Amasa May and Joan Reynolds Faunt, eds., *South Carolina Secedes* (Columbia: University of South Carolina Press, 1960), pp. 76–78.

88. Frank Moore, ed., *The Rebellion Record*, vol. 1 (New York, 1861–1871), p. 203.

89. Dwight Lowell Dumond, ed., *Southern Editorials on Secession* (Gloucester, MA: Peter Smith, 1964), pp. 236, 510.

90. Saunders, ed., *Our National Centennial Jubilee*, p. 163; Michael Kammen, *A Season of Youth* (New York: Alfred A. Knopf, 1978), p. 61.

91. Saunders, ed., *Our National Centennial Jubilee*, p. 289.

92. Ibid., pp. 447–448.

93. Robert G. McCloskey, *American Conservatism in an Age of Enterprise: A Study of William Graham Sumner, Stephen J. Field, and Andrew Carnegie* (Cambridge, MA: Harvard University Press, 1951), ch. 5.

94. Herbert Croly, *The Promise of American Life* (Boston: Northeastern University Press, 1989), pp. 421, 278.

95. John R. Commons, *Races and Immigrants in America* (New York: Macmillan, 1907), pp. 1, 3, 7.

96. Daniel J. Boorstin, *The Genius of American Politics* (Chicago: University of Chicago Press, 1953), pp. 8, 182–183.

97. Ibid., pp. 84, 75, 82, 70, 6, 30.

98. Ibid., p. 117. It is true, of course, as Amy Dru Stanley noted, that the abolitionists did frequently employ images of "suffering Bodies." See her *From Bondage to Contract: Wage Labor, Marriage, and the Market in the Age of Slave Emancipation* (New York: Cambridge University Press, 1998), pp. 22, 25. The difficulty with Boorstin is that he wrote as if the abolitionists said nothing more.

99. Martin Diamond, "The Declaration and the Constitution: Liberty, Democracy, and the Founders," in Nathan Glazer and Irving Kristol, eds., *The American Commonwealth, 1976* (New York: Basic Books, 1976), ch. 2, esp. pp. 47, 49.

100. James Miller, *"Democracy Is in the Streets": From Port Huron to the Siege of Chicago* (New York: Simon and Schuster, 1987), p. 54.

101. *The Port Huron Statement* (Chicago: Charles Kerr, 1999), p. 8.

102. Martin Luther King Jr., "I Have a Dream," in James Melvin Washington, ed., *A Testament of Hope: The Essential Writings of Martin Luther King, Jr.* (New York: Harper & Row, 1986), pp. 217–220.

103. Lyndon Baines Johnson, "To Fulfill These Rights," reprinted in Lee Rainwater and William L. Yancey, *The Moynihan Report and the Politics of Controversy* (Cambridge, MA: MIT Press, 1967), pp. 125–132.

104. Daniel Patrick Moynihan, "The Negro Family: The Case for National Action," reprinted in Rainwater and Yancey, *The Moynihan Report and the Politics of Controversy*, pp. 47, 49, 51.

105. "What We Want, What We Believe: Black Panther Party Platform and Program," in William L. Van Deburg, ed., *Modern Black Nationalism: From Marcus Garvey to Louis Farrakhan* (New York: New York University Press, 1997), pp. 249–251.

106. James Madison, "Speech in Congress Proposing Constitutional Amendments, June 8, 1789," in *James Madison: Writings* (New York: Library of America, 1999), p. 441.

107. Akhil Reed Amar, *The Bill of Rights: Creation and Reconstruction* (New Haven, CT: Yale University Press, 1998), p. 47.

108. Richard C. Cortner, *The Supreme Court and the Second Bill of Rights: The Fourteenth Amendment and the Nationalization of Civil Liberties* (Madison: University of Wisconsin Press, 1981).

Chapter 6. The End of the Social Contract?

1. George Bancroft's fourth of July speech, 1826, at Northampton, Massachusetts, is reprinted in Henry A. Hawken, *Trumpets of Glory: Fourth of July Orations, 1786–1861* (Granby, CT: Salmon Brook Historical Society, 1976), pp. 84, 87.

2. Bancroft's comments were printed in the *Franklin Mercury*, February 24, 1835. Arthur M. Schlesinger Jr. calls attention to this speech in *The Age of Jackson* (Boston: Little, Brown, 1945), p. 164.

3. Joseph Story, *Miscellaneous Writings* (1852) (New York: Da Capo Press, 1972), pp. 743, 750; Joseph Story, *Commentaries on the Constitution of the United States: With a Preliminary Review of the Constitutional History of the Colonies and States, Before the Adoption of the Constitution* (1833) (Boston: Charles C. Little & James Brown, 1851), no. 1912; Story, *Miscellaneous Writings*, p. 615.

4. Story, *Commentaries*, nos. 325–327, 358, 212.

5. Ibid., nos. 344, 347.

6. Abraham Lincoln, "The Perpetuation of Our Political Institutions: Address Before the Springfield Young Men's Lyceum, 1838," in Richard N. Current, ed., *The Political Thought of Abraham Lincoln* (New York: Macmillan, 1967), pp. 11–21.

7. Abraham Lincoln, "Speech in the U.S. House of Representatives on the War with Mexico," in Don E. Fehrenbacher, ed., *Abraham Lincoln: Speeches and Writings, 1832–1858* (New York: Library of America, 1989), p. 167.

8. Current, ed., *Political Thought of Abraham Lincoln*, pp. 45–47.

9. Ibid., pp. 152, 184.

10. Ibid., p. 177.

11. For an overview, see Thomas J. Pressly, "Bullets and Ballots: Lincoln and the 'Right of Revolution,'" *American Historical Review* 67, no. 3 (April 1962): 647–662.

12. Current, ed., *Political Thought of Abraham Lincoln*, p. 123.

13. Ibid., p. 285.

14. John L. O'Sullivan, *Union, Disunion, and Reunion: A Letter to General Franklin Pierce, Ex-President of the United States* (London: 1862), pp. 4, 111, 116.

15. John L. O'Sullivan, *Peace: The Sole Chance Now Left for Reunion* (London: 1863), p. 9.

16. I am drawing upon George M. Fredrickson's fine study *The Inner Civil War: Northern Intellectuals and the Crisis of the Union* (New York: Harper & Row, 1965).

17. George W. Bassett, *A Discourse on the Wickedness and Folly of the Present War*, speech delivered at Ottawa, Illinois, August 11, 1861, pamphlet, Harvard University library.

18. James Freeman Clarke, *Secession, Concession, or Self-Possession: Which?* (Boston: 1861), p. 13.

19. Quoted in Fredrickson, *Inner Civil War*, p. 58.

20. Henry W. Bellows, *Unconditional Loyalty* (New York: Anson D. F. Randolph, 1863), pp. 15, 6, 4.

21. Ibid., p. 10.

22. Charles J. Stillé, *The Historical Development of American Civilization: An Address Delivered Before the Society of the Graduates of Yale College, July 29, 1863* (New Haven, CT: E. Hayes, 1863), p. 4.

23. Horace Bushnell, *Reverses Needed: A Discourse Delivered on the Sunday After the Disaster of Bull Run* (Hartford, CT: L. E. Hunt, 1861), p. 11; Horace Bushnell, *Building Eras in Religion* (New York: Charles Scribner, 1903), p. 311 (the speech in question, "Popular Government by Divine Right," dates from 1864).

24. Bushnell, *Building Eras*, pp. 295, 305; Bushnell, *Reverses Needed*, p. 20.

25. Bushnell, *Building Eras*, pp. 300–301, 307.

26. Bushnell, *Reverses Needed*, p. 16.

27. Ibid.

28. Stillé, *Historical Development of American Civilization*, pp. 13, 14–15.

29. Ibid., pp. 17, 18, 22, 19, 9, 27.

30. Ibid., p. 36.

31. Merrill D. Peterson, *The Jefferson Image in the American Mind* (New York: Oxford University Press, 1960), pp. 222–226.

32. Quoted in Eric F. Goldman, *Rendezvous with Destiny* (New York: Vintage, 1952), p. 68.

33. Joseph P. Thompson, *Revolution Against Free Government Not a Right but a Crime* (New York: Club House, Union Square, 1864), pp. 13–15, 18.

34. Morton Keller, "The Politics of State Constitutional Revision, 1820–1930," in Kermit L. Hall, Harold M. Hyman, and Leon V. Sigal, eds., *The Constitutional Convention as an Amending Device* (Washington, DC: American Historical Association and American Political Science Association, 1981), ch. 2.

35. Peterson, *Jefferson Image*, pp. 266–267.

36. Theodore Roosevelt, *The Strenuous Life* (New York: Century Co., 1901), pp. 18, 254; Theodore Roosevelt, *The Winning of the West: An Account of the Exploration and Settlement of Our Country* (New York: Charles Scribner's Sons, 1926).

37. Roosevelt, *The Strenuous Life*, pp. 66, 71.

38. Elizabeth Cady Stanton, *Suffrage a Natural Right* (Chicago: Open Court, 1894), p. 2.

39. Aileen S. Kraditor, *The Ideas of the Woman Suffrage Movement, 1890–1920* (New York: Columbia University Press, 1965).

40. Amy Dru Stanley, *From Bondage to Contract: Wage Labor, Marriage, and the Market in the Age of Slave Emancipation* (New York: Cambridge University Press, 1998).

41. E. L. Godkin, "The Labor Crisis," *North American Review* 105 (July 1867): 181.

42. Robert C. Bannister, ed., *On Liberty, Society, and Politics: The Essential Essays of William Graham Sumner* (Indianapolis, IN: Liberty Fund, 1992), pp. 169–170, 177, 190, 198, 399–400; William Graham Sumner, *What Social Classes Owe to Each Other* (New York: Harper & Brothers, 1883), pp. 24–25; Bannister, ed., *On Liberty, Society, and Politics*, p. 207.

43. Woodrow Wilson, *Mere Literature and Other Essays* (Port Washington, NY: Kennikat Press, 1965), p. 199.

44. Daniel T. Rodgers, *Contested Truths: Keywords in American Politics Since Independence* (New York: Basic Books, 1987), pp. 112–114, is correct to call attention to the antebellum Protestant colleges with an anti–social contract curriculum. His metaphor of "counterrevolution," however, is perhaps too strong when applied to pre–Civil War America. And, as we have seen, the most prominent Whigs found themselves obliged to come to terms with, rather than reject, the social contract.

45. Roosevelt proclaimed Croly's *The Promise of American Life* "the most profound and illuminating study of our national conditions which has appeared for many years." His review of Croly's *Progressive Democracy* is reprinted in William H. Harbaugh, ed., *The Writings of Theodore Roosevelt* (Indianapolis, IN: Bobbs-Merrill, 1967), pp. 344–352. See also Herbert Croly, *The Promise of American Life* (1909) (Boston: Northeastern University Press, 1989), p. 24.

46. Henry George, *Progress and Poverty* (New York: Robert Schalkenbach Foundation, 1942), pp. 300, 545.

47. Ibid., pp. 390–391; Frederick Jackson Turner, "The Significance of the Frontier in American History," in *History, Frontier, and Section* (Albuquerque: University of New Mexico Press, 1993), pp. 59–91.

48. Stanley, *From Bondage to Contract*, ch. 2.

49. Theodore Roosevelt, *Autobiography* (1913) (New York: Da Capo, 1985), pp. 156, 515; Harbaugh, ed., *Writings of Theodore Roosevelt*, pp. 309–315.

50. George, *Progress and Poverty*, p. 456.

51. John Randolph, in *Proceedings and Debates of the Virginia State Convention of 1829–1830* (Richmond, VA: S. Shepherd, 1830), p. 533.

52. George, *Progress and Poverty*, p. 505.

53. Croly, *Promise of American Life*, pp. 278–279; Herbert Croly, *Progressive Democracy* (1914) (New Brunswick, NJ: Transaction, 1998), pp. 44–45, 129–130.

54. Croly, *Promise of American Life*, pp. 380–381.

55. Thomas Paine, *Agrarian Justice*, in Eric Foner, ed., *Thomas Paine: Collected Writings* (New York: Library of America, 1995), p. 408.

56. Croly, *Promise of American Life*, pp. 26, 420.

57. T. H. Green, *Lectures on the Principles of Political Obligation* (1880) (London: Longmans, Green, 1921), pp. 226–227.

58. L. T. Hobhouse, *Liberalism* (London: Thornton Butterworth, 1911), pp. 95–96.

59. To the generally acknowledged link between Henry George and Progressivism/socialism I can add a personal finding. When I bought a 1942 copy of *Progress and Poverty*, a brochure fell out advertising the next meeting of the Socialist Labor Party, Los Angeles. The scheduled topic was "Post-War Unemployment."

60. Quoted in Eric Foner, *Politics and Ideology in the Age of the Civil War* (New York: Oxford University Press, 1980), pp. 174, 179.

61. Populist Party Platform, July 4, 1892, in Richard Hofstadter, ed., *Great Issues in American History*, vol. 2 (New York: Vintage Books, 1958), pp. 147–153.

62. George, *Progress and Poverty*, p. 320; John L. Thomas, *Alternative America: Henry George, Edward Bellamy, Henry Demarest Lloyd and the Adversary Tradition* (Cambridge, MA: Harvard University Press, 1983), p. 320.

63. George, *Progress and Poverty*, p. 316; see also Henry George's essay "The Warning of the English Strikes," *North American Review* 149 (October 1889): 393: "trades-unions can accomplish nothing large and permanent."

64. Thomas, *Alternative America*, p. 324.

65. See, for example, Thorstein Veblen, *The Theory of Business Enterprise* (New York: Charles Scribner's Sons, 1937), pp. 274, 304, 311–312, 318, 327–331, 338–339, 375–376.

66. William Howard Taft, "Speech of February 22, 1913"; Learned Hand to Francis W. Bird, January 14, 1913. Both sources are quoted in Brad Clarke, *"The True Prosperity of Our Past"* (unpublished Ph.D. dissertation, Brandeis University, 1997), pp. 519–521.

67. Dewey, for instance, denounced "a perversion of the whole ideal of individualism to conform to the practices of a pecuniary culture." John Dewey, *Individualism Old and New* (New York: Capricorn Books, 1962), p. 18.

68. Ibid., p. 89.

69. Ibid., p. 36.

70. Croly, *Progressive Democracy*, ch. 2.

71. In addition to his work on *Individualism Old and New*, see John Dewey's pamphlet *Liberalism and Social Action* (1935) (New York: Capricorn Books, 1963).

72. Croly, *Promise of American Life*, p. 50.

73. Croly, *Progressive Democracy*, p. 338.

74. Ibid., p. 229; Eldon J. Eisenach, *The Lost Promise of Progressivism* (Lawrence: University Press of Kansas, 1994), ch. 3.

75. Harbaugh, ed., *Writings of Theodore Roosevelt*, pp. 271, 272. See also Theodore Roosevelt, "Do You Believe in the Rule of the People?" *The Outlook*, March 9, 1912.

76. Croly, *Promise of American Life*, p. 81.

77. Roosevelt, *Autobiography*, pp. 400, 438, 486, 487.

78. Michael Willrich, *City of Courts: Socializing Justice in Progressive Era Chicago* (New York: Cambridge University Press, 2003).

79. This is not the finding of David Engerman in *Modernization from the Other Shore: American Intellectuals and the Romance of Russian Development* (Cambridge, MA: Harvard University Press, 2003). I do believe, however, that my argument can be legitimately inferred from his evidence.

80. Quoted by Forrest McDonald, *Novus Ordo Seclorum: The Intellectual Origins of the Constitution* (Lawrence: University Press of Kansas, 1985), p. 59n.

81. Merrill Peterson, ed., *Thomas Jefferson: Writings* (New York: Library of America, 1984), pp. 21, 220, 520.

82. John Locke, *Second Treatise of Government*, no. 41.

83. Peterson, ed., *Thomas Jefferson*, p. 880.

84. Foner, ed., *Thomas Paine*, pp. 6–7.

85. Charles F. Adams, ed., *Memoirs of John Quincy Adams*, vol. 10 (New York: AMS Press, 1970), p. 19.

86. Calvin Colton, *The Junius Tracts* (New York: Greeley & McElrath, 1844), p. 76.

87. On the Whigs, see Daniel Walker Howe, *The Political Culture of the American Whigs* (Chicago: University of Chicago Press, 1979). On the Whig-Jacksonian debate, see Lawrence Frederick Kohl, *The Politics of Individualism: Parties and the American Character in the Jacksonian Era* (New York: Oxford University Press, 1989).

88. Robert E. Collins, ed., *Theodore Parker: American Transcendentalist* (Metuchen, NJ: Scarecrow Press, 1973), p. 68.

89. William H. Seward, "The Higher Law," in Daniel Walker Howe, ed., *The American Whigs: An Anthology* (New York: John Wiley, 1973), p. 232.

90. Oliver Wendell Holmes Jr., "Natural Law," in David H. Hollinger and Charles Capper, eds., *The American Intellectual Tradition*, vol. 2, 2nd ed. (New York: Oxford University Press), pp. 128–130.

91. Thurman W. Arnold, *The Symbols of Government* (New Haven, CT: Yale University Press, 1935); Thurman W. Arnold, *The Folklore of Capitalism* (New Haven, CT: Yale University Press, 1937); Richard Hofstadter, *The Age of Reform* (New York: Vintage, 1955), pp. 319–323.

92. Walter Lippmann, *A Preface to Politics* (Ann Arbor: University of Michigan Press, 1962), pp. 152, 158; Walter Lippmann, *Drift and Mastery* (Madison: University of Wisconsin Press, 1985), p. 144.

93. Walter Lippmann, *Public Opinion* (New York: Free Press, 1965), p. 138, ch. 26.

94. Lippmann, *A Preface to Politics*, p. 232.

95. Walter Lippmann, *Essays in the Public Philosophy* (New York: Mentor Books, 1956), p. 137.

96. See, for example, Leo Strauss, *Natural Right and History* (Chicago: University of Chicago Press, 1953).

97. Norman Pollack, ed., *The Populist Mind* (Indianapolis, IN: Bobbs-Merrill, 1967), pp. 217, 220.

98. Ibid., pp. 155–156.

99. Arthur M. Schlesinger Jr., ed., *Writings and Speeches of Eugene V. Debs* (New York: Hermitage Press, 1948), pp. 32, 38, 139, 188, 189, 416, 33, 396, 263, 299, 308.

100. Ibid., p. 297.

101. Woodrow Wilson, *The New Freedom* (Englewood, Cliffs, NJ: Prentice-Hall, 1961), pp. 159, 160.

102. See, for example, Theodore Roosevelt, "The Duties of American Citizenship," January 26, 1893, in Harbaugh, ed., *Writings of Theodore Roosevelt*, pp. 3–16; Theodore Roosevelt, "Duties of the Citizen," April 23, 1910, in *Theodore Roosevelt's Speeches in Europe* (New York: C. S. Hammond & Co., 1910), pp. 1–31.

103. Herbert Hoover, *American Individualism* (1922) (West Branch, IA: Herbert Hoover Presidential Library Association, 1989), p. 47.

104. Herbert Hoover, *The Challenge to Liberty* (1934) (West Branch, IA: Herbert Hoover Presidential Library Association, 1989), pp. 82, 84, 100, 142, 149, 163, 218.

105. Samuel I. Rosenman, ed., *The Public Papers and Addresses of Franklin D. Roosevelt* (New York: Random House, 1938–1950), vol. 1, pp. 742, 753. Sidney Milkis has proven that Franklin Roosevelt played a significant role in editing the Commonwealth Club address. *The President and the Parties: The Transformation of the American Party System Since the New Deal* (New York: Oxford University Press, 1993), pp. 39–42.

106. *Public Papers and Addresses of FDR*, vol. 1, pp. 746, 750, 752.

107. Ibid., vol. 13, pp. 41, 374, 378.

108. Mark Hulliung, *Citizens and Citoyens: Republicans and Liberals in America and France* (Cambridge, MA: Harvard University Press, 2002), ch. 2.

109. R. Shep Melnick, *Between the Lines: Interpreting Welfare Rights* (Washington, DC: The Brookings Institution, 1994).

110. Mary Ann Glendon, *Rights Talk: The Impoverishment of Political Discourse* (New York: Free Press, 1991), p. 176.

111. John Rawls, *A Theory of Justice* (Cambridge, MA: Harvard University Press, 1971), pp. 16, 112, 114, 115, 116. For a discussion of Rawls from the standpoint of someone sympathetic to Locke, see Michael Zuckert, *Launching Liberalism: On Lockean Political Philosophy* (Lawrence: University Press of Kansas, 2002), ch. 12. For a historical and critical overview, see John Dunn, "Contractualism," in *The History of Political Theory and Other Essays* (Cambridge: Cambridge University Press, 1996), ch. 3.

112. Dewey, *Individualism Old and New*, p. 16.

Index

Gordon anti-Catholic riots of 1780, 121
Greeley, Horace, 98, 100, 179, 183
Green, T. H., 187–188
Grotius, Hugo, 9, 11, 16–18, 20, 23,
    25–26, 30, 38, 43–47, 54, 57–59,
    85–91, 94–95, 101, 123, 144, 162,
    190, 195
Grow, Galusha, 100
Guizot, François, 182

Haiti, 146
Hamilton, Alexander, 5, 28–32, 36,
    39–40, 114–115, 181–182. *See also*
    Federalist; Federalists
Hammond, James Henry, 57–58, 63, 130
Hand, Learned, 189
Hardin, Benjamin, 159
Harper, William, 58–59, 63, 129–130,
    160
Harrington, James, 25
Hartz, Louis, 8, 108–109
Hawthorne, Nathaniel, 68, 124
Hayden, Tom, 169
Hayne, Robert, 73, 129–130
Hegel, G. W. F., 6, 193, 204
Henry, Patrick, 31, 34, 193
Henshaw, David, 65
higher law, 195–199
Hildreth, Richard, 75, 150
Hill, Benjamin, 63
historicism, 6, 175–176
    European, 189
    German, 175–176
Hobbes, Thomas, 12, 20, 123, 190
Hobhouse, L. T., 187–188
Holmes, Oliver Wendell, Jr., 197
Homer, 99
Homestead Act, 84, 91–93, 96–97,
    99–101. *See also* agrarians
Hoover, Herbert, 201
Hopkins, Stephen, 13
Horace, 91
House of Commons, 110
House of Representatives, 83, 147, 177
Howard University, 170
human nature, 16, 68, 194

human rights, 71, 97, 136, 151, 156, 158,
    164, 178, 181, 192, 201, 205
Hume, David, 13–14, 15, 37, 72, 101,
    176, 195
Hutcheson, Francis, 21
Hutchinson, Thomas, 12, 15, 17

inclusion, 142, 147, 152–153, 156–158,
    164, 169, 172
Independent Treasury, 153
India, 105, 132
Indians (Native Americans), 53, 79, 102,
    184, 193–194
individualism, 81, 188–191, 202
individual rights, 171, 201
industrial age, 190, 202
international law, 143

Jackson, Andrew, 53, 74, 97–98, 153
    King Andrew the First, 163
Jacksonians, 5–6, 61, 64–65, 82, 96,
    124–125, 146, 156–157, 163, 175,
    187, 194, 200
Jacksonian Democrats, 65
Jacobins, 125, 127, 134, 139, 146–147,
    150
James II (king of England), 17, 19–20, 56,
    138, 144
James, William, 199
Jay, John, 37, 51. *See also Federalist;*
    Federalists
Jefferson, Thomas, 3, 9, 22, 57, 79, 200
    Adams family and, 119–120
    agrarians and, 76–77, 89, 92–92, 97,
        186
    Declaration of Independence, 143–146,
        152–153, 157–158, 160–161,
        164–166
    Indians, 193–194
    as Jacobin, 134
    on John Taylor, 54
    legacy of, 175–176, 178, 181–183,
        185
    Locke and, 26, 65, 75, 194
    Paine and, 65, 145–146
    religion 34, 67

of justice, 204
of right, 106
See also first principles; fundamental
    principles; original principles;
    political principles; revolution
    principles
private property, 82, 84, 86, 89, 91,
    94–95, 102–104, 106, 188, 201
Progressive age, 167, 175
Progressives, 9, 107, 134, 137, 157, 173,
    187–190, 193, 197, 204–205
    Bull Moose, 185, 192, 201
    Locke and, 186, 189–190
    New Freedom, 136, 158, 191, 198,
        201
    New Nationalists, 167, 186, 191–192,
        198, 201
property rights, 29, 62, 87, 136, 167,
    178, 192, 201
Protestant Reformation, 123
Publicola, 118, 120, 122. See also Adams,
    John Quincy
Publius, 32. See also Federalist;
    Federalists; Hamilton, Alexander;
    Jay, John; Madison, James
Pufendorf, Samuel, 2, 9, 11, 16–22, 25,
    30–31, 38, 40–41, 43–44, 46–47,
    54, 57–59, 69–70, 85, 87–89,
    94–95, 101, 122–123, 144–145,
    162, 175–176, 186, 190, 195. See
    also social contract
Puritan Revolution, 3, 4, 17, 22, 145

race, 79–80, 82, 90, 123, 132, 167,
    169–171, 192
racism, 131, 167, 183–184, 192–193,
    204
radicalism, 5, 39, 67, 78, 83–84, 91, 98,
    125, 167, 169, 178
Randolph, John, 162, 186
ratification, 5, 27, 29–30, 45, 52, 171,
    196. See also popular sovereignty
Rawls, John, 204
Reconstruction, 158
religion, 16, 34–35, 48, 51, 93, 111–112,
    129, 132, 177, 180, 195, 205

religious freedom. See freedom, of religion
representative government, 175
Republican party, 1, 5, 63, 75, 99–100,
    129, 155–156, 162, 176–178, 184,
    186, 203
republican virtue, 131
revolutionary ideology, 7–8, 91, 114
revolution principles, 22–4, 32, 44,
    47–48, 55, 74, 79–80, 82, 84–85,
    95, 102, 107, 116, 137, 139, 146,
    154, 178, 181–182. See also
    Jefferson, Thomas, revolution
    principles; Locke, John, revolution
    principles
Rhode Island, 13, 73–74
    Charter of 1636, 73
Ricardo, David, 102
Rich, Charles, 148
rights, 1, 17, 25, 48, 56–57, 62, 66, 70,
    72, 76, 86, 90, 96, 98–102, 113,
    126, 144, 149, 153, 159, 164, 174,
    178, 191, 197, 200
    to bear arms, 5
    of conscience, 35, 48–49
    to emigrate, 40–41
    of Englishmen, 110, 116, 123, 145
    to land, 77, 81, 85, 92, 96, 99, 155,
        188 (see also agrarians)
    to live, 98, 197
    of man, 7, 24, 65, 78–80, 82–84, 87,
        89, 91, 99, 116, 119–120, 123, 139,
        142, 168
    to revolution, 5–6, 33, 39–40, 63–64,
        73, 145, 158, 171, 176–177, 179,
        182
    to secede, 179–180 (see also secession)
    to self-defense, 12, 39, 67
    of self-government, 60, 164, 179 (see
        also popular sovereignty)
    of slavery, 69 (see also slavery)
    to vote, 49, 132, 152
    of women, 162
    See also civil rights; equal rights;
        human rights; individual rights;
        natural rights; political rights;
        property rights; states' rights